What is Shi'i Islam?

For the public at large Shi'ism often implies a host of confused representations, suggesting more often than not obscurantism, intolerance, political violence and other ignominies running hot or cold in response to world events. In fact for many people, Shi'ism stands for "radical Islam", or — worse — "Islamic terrorism". In some respects, nothing is more familiar than Shi'ism, and yet nothing is more misunderstood. For some twenty years the media have increased their coverage of the phenomenon. Never, or only rarely, do they formulate the question we ask here: what is Shi'ism? What is this belief that inspires millions of people dispersed throughout the world?

This book provides a broad-based introduction to Shi'i Islam. It examines what the Shi'i believe, how they see themselves and how they view the world. It includes a thorough examination of doctrine, philosophy, the Shi'i approach to the Qur'an and the historical evolution of Shi'ism as a branch of Islam. Too often, and too quickly, the conclusion is drawn that Shi'ism is a marginal heretical sect, fundamentally alien to the deeper truth of the great religion of Islam, thrust by historical accident onto the political stage. Shi'ism either speaks the truth of Islam, meaning that it is a truth of terror, or it is entirely foreign to Islam and, therefore, merits outright rejection, as Islamic fundamentalists and some individuals repeatedly claim. This book intends to explain why such common misunderstandings of Shi'ism have taken root.

Written in an accessible format and providing a thorough overview of Shi'ism, this book will be an essential text for students and scholars of Islamic Studies or Iranian Studies.

Mohammad Ali Amir-Moezzi is Professor at the École Pratique des Hautes Études, Sorbonne, France.

Christian Jambet is Professor at the École Pratique des Hautes Études, Sorbonne, France.

Routledge Persian and Shi'i Studies

Series editor: Andrew Newman, University of Edinburgh

Editorial Board: Dr Robert Gleave, Department of Religious Studies, University of Bristol; Dr Marco Salati, Faculty of Oriental Studies, University of Venice, Italy; Dr Kazuo Morimoto, Institute of Oriental Culture, University of Tokyo, Japan; Dr Maria Szuppe, CNRS, Paris, France; Mr Rasul Ja'fariyan, Library of Iranian and Islamic History, Qum, Iran; Dr Mansur Sefatgul, Department of History, University of Tehran, Iran.

What is Shi'i Islam?
An Introduction

Mohammad Ali Amir-Moezzi and Christian Jambet

Translated by Kenneth Casler and Eric Ormsby

 Routledge
Taylor & Francis Group

LONDON AND NEW YORK

First published in English 2018
by Routledge
2 Park Square, Milton Park, Abingdon, Oxon OX14 4RN

and by Routledge
711 Third Avenue, New York, NY 10017

Routledge is an imprint of the Taylor & Francis Group, an informa business

Qu'est-ce que le shi'isme? By Mohammad Ali Amir-Moezzi and
Christian Jambet

© Librairie Artheme Fayard, 2004
Translated by Kenneth Casler and Eric Ormsby

Published in French by Fayard 2004

British Library Cataloguing in Publication Data
A catalogue record for this book is available from the British Library

Library of Congress Cataloging in Publication Data
Names: Amir-Moezzi, Mohammad Ali, author. | Jambet, Christian, author. |
Casler, Kenneth, translator. | Ormsby, Eric, translator.
Title: What is Shi'i Islam? : an introduction / Mohammad-Ali Amir-Moezzi
and Christian Jambet ; translated by Kenneth Casler and Eric Ormsby.
Other titles: Qu'est-ce que le shi'isme? English
Description: New York, NY : Routledge, 2018. | Series: Routledge Persian
and Shi'i studies series ; v. 3 | Includes bibliographical references and index.
Identifiers: LCCN 2017052878| ISBN 9781138093706 (hbk) |
ISBN 9781138093737 (pbk) | ISBN 9781315106441 (ebk)
Subjects: LCSH: Shi'ah. | Shi'ites. | Shi'ah--Doctrine.
Classification: LCC BP193.5 .A4513 2018 | DDC 297.8/2--dc23
LC record available at https://lccn.loc.gov/2017052878

ISBN: 978-1-138-09370-6 (hbk)
ISBN: 978-1-138-09373-7 (pbk)
ISBN: 978-1-315-10644-1 (ebk)

Typeset in Bembo
by Taylor & Francis Books

Contents

Illustrations

Figure

Map

Note

We have chosen not to transliterate Arabic or Persian terms using the conventional diacritical systems but, rather, to adopt a simplified transliteration in order to simplify matters for non-specialist readers without, however, impeding recognition of words and names by the specialist.

For the non-specialist, here are a few simple pronunciation guidelines. *Kh* resembles the Spanish *jota* or the German *ch*. S is always hard; *gh* is pronounced like a guttural *r*, and *r* like a rolled *r*. Q is pronounced gutturally.

Dates are ordinarily provided in both the Hijra and Gregorian calendars, respectively. If the word "Shi'ism" is not qualified, it refers to Twelver or Imami Shi'ism. With regard to proper names, sometimes we use the Arabic article *al*, sometimes not. Thus the reader will encounter both al-Husayn and Husayn. So too with *b*. or *ibn*: both mean "son of" as in 'Ali b. Abi Talib = 'Ali, son of Abi Talib.

In the bibliography at the end of each part, we only list publications in European languages. Readers of Arabic or other languages of Islam will find useful bibliographies in these languages in the works listed. Our bibliographies are meant to complement the footnotes in chapters and have been kept to a minimum. With a few exceptions, we make scant use of articles from specialist reference works; for more details concerning the main figures, historical events, technical topics, geographical places, titles of publications and so on, we recommend the entries in *The Encyclopaedia of Islam, Encyclopaedia Iranica, The Cambridge History of Arabic Literature, The Cambridge History of Iran, The Encyclopaedia of Religion*, etc. As a rule, we do not provide bibliographical references to articles from such publications or from generally accessible reference works.

Preface

At the time of the first publication of this book in 2004, the Western world was much less interested in Shi'ism than it is today. Since then, more and more scientific works, books and articles have appeared on the subject. One of the latter, *Shi'i Esotericism, its Roots and Developments*, M. A. Amir-Moezzi *et al.* (eds.), Brepols, 2017 (857 p.), shows clearly that interest in this minority branch of Islam goes far beyond the circle of Islamicist scholars. The Shia's themselves, no doubt exasperated by the violence of Sunni extremist movements against them, are increasingly feeling their own religious identity and are seeking, more than ever, to claim and protect the unity and power of their community. These last years, the mourning ceremonies of 'Ashura in Karbala in Iraq have brought together between 15 and 20million faithful, more than four times the pilgrims in Mecca, while the Shia's represent only one-fifth of the Muslims!

This is undoubtedly one of the reasons for the success of this book, perhaps the first synthesis of the Shi'i religion for many years and accessible to a large but non-specialized public. It has undergone several re-editions in France before appearing in 2014 in pocket edition, objective proof of its popularity. We are deeply grateful for this and thank scholars, students, researchers and those who are simply curious for the great interest they have given to our work.

Today, we are also very deeply happy with the publication of the English translation of our book. We warmly thank its translators, Kenneth Casler and Eric Ormsby, as well as the Institute of Ismaili Studies (London) for funding this translation. We also warmly thank our friend and colleague Prof. Andrew J. Newman for accepting this translation in the Persian and Shi'i Studies series, which he edits in the old and prestigious publishing house Routledge.

Mohammad Ali Amir-Moezzi (MAAM) & Christian Jambet (CJ)

Introduction

The title of a book should be self-explanatory, particularly if it is formulated as a question. It should require no further justification, except perhaps to reassure the reader that the authors will provide an answer. In any event, it may be useful if we briefly outline our intentions here at the outset.

For some time we have studied the religion, civilization and philosophy of Islam – more precisely Shi'i Islam or Shi'ism[1] – a vast domain of beliefs and narratives. In passionate debate with non-specialists, we have often encountered wry smiles, irony, even a whiff of fear, as though Shi'ism were something shocking, something sulphurous or perhaps even evil. Our students, who share our curiosity, are quick to admit that Shi'ism is worthy of scientific attention. But for the public at large, Shi'ism more usually implies a host of confused representations, suggesting more often than not obscurantism, intolerance, political violence and other ignominies running hot or cold in response to world events. For most people, in fact, Shi'ism stands for "radical Islam", or – worse – "Islamic terrorism".

The Western world woke up to the existence of the Shia when the Iranian Islamic Revolution overthrew the last Shah in 1978–1979. Collective memory continues to brim with powerful images of that revolution: the exalted masses in Tehran awaiting the return of Ayatollah Khomeini; the appearance on our television screens of turbaned dignitaries from a bygone age; women shrouded in veils; crowds vociferous in their hatred of the Great Satan; the return of a great nation to an age of theology and religious absolutism; the political condemnation of writers and poets; the banning of what we in the West consider to be essential freedoms. Nothing can erase these images, which still trigger strong emotions and trick us into thinking that we understand what is going on. But images do not permit us to engage with, let alone comprehend, the phenomena they represent.

And now, in Iraq, Syria and Yemen, the Shia are again the focus of attention. New images combine with old: mass pilgrimages to holy sites and cities; dignitaries and pilgrims assassinated in religious sanctuaries; entire cities under absolutist moral authority; disturbing silence and worrying political anticipation. In some respects, nothing is more familiar than Shi'ism, and nothing is more misunderstood. For some twenty years, the media have increased their coverage of the phenomenon. Never, or only rarely, do they formulate the question we ask here: what is Shi'ism? What is this belief that inspires millions and millions of people dispersed throughout the world?

Excessive simplification of the issues has given rise to a twofold illusion. On the one hand, Shi'ism is reduced to a narrow political notion as if, since time imme-morial, it has represented little more than a political ideology focused on the conquest of the state and the formation of a strict Islamic Republic. The forgotten role the Shia once played in the Middle East – and will no doubt play again in the future – has driven its long and colourful history into the shadows, silencing its wonderfully complex beliefs and ideas. On the other hand, Shi'ism is seen rather surprisingly as "another" Islam, as something that does not in fact belong to Islam at all; at least not to the true, orthodox Islam. It is well known that Shi'i and Sunni doctrines are different. But too often, and too quickly, the conclusion is drawn that Shi'ism is a marginal heretical sect, fundamentally alien to the deeper truth of the great religion of Islam, thrust by historical accident onto the political stage. Shi'ism either speaks the truth of Islam, meaning that it is a truth of terror; or it is entirely foreign to Islam and, therefore, merits outright rejection, as Islamic fundamentalists and individuals too clever by half repeatedly claim.

Our intention here is not to mount arguments against such simplifications. Rather we will attempt to explain why they have taken root in the first place in the minds of a learned public. This effort will require – in as few pages as possible – a genealogy and history of the ideas which transformed a deeply spiritual belief – the original Shi'ism – into its exact opposite: a form of political power. (When we say "original Shi'ism", our reference is to the thoughts and practices found in the earliest texts available to us.) Our inquiry will show that Shi'ism is not a phenomenon without flaws. It is torn by internal strife, not only between factions and rival groups but also in the outlook and experiences of individual Shi'i scholars; it is torn by its own conflicts between a spiritual, metaphysical pole and a legal pole, which today are the drivers of a particular ideology and religious regime in Iran.

Amid the heat of Iran's Islamic Revolution, Michel Foucault published sev-eral sensational articles in which he spoke of a "religious political programme". His work drew attention to an important fact: an Islamic spirituality had proved itself capable of fomenting a political movement, which in turn could not be explained by the usual historical causes (i.e. material, social and economic factors). Religion had ceased to be a shallow ideology and had moved to the very core of a genuine historical process. Foucault's idea was not new, but it had an impact on Western public opinion, which had become increasingly forgetful of its own religious past and ignorant of the impact of these traditions in other parts of the world. At the same time, his phraseology obscured the very object it sought to clarify. Yes, the Shi'ism of the mullahs had become a religiously inspired political movement. But how did this conjunction of dis-cordant notions – religion and politics – come to be? Is there not a Shi'i spiri-tuality that is perhaps resistant to any form of politics? Foucault offered no answers to such fundamental questions.

Whether we as authors have any claim to originality will be for the reader to decide. We believe the project itself embodies its own originality. We will offer an explanation of what Shi'ism is, refraining from a discussion of what certain Shia either said or did. It is in this regard that our book differs from others that provide helpful insights into Shi'i Islam (cf. the works of Said Amir Arjomand, Heinz Halm, Moojan Momem and Yann Richard). When specialists narrate the story of Shi'ism's various currents, they often leave the many details of its doctrines in the dark. They forget to pose the one question that might legitimately be asked: what do the Shia really think and believe? How do they see the world? How do they see themselves? We propose to focus our attention on the particulars of Shi'i thought and on the inner workings of the Shi'i mind. We will take a middle road between existing general works and more specialized studies (e.g. those of Jean Calmard, Etan Kohlberg, Wilfred Madelung and others).

We do not aim to provide a historical analysis of events in the Islamic world, beginning with the Great Discord – the principal cause of division in Islam as early as its first century – and continuing to the present day. Nor will we narrate the history of Sunni and Shi'i caliphates from the rise of the Umayyads to the decline of the Ottomans. We will not tell the stories of the Abbasids, the Fatimids or the minor dynasties that ruled the House of Islam. And we will not tell the history of modern Islam or the history of the economic and political events that have left a mark on Islamic lands where Shi'ism is dominant. We will not present an anthropology of the mourning festivals and rituals or provide a description of the daily lives of the clerics and the faithful. We will not discuss controversies about the veil or education in religious schools. There are many excellent books on these topics. Instead, we will turn our attention to the very heart and soul of Shi'ism; we will explore its innermost spirit, and as far as we are able, we will reconstruct its various religious truths.

In our view, it is important to emphasize the religious fact of Islam per se. Once upon a time, Shi'ism played a crucial role in the history of empires; but above all else, it was – and is today – a religion; a religion revealed to a prophet, Muhammad; a religion whose revealed essence is communicated through the letters, the verses and the suras of the Qur'an. The Holy Book is the foundation of the religious fact of Islam. But, as the reader will discover, the Holy Book itself is problematic. A fundamental feature of Shi'ism is its approach to and questioning of the Holy Book itself, both in terms of its existence and its composition. Our study will explore the numerous complex doctrines that gradually gave rise to Shi'ism or, more accurately, to several Shi'isms. We argue that an understanding of what the Shia think is fundamental to the analysis and comprehension of what they decide, do, experience and endure.

Does this mean that historical considerations are absent from our work? Not at all. The evolution of religious doctrines, rituals and theories – theology, jurisprudence, philosophy and expressions of piety – is very much part of social history. In fact, the evolution of doctrine offers a valuable gloss on history. It provides evidence for how the faithful – and the learned elite, well schooled in the wisdom of books – came to support a given political position. In our view, the key to social and political history is nearly always found in the history of religion. It provides a backdrop, explains the structure of social and political forms, and establishes the horizon for a vision of the world. But this only appears to be a paradox. The study of Shi'ism as a religious phenomenon is not at all inconsistent with the study of the life of Shi'i communities. On the contrary, it helps to explain community life more accurately. For this reason, our approach combines the methods of history – specifically the history of texts – and the methods of phenomenology – the phenomenology of the Shi'i mind. In our view, this is neither impossible nor absurd. Our method takes the middle path between a historicism that neglects fundamental spirituality and a phenomenology that ignores history.

As always, it is imperative to acknowledge the decisive contribution of Henry Corbin in the study of Shi'i spirituality. Nevertheless, we feel obliged to explain how and why our work stands apart from his. In 1971, Corbin published the first volume of his *En islam iranien*. It was the first publication providing an educated audience with access to the doctrines of Twelver Shi'ism. Until then Corbin's work as a philosopher and an Orientalist had remained the preserve of specialists. Aside from his great work, *Creative Imagination in the Sufism of Ibn 'Arabi* and certain chapters of his *History of Islamic Philosophy*, very few people were familiar with his vast pioneering work in the field of spiritual Islam. A fortiori, Corbin's tireless study of Shi'ism was known to only a handful of experts despite his incessant – if occasionally disillusioned – efforts to attract the interest of his fellow philosophers.

In 1971, volume one of *En islam iranien* finally revealed Shi'ism to a broader audience. Corbin's arguments are difficult to summarize but a few remarks may prove helpful. He argued that in contrast to the doctrines of Sunni Islam, Shi'ism never confuses political power and religious authority. It always maintains a healthy distance between the history of political events and the history of spiritual phenomena. He also argued that the imam deeply venerated by the Shi'i faithful represents a non-political focus of attention in Islam and provides an antidote to the temptations of secularization and involvement in historical events. In short the imam protects against the profanation of man's spiritual destiny. When the Iranian Revolution erupted in 1979, barely eight years after the publication of Corbin's magnum opus, and only a few days after he died, it appeared to sound the death knell to this argument. Who can say what thoughts the Iranian revolution might have inspired in Corbin? In the words of Hegel, philosophy always arrives too late.

This is not the place to debate whether Corbin erred in his analysis. Moreover, it is hardly a question of right or wrong. Corbin never held illusions about Shi'i clerics; he understood them all too well. His intention was to explain the "philosophical and spiritual aspects" of Shi'ism. He was not interested in the theological and legal schools, which in his opinion misrepresented "the essence of Shi'ism". The fact that the clamour of history may have obscured a few great philosophers and spiritual masters would scarcely have surprised him. Such, he knew, is the pattern of all human history. For Corbin, the living essence of spiritual Islam was a rare, hidden and living reality in the hearts of the faithful. Everything else was harmful and useless shadow play. Indeed, Corbin may have erred to excess on the side of essentialism.

We who have the doubtful privilege of witnessing recent events, having the great gift of hindsight, must now rise to a challenge that Corbin did not have either the time or the opportunity to confront. While remaining faithful to his phenomenological analyses, we too must face up to history and in so doing distance ourselves from him on occasion. We must endeavour to refashion the history of Shi'i thought and, at the outset, include in our account schools of thought that Corbin left by the wayside, not wilfully but because he felt so strongly that any scholar's life is simply too brief to appease the yearning for matters of the spirit. But despite our seeming disloyalty, we remain faithful to the example Corbin has bequeathed us; we do so by attempting to understand how what he admired so deeply in Shi'ism was transformed into its very opposite, which he vehemently opposed, along the lines of Wahhabi Sunnism (and we see where that has led!) – that is, into what he most abhorred: the clergy in power.

A further point of method must be noted. We have made considerable use of original sources. Despite their antiquity, many of these sources came into being rather late, at least with respect to the origins of Islam, Muhammad's prophecies and the first imams. Like it or not, we are dependent on a vast corpus of texts, many written long after their authors pronounced the words attributed to them. As stated, it is not our intent to resurrect the "truth" of original Islam, but rather to recover the truth of Shi'ism's representation of Islam in concrete terms and as it was lived. After all, the phenomenon later known as Shi'ism was in fact the first movement of thought and action to take shape in the years immediately following the death of the Prophet Muhammad. By a strange quirk of history, Sunnism – mainstream Islam today – achieved its inner coherence in opposition to Shi'ism: when it affirmed the authority of Muhammad's successors, the first three caliphs; when it developed a science for authenticating Islamic acts and sayings (the hadith); when it developed a body of theoretical practices under the caliphate of 'Uthman and with the decisive contributions of Ibn Hanbal. The history of the rupture between Shi'ism and Sunnism has been told many times. Our approach begins with the texts as they exist, without pronouncing judgment on them, simply taking them as the starting point for our argument.

Finally it is necessary to recall a few particular facts. Islam is not a unified religion with a central magisterium. It knows neither orthodoxies nor heresies such as an organized Church might assert. In Islam the main division is between Sunnism and Shi'ism. Each branch claims to be the true orthodoxy. But Sunnism itself is protean in form. There is little in common between a literalist Hanbali scholar bound to a scrupulous respect of religious law and a mystic meditating the work of Ibn 'Arabi. There are few similarities between a

Hanbali mystic such as the marvellous Sufi al-Ansari, whose tomb in Herat, Afghanistan, was recently desecrated by the Taliban, and those same ignorant and fanatical Hanbalis who profaned his tomb, blithely unaware that it was a place of pilgrimage for their own religious brethren! There is more affinity between the spiritual exaltation of a Sunni or Sufi poet and the beliefs of a Shia rapt in the love of his inner imam than between the doctrinaire experts of an Islamic State fulminating from rival "camps". The essential differences lie elsewhere.

Whatever the depth of Sunni feelings for the Prophet's family, there is no question of granting its members a divine calling either equal or superior to the Prophet's own. Every Sunni venerates 'Ali ibn Abi Talib, his wife Fatima and their sons Hasan and Husayn, grandsons of the Prophet. With the exception of the Wahhabis, who with their political power and propaganda stand apart from other Muslims, no Sunni would tolerate expressions of hatred and anathema discrediting the saints of Islam. But Sunnis do not focus their devotion on the saints or venerate them to the degree that even the most humble of the Shi'i faithful express. For the Sunnis, who direct their devotion and meditation elsewhere, the saints of Islam are not manifestations of God. Sunni Islam reproves, indeed condemns, any form of association or confusion of God with his creatures. By contrast all Shia, whatever their internal divergences, unite around a living cult of the imams who descend from the family of the Prophet.

It is important to note that the Sunni and Shi'i worlds do not represent two disconnected, geographically separate communities. Both exist side by side around the globe. Admittedly Shi'ism is virtually absent from the Maghreb (though some spiritual inheritances are worth closer attention in this regard). And Shi'ism is generally absent from "Western" Islam. But it is prevalent in its traditional lands in the Near East and Middle East, from the Lebanon to Iraq and from Iran to Bahrain. It has a strong presence in Muslim Asia, from the Caucasus to India, and in the Arabian Peninsula, for example, in Yemen. The Shi'i diaspora extends even into Africa.

As for the history of Shi'ism, we will follow its broad outlines using the periods established by Henry Corbin. The first period commences with the life of the imams (the existence of a close circle of followers and a growing "party" of 'Ali). It ends with the "Major Occultation" of the Twelfth Imam (329/940). The second period extends from the "occultation" through to the 13th/17th century. During this period the great works of the Twelver Shi'i tradition were written – the period of the doctors of the Law and the theologians, the philosophers and the jurists. The third period includes the fall of Baghdad and the Mongol invasion that toppled the Abbasid capital, and it extends through to the adoption of Shi'ism as the Iranian state religion in the 10th/16th century. It was a prolific period in terms of Shi'i doctrinal and mystical writings, and it witnessed a confluence of the spiritual currents of Shi'ism and the great ideas of Sunnism, which resulted in many significant works. The fourth and final period begins with the reign of the Safavids in Iran. It too witnessed a flourishing of Shi'i philosophy and many dazzling expressions of culture and civilization. It also witnessed the accelerated development of a particular tendency at the very heart of Shi'ism; namely, the progressive evolution of an ideology that led first to Shi'ism becoming an instrument of state power and then to the emergence of political Shi'ism, itself the culmination of the whole long history of those earlier periods. In the present work, we will describe and analyze this evolution.

Our work has the perhaps impossible task of dealing with all four of these great historical periods and demonstrating, among other things, how a lateral approach may lead in some way from an esoteric and mystical Shi'ism, such as it appears in the foundational texts, to the temporary triumph of a legalistic and rationalistic Shi'ism only to culminate at the end in a political form of Shi'ism. And yet another tendency, no less lateral, stands in opposition to this ideological tendency: Shi'i wisdom, the wisdom of an esoteric, philosophical and mystical Shi'ism.

Is there any need to add that our work is in no way intended to be either apologetic or derogatory? In the pages that follow we have only one aim, and that is to enhance understanding in some small measure.

We would not have been able to realize such a project without the staunch support which our friend Olivier Bétourné has given us through his advice, his trust and his reading of the text, for all of which we are deeply grateful.

Note

1 Shi'ism is also spelled Shiism. We prefer to use "Shi'ism" in order to keep faith with a long scholarly tradition and also because this spelling makes the Arabic origins of the word Shi'a clear, conveying the meaning "party", "group of faithful", with an English ending added on. Arab-speaking Sunni Muslims (*ahl al-sunna*) commonly refer to the Shia as *al-shi'a*, which carries a negative connotation. The Shia themselves use different terms in self-reference. Shi'ism, spelled in this way, has only one justification: to refer to its traditional use in Orientalism.

Bibliography

Some general works

M.A. Amir-Moezzi, *L'islam degli sciiti. Dalla saggezza mistica alla tentazione politica*, Bologna: EDB, 2016.

M.A. Amir-Moezzi & P. Lory, *Petite histoire de l'islam*, Paris: Librio, 2007.

Sadir Amir Arjomand, *The Shadow of God and the Hidden Imam*, Chicago: University of Chicago Press, 1984.

L. Capezzone & M. Salati, *L'Islam sciita. Storia di una minoranza*, Roma: Lavoro, 2006.

William C. Chittick, *A Shi'ite Anthology*, Albany, NY: State University of New York Press, 1981.

F. Daftary, *A History of Shi'i Islam*, London: I.B. Tauris, 2014.

F. Daftary & G. Miskinzoda (eds), *The Study of Shi'i Islam: History, Theology and Law*, London: I.B. Tauris, 2014.

Dwight M. Donaldson, *The Shi'ite Religion. A History of Islam in Persia and Irak*, London: Luzak and Company, 1933.

Graham Fuller & Francke Rend, *The Arab Shi'a: the Forgotten Muslims*, Basingstoke: Palgrave Macmillan, 1999.

Geneviève Gobillot, *Les Chiites*, Belgium: Brepols, 1998.

Najam Haider, *Shi'i Islam. An Introduction*, Cambridge: Cambridge University Press, 2014.

Heinz Halm, *Die Schia*, Darmstadt: Wissenschaftliche Buchgesellschaft, 1988.

Heinz Halm, *Der schiitische Islam. Von der Religion zur Revolution*, Munich: C.H. Beck, 1994. [*Shi'a Islam: From Religion to Revolution*, English trans. by A. Brown, Princeton, NJ: Wiener, 1997.]

John Hollister, *The Shi'a of India*, London: Luzac and Company, 1953.

S. Jafri & M. Hussain, *The Origins and Early Development of Shi'a Islam*, London: Longmans, 1979.

E. Kohlberg (ed.), *Shi'ism*, Aldershot: Ashgate, 2003.

Moojan Momen, *An Introduction to Shi'i Islam*, New Haven, CT: Yale University Press, 1985.

Yitzhak Nakash, *The Shi'is of Iraq*, Princeton, NJ: Princeton University Press, 1994.

Monika Pohl-Schoberlein, *Die schiitische Gemeinschaft des Südlibanon (Jabal 'Amil) innerhalb des libanesischen konfessionellen Systems*, Berlin: K. Schwarz, 1986.

Yann Richard, *L'Islam chi'ite: croyances et ideologies*, Paris: Fayard, 1991.

Sayid A. Rizvi, *A Socio-Intellectual History of the Isna 'Ashari Shi'is in India*, Canberra: Ma'rifat Publishing House, 1986.

Biancamaria Scarcia Amoretti, *Sciiti nel mondo*, Rome: Jouvence, 1994.

Jafar Sobhani, *Doctrines of Shi'i Islam*, trans. Reza Shah Kazemi, London: I.B. Tauris, 2001. [The author is a Shi'i religious scholar.]

Rudolf Strothmann, *Die Zwölfer-Schi'a. Zwei Religionsgeschichtliche Charakterbilder aus der Mongolenzeit*, Leipzig: Harrassowitz, 1926.

Muhammad Husayn Tabataba'i, *Shiite Islam*, trans. Seyyed Hossein Nasr, Albany, NY: State University of New York, 1977. [The author is a Shi'i religious scholar.]

C. Turner & P. Luft (eds), *Shi'ism: Critical Concepts in Islamic Studies*, Abingdon: Routledge, 2007.

Jacques Weulersse, *Le Pays des Alouites*, 2 vols, Tours: Arrault, 1940.

Part I

Doctrinal foundations: The early beginnings of Shi'ism

1 Origins and conceptions of the world

Shi'ism is the oldest religious current in Islam, for what may be called its core principle dates from the time when the problem of succession to the Prophet Muhammad first arose. Shi'ism is the largest of the Muslim minority movements and is considered by the "orthodox" Sunni majority to be Islam's most significant "heterodoxy"; that is, "heresy". To be sure, the Shia themselves hold their doctrine to be the supreme "orthodoxy" of Islam.

The Arabic word *shi'a* – meaning party, faction, faithful – came to be used gradually as an antonomasiac designation of what appears to have been the first of several political-religious "parties" to emerge within the Muslim community; it was the party of those who claimed the exclusive right of 'Ali b. Abi Talib, cousin and son-in-law of the Prophet, and of his descendants, to guide the community in spiritual and worldly matters. According to the tradition, at the time of Muhammad's death in 11/632, two different conceptions of who should succeed the Prophet collided. A majority of Muslims claimed that Muhammad had not clearly designated his successor and resorted, therefore, to the ancestral tradition of electing a tribal ruler. Thus, a counsel of the Prophet's Companions, together with influential members of the most powerful clans of the Meccan tribes, appointed a venerable figure who was advanced in years and came from Muhammad's own tribe of the Quraysh. Their choice fell on Abu Bakr, the Prophet's old Companion and one of his several fathers-in-law. Accordingly, Abu Bakr became the first caliph (*khalifa*) of the new community (the technical meaning of the title seems to have developed later), and thus his followers are the ancestors of those later designated as "Sunnis".

The followers of 'Ali were on the opposing side. They maintained that Muhammad had clearly designated 'Ali as his successor. He had done so, they argued, on several occasions in various ways, directly and indirectly. In their view it could hardly have been otherwise: how could the Prophet have left the important matter of his successor in abeyance? Could he have been so indifferent to the future leadership of his community as to leave it in uncertainty and confusion? This would be contrary to the very spirit of the Qur'an, in accord with which the successors of the great prophets of the past had been chosen from among the closest family members, who were privileged by blood ties as well as by initiation into the mysteries of their religion. True, the Qur'an does recommend seeking counsel in certain instances, but never in matters concerning the succession of prophets, which is fundamentally an issue of divine election. As far as his followers – those later called Shia – were concerned, 'Ali was this chosen heir, designated by Muhammad and confirmed by the Qur'an. In this instance, 'Ali's youth – a dissuading handicap for the adherents of ancestral tribal customs – was not of any particular importance. We will return to this point later. 'Ali is thus deemed by Shia to be their first imam (guide, leader, chieftain; like the term "caliph", the technical meaning of the word *imam* came much later). The concept of imam referred to the true leader of the community, even if he did not effectively hold power. and as we shall see, the figure of the imam will become the central notion in the Shi'i religion, which never employs the term "caliph" to designate its leader.

Thus Shi'ism is as old as the dispute over who should succeed the Prophet of Islam. Even so, it cannot be reduced to this alone. The Alid claim of legitimacy is just the starting point for monumental doctrinal developments in which the central issue of the "prophetic inheritance" acquires numerous complex meanings. These in turn shed light on important historical events. For this reason, though it may seem odd at first, we find it more apt and more illuminating to present the doctrinal issues in all their specificity before dealing with historical events. In the case of Shi'ism – and no doubt in all religious systems which base their legitimacy on ideas, practices and texts held to be sacred – doctrinal history goes hand in hand with general history, if indeed it does not shape that history to a large extent. When the essential aim is to reveal the true meaning of sacred things, when the mode of understanding and the mode of being impact on and co-determine one another, what is experienced becomes an essentially hermeneutic situation. Thus, the beliefs, the articles of faith and the very ideas will have as their fundamental mission the revealing of the true but hidden meaning of existence. Relying on historical and critical method, our aim is nothing less than to restore to historical events their inherent density, which often goes unrecognized.

What, then, are the specifics, the spiritual bases, of Shi'ism? What doctrinal characteristics distinguish it from other Islamic religious movements? When we consider the texts, the oldest sources that have come down to us (compiled for the most part between 250/864 and 350/961), it quickly becomes clear just how very rich and teeming – indeed, at times, chaotic – the Shi'i religion actually is. The divers origins out of which these ideas emerged or, indeed, even the profusion of tendencies that have become discernible over time, do not explain everything.

The earliest extant texts reveal Shi'ism to be a vast and amazingly complex edifice. Theology and Qur'anic exegesis rub shoulders with esotericism; jurisprudence exists side by side with magic; cosmogonic myths coexist with devotional practices. For reasons to do with certain teachings, information can be dispersed quite intentionally; the narrative of chapters can appear confused, the plot broken. Moreover, the sheer volume of texts may momentarily frustrate the researcher who struggles to impose cohesion and clarity. Teachings are frequently presented piecemeal in countless texts and in traditions (hadith) dating back to the time of the imams. They require an effort of collection, compilation and classification in order to clarify a single idea in its entirety.

True, the extraordinary range of doctrinal developments, the striking abundance of Shi'i literature in so many areas (exegesis, theology, mysticism, law, philosophy, historiography) or, indeed, the sheer intellectual force of so many different authors offer objective if implicit proof of a fundamental coherence, even though at times it may seem hard to discern. The following synthesis, the fruit of many years of study and the scrutiny of thousands of pages, represents an attempt to draw out this underlying coherence, thereby making possible a better comprehension both of structural features and of points of detail.

The central axis around which all Shi'i doctrine revolves is the figure of the imam. In Sunni Islam the term has no particular importance; it can designate a chief, a ruler, a religious scholar or a prayer leader. But for the Shia it is a sacred title. Simplified to the extreme, Shi'ism might even be termed predominantly an "imamology". In every respect – from theology to ethics, law, exegesis, cosmology, ritual and eschatology – every aspect of doctrine, every principle of faith derives in the final analysis from a conception of the imam as the "Guide" and has no meaning apart from him. Shi'ism itself is ordered around a dual conception of the world. We will see how the figure of the imam is ever-present in all of Shi'ism's different manifestations and serves as its true centre of gravity.

A dual vision

All reality, from the highest to the most trivial, has at least two aspects: a manifest or visible one (in Arabic, *zahir*) and a secret or hidden one (*batin*), concealed under visible reality and capable of containing even more hidden levels (*batin al-batin*). This dialectic of the manifest and the hidden (the exoteric and the esoteric) – the two are distinct, yet interdependent – expresses a basic article of faith ever-present in the minds of thinkers and the learned elite but also pervading the beliefs of the masses of the faithful. How does this dialectic express itself in the different religious disciplines?

We turn first to its expressions in theology. God encompasses two levels of being, two ontological planes. The first is Essence, considered incomprehensible, unimaginable, beyond all knowledge and thought. This hidden esoteric level of God is the absolute unknowable "abscondity" of God. But if the matter went no further, there would be no relationship, no possible communication between the Creator and his creatures. Therefore, God in His Goodness caused to be born in His own Being another level: the level of Names and Attributes through which He reveals Himself and makes Himself known. This revealed exoteric level of God is no longer "God the Unknowable", but "God the Unknown", or God "Who desires to be known". It recalls the *Deus absconditus* and *Deus revelatus* of medieval Christian theology. Names and Attributes function in creation through vehicles and divine Instruments, that are the physical places of God's manifestation in so many theophanies. The most important theophany, the highest locus of revelation of the divine Names – that is, what can be known about God – is a metaphysical being that various Shi'i authors at different periods called the Imam in Heaven[1]: the Imam of Light, the Cosmic Man. This refers to the Imam (always upper-case "I") in his universal ontological acceptation. Knowledge of his reality is thus equivalent to what can be known about God, since the true revealed God – He who manifests what can be manifested in God – is the Cosmic Imam.

The Cosmic Imam in turn also possesses a hidden dimension and a manifest aspect. His esoteric aspect – his unrevealed face – is precisely his metaphysical cosmic aspect – "in the heavens" is the formulation of the earliest sources. His exoteric aspect – his physical manifestation in the visible world – is expressed in the historic imams (lower-case "i") who live in the various time cycles of sacred History. These considerations point us in the direction of another discipline: prophetology.

The Shia believe that each great prophet, each messenger from above, is accompanied in his mission by one or more imams. It has been so since Adam, the First Man and the first prophet, until Muhammad, the "Seal of the Prophesy", by way of many others: Enoch, Noah, Abraham, Joseph, Moses, Solomon or Jesus, among others. Throughout all the many cycles, the great messengers and great imams have been connected by an uninterrupted chain of prophets, imams and minor saints who form the great family of the "Friends of God" (*awliya'*, plural of *wali*), those who possess and transmit the divine Covenant, the *walaya* – a central tenet of Shi'ism which refers, among other things, to the imamate. They are the physical places of manifestation of the archetypal Cosmic Imam, his revealed face. Thus knowledge of what is knowable in God, the supreme mystery of being, begins with knowledge of the man of God or, more precisely, the Man-God, for he is the theophanic man. Knowledge of whom results in knowledge of universal Man, the mirror wherein the divine Names and Attributes find their reflection.

Why is this so? The "Friends of God" transmit to mankind the Word of God. At particular moments in time the Word of God is revealed through Books, Holy Scriptures, brought by the great law-giving prophets, those the Qur'an describes as "endowed with firm determination" (*ulu'l-'azm*). Though lists of names may vary, the most frequently named prophets are Noah, Abraham, Moses, Jesus and Muhammad.[2] Furthermore, since the Revelation appeared in the form of a Book, the divine Word has both a manifest exoteric aspect and a secret esoteric aspect: a "letter" beneath which the "spirit" lies concealed. Of course, the prophet-messenger knows both levels. However his mission is to transmit the letter of the Revelation – the exoteric level, "that which has descended" (*al-tanzil*) – to the greatest number of people, to the ordinary faithful of his community. As we pointed out above, a prophet is accompanied in his mission by one or more imams.[3] By virtue of a strict parallelism and complementarity, the imam's mission lies precisely in revealing the secret of its origin (*ta'wil*), not to all but to a small number of initiates, the elite of the community. The Shia thus affirm their minority position in the community as a sign of election. Without the imam's initiatory teachings, the text of the Revelation will not convey its full depth; it is a letter whose spirit remains unknown. This is why the Qur'an is called the silent Book, the mute Guide, and why the imam is called the speaking Qur'an. Though the Prophet, of course, knows both levels, he remains the messenger of the exoteric aspect of the faith or of that exoteric religion which Shi'i technical terminology designates as *islam* (literally submission, or submission to the letter of the Revelation), which makes the ordinary faithful *muslims* (those who submit or "muslims"). Parallel to this, the imam is the messenger of the esoteric aspect of the Revelation, the initiator of the spiritual religion that lies hidden beneath the letter, known technically as *iman*, literally "faith". Therefore, the people of the faith – the "faithful believers" or *mu'min* – are those initiated into the secrets of the religion; the men of the esoteric; the followers of the imams; in a word, the "shia". This is why all religions have had their majority "muslims" and their minority "shia"; a throng of "exoteric folk" incapable of profundity, and an elite made up of the "people of the esoteric" initiated into the spiritual layers of the faith. Historical Shia, descending from historical Islam, are thus the final link in a long initiatory chain tracing its origin back to Adam and to the initiated "shia" of his imam Seth.[4] What then is the initiatory teaching of these successive imams? Its ultimate message is the unveiling of the mysteries of God, of man and of the world; that is, in Shi'i terms, the mysteries of the Imam: Man manifesting in creation the revealed God, the Secret of Secrets in all religions. The historical, the earthly imams are, so to speak, keepers and transmitters of a secret, the essence of which is very precisely the metaphysical Imam.

This dual conception of the world can be delineated on a table of "terms of complementarity" based on the dialectic of the manifest and the hidden.

Manifest	*Hidden*
exoteric (*zahir*)	esoteric (*batin*)
Names and Attributes	Essence
Prophet (*rasul, nabi*)	*Imam/wali*
Prophecy (*nubuwwa*)	Imamate/*walaya*
letter of the Revelation (*tanzil*)	spiritual hermeneutic (*ta'wil*)
submission to the exoteric (*islam*)	initiation into the esoteric religion (*iman*)
majority/ordinary masses	minority/elite

A dualistic vision

In Shi'ism, alongside this dual conception, another fundamental belief exists. It is a dualistic vision of the world. The history of creation is the history of a cosmic struggle between the forces of Good and Evil, between light and darkness. Given the central role of initiation and knowledge in Shi'ism, as we have just seen, it can be affirmed that knowledge is the Good and ignorance the Evil. The struggle between the respective forces of these two universal but antagonistic powers is woven into the very fabric of life.

According to cosmogonic traditions, the characteristic feature of the Creation from the very beginning is the battle between the opposing Armies of cosmic Intelligence (*al-'aql*) and cosmic Ignorance (*al-jahl*). These, in turn, are symbols and archetypes of the Imam and his followers on the one side and of the Enemy of the Imam and his henchmen on the other. This primeval struggle has an echo in every age and in every historical cycle throughout all time. It pits the Friends of God (i.e. the prophets and the imams) and their faithful followers against the forces of Ignorance. Using Qur'anic expressions, Shi'i texts tell of the constant struggle between the People of the Right (*ashab al-yamin*) and the People of the Left (*ashab al-shimal*). According to the theories of complex, if not obscure, cycles, the world has experienced two kinds of government since its creation: the government of God under which the prophets and the imams – Guides of Light and Justice – have been able to teach their esoteric truths openly; and the government of Satan under which the practice and teaching of truths has necessarily remained secret because the world is under the influence of the Guides of darkness and injustice. As Satan is the adversary (*didd*) of Adam, the history of Adamic humanity has been marked by adversity and the brutality of the demonic forces of Ignorance. Such forces represent the majority and are always dominant throughout Adamic time; they relegate the minority – the persecuted initiates – to the periphery and isolation. Such circumstances will reign until the End of Time, until the advent of the Mahdi, the eschatological Saviour who will overcome the forces of Evil once and for all. This is because with the advent of every religion, the Guides of Injustice usurp power, and a majority emerges in the community that refuses to believe in the existence of a hidden meaning beneath the letter even though that majority lives in subjugation to the letter of religion. Under the authority of the Guides of Ignorance, the majority abandons the most meaningful aspects of its religion and condemns itself to decadence and violence.

The Adversaries, that is, the Enemy of the imam and his followers – to use the technical terms of Shi'ism – are not necessarily pagans or unbelievers or followers of other religions. Neither the Israelites who betrayed Moses by worshipping the Golden Calf nor the Companions of Muhammad who refused the election of 'Ali were non-Jews or non-Muslims; rather, they were those who rejected the esoteric aspect of religion (*walaya*) when they rejected the initiated Guide and the Imam, who is his herald. The Shia call these adversaries the people of the exoteric – the people of appearances – or the people of the surface (*ahl al-zahir*, depending on the different meanings of *zahir*); in short, people in thrall to the literal meaning of religion, Muslims who have gone astray (*muslim dall*). From a strict doctrinal point of view, an initiated Shia will feel much closer to a Jewish or Christian "shia" – that is, a person initiated into the arcana of Judaism and Christianity – than to an exoteric Sunni Muslim, who is seen as an adversary. Furthermore, most of the early texts praise the Shia in a general way, while some do make a distinction between "true Shia" – that is, those few who have been initiated into the teachings of the imams – and "surface Shia" – that is, the many who have only a superficial knowledge of the doctrines and who can easily fall into error.

Within such a context of fierce and stubborn struggle which pits the forces of initiation and counter-initiation against one another – the result of a radically dualistic conception of the world – two important factors must be considered. The first is discretion. In order to protect his life and ensure his own safety and that of his Guide and fellow companions, as well as the integrity of his doctrine, he must practise discretion. To protect what is secret, the discipline of the arcana (usually termed *taqiyya* and *kitman*) is a canonical obligation for the Shia. For Adamic humanity, under the rule of Satan, the revelation of secret teachings provokes not only incredulity and derision but also incomprehension, denunciation, persecution and violence.

Then there is something else, something arising from the realm of feeling, from a profound intention, whose essential character is accentuated with tireless repetition in the texts: the believing Shia is constantly summoned to an undying love, to an unassailable loyalty and utter submission to his imam – in short, to all the virtues required of a disciple with respect to his master. The term used to name this deep emotion, which transforms faith into a transformative inner experience, is, yet again, *walaya* – a term we have evoked above more than once.

The believer is urged, at the same time, to detach himself from the imam's adversaries and to practice *bara'a*. In a world dominated by war and its pressures, a sacred alliance (*walaya*) between the initiatory Guide and the knowledge he transmits can only be achieved if it involves a "sacred" separation (*bara'a*) from the people whose sole aim is to destroy true knowledge and its possessors. In this conception of the world, no neutrality is possible. Whether he wishes it or not – whether he even knows it or not – every human being takes part in this war. He either deliberately joins the forces of knowledge or he supports the forces of Ignorance, willingly or – by remaining indifferent or adopting a neutral stance – unwillingly.

This dualistic vision can also be formulated in terms of a dialectic of Good and Evil as shown in these opposites:

Good/Knowledge	*Evil/Ignorance*
Cosmic Intelligence (*al-'aql*)	Cosmic Ignorance (*al-jahl*)
The Imam and his followers	The Imam's Enemy (*'aduww*) and his henchmen
Guides of light, justice, direction	Guides of darkness, injustice, misdirection
People of the Right	People of the Left
Love/Alliance (*walaya*)	Separation/Hate (*bara'a*)

This twofold conception of the world appears to be a particular characteristic of Shi'i faith. The dual notion of reality, expressed in "complementary pairings", can be shown in terms of a vertical axis symbolizing initiation, for the transition from the manifest to the hidden, from the exoteric to the esoteric, by the intermediary of the imam's sacred teachings brings one closer to the Divine and to an understanding of the mysteries of being. So too in this dualistic vision of the world can we can use a horizontal axis, symbolizing struggle, to illustrate the "oppositional pairings" locked in a universal and timeless conflict between knowledge and ignorance.

Iniation and struggle – the entire historical destiny of Shi'ism can be understood as a tension between these two constants which are all its own. For Shi'ism, initiation determines the spirituality of humanity, while struggle determines its history. The believer is constantly summoned to maintain his equilibrium at the very point where these two intersect. As now must be obvious, the role of the imam is seen to be everywhere both fundamental and axial. He transmits through his person and his knowledge the secret truths; he is the Master Initiator and the ruler of the forces of knowledge; he prevents the ruination of the world by the forces of darkness. In his many dimensions, the imam is truly the Alpha and the Omega of Shi'ism.

Notes

1 Also referred to as "Ali in Heaven". 'Ali is the supreme Imam. The term signifies the archetypal, metaphysical Imam, as well as the highest terrestrial manifestation of the "historical Ali". We will return to this point later.
2 Adam sometimes tops the list.
3 Again sources differ on names. The most common lists give Sem as imam of Noah; Ismael with Abraham; Aaron or Joshua with Moses; Simon, John or all of the Apostles with Jesus; and of course, 'Ali and his descendants with Muhammad.
4 There is a distinction within Shi'ism between superficial Shia and true Shia, in other words between those who are content with the exoteric aspects of the imam's teachings and those who desire to embrace the hidden aspects of his teachings: in short, exoteric Shia and esoteric Shia.

2   The early beginnings of Shi'ism

The saints and the main branches

In Shi'ism the principal object of devotion is a small group of individuals which includes the Prophet Muhammad, his daughter Fatima, his son-in-law 'Ali and the imams who descend from these two[1] (see the genealogy below). Disagreement amongst Shia over the lineage and actual number of imams has always been rife. As we shall see, Shi'ism splintered into numerous schisms, movements and currents, only three of which survive today. Together they form Shi'ism's most important spiritual communities. Our discussion in the preceding chapter allows us now to gauge the religious significance of the historical imams and to assess their weight in the scales of the sacred.

Authentic objects of mystical love, the historical imams are the focus of deep popular devotion for ordinary people and objects of contemplation for thinkers and the learned. Their supposed dates of birth are religious holidays, just as the anniversaries of their deaths are days of mourning. The faithful look to their tombs as places of pilgrimage; the cities where they are interred are holy. The teachings attributed to them in the vast Shi'i canon of writings have been tirelessly read, copied, commented on and meditated across the centuries up to our own time. Although the main branches of Shi'ism have always sought to venerate the figures of the Prophet and the imam in equal measure, study of these sources as well as of popular beliefs reveals that the role of the imam is superior to that of the Prophet. And for good reason.

First, as we have seen, Shi'ism is above all an imamology, a religion centred on the person of the imam. Then, even though the manifest and the hidden – the exoteric and the esoteric – are complementary, they are not of equal importance. The exoteric is the bedrock on which the esoteric lies, but the esoteric gives life and meaning as well as direction and importance to the exoteric. Indeed the spirit can exist without the letter, but the letter is dead without the spirit. In this perspective, the Prophet is the messenger of the letter and the imam is the messenger of the spirit.

We must look more closely at the lineage of the imams. The basic principles governing the imamate – knowledge (*'ilm*) and explicit investiture by the previous imam (*nass*) – seem to have emerged very early. Yet it must be noted that as each imam passed away, there was disagreement over the identity of his successor and next imam. Such discord resulted in the emergence of new sects, all the more so since the early dogmas, doctrines and practices of the religion had not been sharply delineated. Some followers simply denied the death of a particular imam, claiming he had been "occulted" and was destined to appear again at some later time as the messianic "Saviour".

The historical records and the heresiographical accounts speak of over one hundred such sects in the early centuries of the Hijra. Most were short-lived, though some of their doctrines were incorporated in surviving movements. In what follows we will concentrate on the main branches still in existence today.

The lineage of the imams

1 'Ali, son of Abu Talib

'Ali is the cousin and son-in-law of the Prophet Muhammad; he is the husband of Fatima and the father of Hasan and Husayn. 'Ali is the first imam of the Shia and the fourth caliph of the Muslims (35–40/656–661). According to the traditional narratives of the historical and hagiographic record, 'Ali was one of the most remarkable and colourful personalities of early Islam. Perhaps the first convert of Arabia's nascent religion, even as a child he was the closest of Muhammad's Companions. Muhammad himself was orphaned at a young age and welcomed into the household of his paternal uncle Abu Talib, 'Ali's father. When Abu Talib faced ruin and poverty, Muhammad adopted 'Ali. As Islam gathered strength, 'Ali's fame spread, fostered by his early conversion, celebrated bravery and military exploits. Fighting alongside Muhammad, he showed unstinting loyalty to the new Arab prophet. He ranked among the few learned individuals in Mecca, winning admiration for his wisdom, his eloquence and his abilities as an orator. He became one of Muhammad's first scribes, recording his Qur'anic revelations and working for him on worldly affairs.

As we observed earlier when discussing the Prophet's succession, there are diverging Sunni and Shi'i versions of what happened in the period immediately following the Prophet's death. The Shia claim that on several occasions and quite unambiguously, Muhammad designated 'Ali as his successor. One such instance was on 18 Dhu'l-Hijja 10/16 March 632, shortly after the Prophet's "farewell pilgrimage", not long before his death, near Ghadir Khumm between Mecca and Medina. For this reason Ghadir Khumm is one of the greatest Shi'i religious festivals: it celebrates 'Ali's official investiture.[2] In fact, 'Ali only became caliph some twenty-four years after Muhammad's death. In the opinion of the Shia, the election of each of 'Ali's three predecessors – Abu Bakr, 'Umar and 'Uthman – represented a virtual coup d'état on each occasion. By excluding 'Ali from power, the three caliphs came to be seen as usurpers, traitors to Muhammad and his calling.[3]

'Ali's caliphate was a period of extreme crisis. No sooner had Muhammad died than Arabia and the Muslim community experienced a string of civil wars and fratricidal conflicts, and these coincided with the Great Conquests under 'Umar's caliphate. At this time, 'Ali apparently sat on the sidelines, teaching and leading a life of renunciation. His two predecessors had died violent deaths. 'Ali, pressured by his followers to assume power, had to deal with bloody conflicts during the five years of his caliphate on three fronts: 1) against his usual enemies, the Prophet's old Companions led by Muhammad's widow 'A'isha (the Battle of the Camel); 2) against the Kharijites, 'Ali's disillusioned followers who had become his fiercest adversaries (the Battle of Nahrawan); 3) and against the Umayyad family, which had become increasingly influential in Syria under Mu'awiya, the family patriarch (the Battle of Siffin). According to tradition, 'Ali was assassinated by a Kharijite on 21 Ramadan 40/28 January 661, and he was laid to rest in Najaf, Iraq. His mausoleum in this shrine city is arguably one of the most important of Shi'i pilgrimage sites, though some followers venerate other places as his tomb. 'Ali's death brought Mu'awiya, the head of the Umayyad family, to power, thus establishing Islam's first dynasty.

Even during the Prophet's lifetime, 'Ali stood out as a remarkable personality. Indeed, he was the only person whose name was associated with an astonishing expression: the "religion of 'Ali" (*din 'Ali*). Based on philological studies of the different types of sources and passages in which the expression is found and on a historical analysis of the religious and anthropological context of early Islam, this expression seems to reflect several principles of faith rooted in pre-Islamic ancestral beliefs (still strong at the time) even more than in Qur'anic doctrines; this involves a certain "cult of kinship" prevalent at the time. Thus, in accord with old Arab notions, privileged ties of kinship created a kind of spiritual identity between Muhammad and 'Ali: they were first cousins, which by tribal tradition was the noblest of family relations; Muhammad was the adopted son of 'Ali's father and 'Ali himself became Muhammad's adopted son. At the time of the solemn brotherhood (*mu'akhat*) sealed by the Prophet with different Muslims, Muhammad himself chose 'Ali for his "brother". They no doubt ceremoniously mingled their blood, thus establishing the mystical bond of "blood brotherhood" between them. Muhammad also gave 'Ali his daughter Fatima in marriage so that 'Ali became the father of the Prophet's two grandsons, Hasan and Husayn, his only male descendants. Muhammad considered all four his Holy Family; they are *Ahl al-bayt* (the People of the Prophet's Household). He would have regularly performed *tahnik*, the sacred rite of letting his spittle flow into their mouths in order to transmit his charisma, spiritual virtues, initiatory knowledge and supernatural powers. These various facts established 'Ali as a figure who shared in the sacredness of Muhammad, making him – at least as far as the followers of the religion bearing his name were concerned (who constituted the earliest kernel of what would become Shi'ism) – as a matter of course the one legitimate successor to the Prophet.

Very quickly, probably right after the Prophet's death (and doubtless for all the reasons that have been suggested), 'Ali's followers set in motion a process of glorification that gradually transformed the historical person into a figure as heroic as he was tragic, and of increasingly cosmic dimensions. 'Ali, the supreme imam and legitimate "father" of all successive imams, fulfils the meaning of the term imam in its two acceptations: the historical earthly imam and the cosmic metaphysical Imam; the esoteric face of the former at the same time as the revealed Face of God. It helped that in the Qur'an, the name al-Ali (the Most High, the Supreme) was one of God's own. For some of his followers (whom the heresiographers vilified as "extremists" in a somewhat forced manner) but also within more moderate circles, 'Ali, in the tradition of all imams, is a "theophanic" being, a locus of manifestation of the revealed God. He is the supreme reality of everything that is divine in the universe as the personification of the Cosmic Imam who is concealed in every theophany. This explains why, in Shi'i mystical consciousness, 'Ali and all the imams of his issue are indeed the ultimate spiritual guides and initiatory exemplars; at the same time, they form the supreme horizon of that inner journey which transforms the humble believer into a Friend of God. This is why even some of 'Ali's disciples – Salman the Persian, Kumayl ibn Ziyad, Miqdad or Abu Dharr al-Ghifari – enjoy immense respect and are considered "the pillars" of Shi'ism.

Even within Sunni spirituality 'Ali enjoys exceptional prestige. Respected for his proximity to the Prophet and as the father of Muhammad's male descendants through Fatima, he stands as a model of wisdom, piety, knowledge and spirituality. In the mystical writings he is quoted more often than any of Muhammad's Companions. He is at the source of almost all the initiatory chains of transmission and of the lineage of the spiritual masters in the overwhelming majority of Sufi brotherhoods; he is also seen as the initiator of a large number of the elements, rituals and institutions of Sufism. He is thus one of the central figures in Muslim spirituality at large.

In addition to the many aphorisms, traditions, sage dicta or even mystical texts attributed to him in all sorts of works, two books are attributed to him: the famous *Nahj al-balagha* ("The Way of Spiritual Maturity" or "Peaks of Eloquence"), one of Shi'ism's most venerated texts – a compendium of advice, letters, aphorisms and sermons compiled by Sharif Radi (d. 406/1016) which has inspired countless commentaries from various perspectives (theological, mystical, philosophical, political, etc.); and next, a collection of poems, *Diwan*, much of which is certainly apocryphal.

'Ali's first wife, Fatima, is the most venerated of feminine Shi'i saints. While she lived, 'Ali took no other wives – an unusual thing at the time. Daughter of Muhammad and Khadija, the Prophet's first wife (and greatly admired in her own right), Fatima is depicted in hagiographic records as particularly close to her father. Her fragrance, said Muhammad, recalled the sweet smells of paradise he encountered on his heavenly ascents. In 11/633, barely a year after Muhammad's death, Fatima also passed away, still quite young, of a broken heart. In Medina three burial sites are venerated in her name; due to uncertainty, all three are considered her tomb.

For the Shia, Fatima is far more than an ideal of piety, courage and obedience to her father and husband. She is also the "mother" of the entire line of imams. Better still, she represents what links Muhammad to 'Ali, the letter to the spirit, the exoteric to the esoteric. This is the origin of one of her most celebrated names: the Confluence of Two Lights (*majma' al-nurayn*), those of Prophecy and the Imamate. She has many other names as well: Sovereign of Women, Most Supreme of Free Women, the Radiant (*al-zahra*), and the Virgin (*batul*). The latter invokes a constant parallel between Fatima and Mary, mother of Jesus. Both are women of light and miracles, models of pure devotion and timeless adoration, paragons of womanhood in the noblest sense, at the very heart of a Sacred Family, mothers of divine sons who have been sacrificed, and the symbols of a suffering that hallows.

2 Al-Hasan, son of 'Ali

Ali and Fatima's two sons, al-Hasan and al-Husayn, the second and third imams, are first and foremost the subjects of delightful little anecdotes that illustrate the moving love brimming with tenderness which the Prophet, their grandfather, lavished upon them. Shi'i and Sunni texts alike record, for example, how Muhammad allowed them to climb onto his back when he prostrated himself in prayer or how, during an important public sermon, he stepped down from the pulpit to pick up little Hasan who, tripping on his tunic, had taken a hard fall. According to tradition, the Prophet took his two grandsons and their parents under his broad mantle as a way of declaring them free of blemish, free of sin. They became known as the "Five People of the Mantle" (*ahl al-kisa* in Arabic, *panj tan-e al-e 'aba* in Persian), who form the sacred Pentade of Shi'ism: Muhammad, 'Ali, Fatima, Hasan and Husayn. They are those whose ontological reality forms part of the great mysteries; and whose names, derivatives of God's, constitute the secret knowledge transmitted by God to Adam at the creation of the world.[4]

A few days after 'Ali's assassination, Hasan's followers in Kufa (Iraq) proclaimed him caliph. Almost immediately he came face-to-face with the hostility of Mu'awiya, his father 'Ali's erstwhile and powerful enemy. Hasan was doubtless well aware of the imbalance of forces at hand and quickly abdicated. Drawing on sources from all sides of the debate, there are several interpretations of his abdication. Imam Hasan posed several conditions for his abdication, which initially appeared acceptable to the Umayyad caliph, at least for a while. Among these were that the Umayyad authorities should cease cursing 'Ali from the pulpit; that Mu'awiya should desist from persecuting 'Ali's followers; and that Hasan himself be made a public grant of funds from the Kufa treasury. His other motives, as provided by the sources, are also plausible: in addition to the realization that his troops lacked strength, the imam seemed in principle well disposed to maintaining concord and avoiding bloodshed. He was disgusted by the violence and the lies of politics. Even so, in the eyes of his followers, neither his abdication in favour of Mu'awiya nor his great affection for women (attested by his countless wives and concubines) jeopardized his position as imam. Following a long illness, Hasan died sometime around 49/669–670 (other dates are given). According to Shi'i tradition, which always prefers its imams to die a martyr's death, the cause of death was poisoning attributable to one of Hasan's wives, who had come under the influence of Mu'awiya. The latter saw in Hasan a dangerous rival to his son Yazid, recently enthroned as the second Umayyad caliph. Hasan was laid to rest in the Jannat al-Baqi' cemetery in Medina.

3 Al-Husayn, son of 'Ali

The tragic destiny of the "Martyr of Karbala", the second of 'Ali's two sons and the youngest of the Five People of the Mantle, denotes a turning point in the history of Shi'ism. Although some historians – alongside some revolutionary Shi'i factions and other Muslims as well – use the example of al-Husayn to present Shi'ism as a fundamentally political and anti-establishment movement, a closer reading of the sources which discuss the events and the figure of Imam Husayn suggests something rather more complex. (Such a reading also provides hard evidence, if it were needed, of the way in which politics uses documents and events out of context to "instrumentalize" religious phenomena for ideological purposes.)

Given the depth of the tragedy – the massacre of Muhammad's beloved grandson and virtually his entire family by the leaders of the Muslim community scarcely fifty years after the Prophet's death – every methodological precaution must be taken to present objectively and accurately the historical circumstances leading to the Karbala massacre. The source material must scrupulously reflect the different attitudes and traditions; more recent findings must be separated from older information; clear distinctions must be made between emotional accounts and the ideological biases of their authors, and so forth.

The conclusion that can be drawn is that Husayn probably had no intention of seizing power. Granted, when his brother Hasan died, Husayn refused allegiance to Yazid I, son of Mu'awiya, for at least two reasons: first, he was against the founding of a hereditary dynasty; and second, he was opposed to the investiture of a person whose debauchery and cruelty are confirmed by every source, regardless of religious or political affiliation. There is no proof, however, that Husayn planned an armed rebellion against the Umayyad army.

In 61/680, with a few dozen family members, including women and children, Husayn left Mecca, to which he had withdrawn, for Kufa. At the request of local followers, he set out to take charge of the community there. A member of the advance party, his cousin Muslim ibn 'Aqil appears to have provoked hostilities upon his arrival in Kufa, fomenting an armed insurrection, which was quickly and severely suppressed by the Umayyad authorities. Muslim himself was killed. One week later, Imam Husayn, his family and companions, under close surveillance, arrived in nearby Karbala. They were met by the army of Ibn Ziyad, the Umayyad governor of Iraq, which was growing ever more threatening. Husayn's sermons and letters from the period show that he was indeed aware of his position as imam and that he believed Yazid to be unfit to serve as caliph. They also show that he knew his cause to be lost. For this reason, he sought to resolve his differences with the Umayyad authorities through negotiation.

The negotiations failed for reasons that are poorly understood, though probably because Ibn Ziyad and his advisors remained intransigent. They seemed particularly determined to impose humiliating conditions of surrender on the Prophet's grandson, family and followers. After they had been made to suffer several days of horrible thirst, the battle began on 9 Muharram 61/ 9 October 680, culminating in an uneven fight and a massacre the following day (10 Muharram). Though Husayn and his retinue – wives, children, brothers, nephews and cousins – resisted for several hours, they were finally killed indiscriminately without regard for age or gender. Husayn himself lost his wives, his children, his brothers, nephews and cousins before being decapitated and his body trampled by enemy horses. Tradition puts the number of deaths at seventy-two (the so-called Karbala martyrs). Imam Husayn's camp was thoroughly pillaged. The survivors – who included his sister Zaynab and, miraculously, his youngest son Ali – were taken to Damascus and paraded before the caliph. They showed exemplary courage and dignity. According to tradition, Husayn's body was buried in Karbala itself.[5] Thus today, for Shia everywhere, 9 and 10 Muharram, known as Tasu'a and 'Ashura, are days of the greatest sorrow. Karbala became a site of the most impressive of pilgrimages, and the third imam, Husayn, the emblematic martyr of Shi'ism.[6]

Thanks to his inspiring exploits, Husayn, the most venerated of the Prophet's grandsons, became a model for the Shia as well as for the whole community of Muslims, revered for his refusal to be humiliated, his bravery in suffering, his dignity and his contempt for death. To be sure, for some believers, Husayn had not died at all, nor had he experienced suffering on the battlefield since God had carried him away to heaven before the battle began. This minority doctrine has been forgotten with the passage of time.

Husayn soon became an archetype for all political and social activists, in particular those who believed it necessary to rise up against corrupt and unjust rulers. Yet neither the early Shi'i literature nor the accounts of the imams descending directly from him portray Husayn as an insurgent against Umayyad authority. He is always presented as a Friend of God (*wali*), boldly fulfilling his destiny in accordance with the will of the Beloved (i.e. God). Like Abraham, who was prepared to accomplish God's will by sacrificing his son, Husayn's deed was soon regarded as "the Glorious Sacrifice", to use the Qur'anic interpretation (37:107). According to such traditions, Husayn as a theophanic being, a fully initiated sage having knowledge of the past, present and future, was fully aware of his tragic destiny. Nevertheless, he made of himself and his loved ones a sacrifice to God in order to give life to the religion of the spirit; by unifying his followers around his deeds and their poignant outcome, he reaffirmed their community and gave it a real identity. At the same time he unmasked the "Enemies", the rulers of the dark forces of Ignorance, the very same forces claiming to be the guardians of the religion of the majority. His sacrifice proved, as is always the case at the very core of a religion and its history, that a mob of ignoramuses persecutes a handful of the elect. In the eyes of the faithful, the drama of Karbala becomes the most tragic illustration of Shi'ism's dualistic vision of the world.[7]

Karbala seems to have represented a decisive turning point in the political attitudes of the imams who descended from Husayn and in their position with respect to power, especially for those who later shaped Imami Twelver Shi'ism.

From this moment on, Shi'i imams adopt a quietist attitude, leaving to God alone the hour of their ultimate victory in the world. The technical expression for this attitude is *qu'ud*, literally "sitting" or "staying put", as opposed to *qiyam* (revolt) or *khuruj* (coming out; i.e. insurrection). If we believe the many Shi'i accounts which came into existence much later, it appears that after Karbala the imams realized – and endeavoured to persuade their disciples – that the period of harmony between worldly and spiritual powers that had prevailed during the life of the Prophet was now gone *forever*. They apparently concluded that the religious realm (in the sense of the "true religion", *din al-haqq*; i.e. the religion of the imams, Shi'ism) and the political realm had now become *forever* irreconcilable. We stress "forever" because, according to Shi'i belief, the "ideal city" under a just ruler will only be achieved at the End of Time (*akhir al-zaman*) with the advent of the Mahdi, the eschatological Saviour, the twelfth and last imam, the Hidden Imam (see below).

Everything seems to indicate that for Imami (Twelver) Shi'ism after the events at Karbala, all political attitudes and protestations are projected into a messianic future, crystallized in the figure of the Hidden Imam and his triumphal return: He alone is the "just ruler", the sole being legitimately equipped to do battle with the unjust, avenge the downtrodden and establish a world of knowledge and justice. Until his coming again, the world will be governed by the unjust, and any attempts at rebellion, however well founded, are irrevocably destined to fail.

In order to preserve the purity of his faith, the Imami believer is instructed to submit to this general state of affairs: an unwaveringly quietist political attitude is required for the preservation of his faith. An entire series of traditions, traceable to various imams and recorded in Shi'i canonical writings, emphasizes this separation of the worldly and spiritual realms. The faithful are forbidden to seek power or to collaborate with men of power: "Beware of those who command and promote themselves as leaders. As God is my Witness, the man behind whom the sound of [his partisans'] sandals rises will perish and cause to perish". Thus the faithful are forbidden to rise up against the powers of this world. In the current cycle of history, the ignorant majority are ruled by the unjust. The minority of true initiated believers should not attempt to overthrow this order until the coming of the Saviour: "The dust settles on him who raises it" (i.e. the rebel will be the victim of his own rebellion). "Any banner raised before the Imam of the Resurrection (the Hidden Imam) belongs to a rebel against God." "None among the Shia has rebelled, or will rebel, even against oppression or to defend a just cause, lest a great calamity tear him up by the roots. And so shall it be until the return of the Imam of the Resurrection. The rebellion of one of us will only provoke more suffering for us, the Imams, and for our followers."

In short, these texts ban all political activity by the faithful. Later imams will make genuine efforts to remain aloof from the dangers of political life, more or less successfully. Nevertheless, as we shall see, because of their religious function and position, several would become caught up in the struggles of history, virtually against their will. In any case, it is significant that the imams, in an allusion to their political quietism, will take on the title of *al-qa'id* (the sitting imam) in contrast to the Saviour who is called *al-qa'im* (the standing Imam; i.e. he who stands up and opposes injustice).[8]

Al-Husayn's martyrdom and its consequences gradually became a cultural and religious focal point. The mourning rituals for Husayn absorbed and perpetuated the ancient funeral rites performed for the young and valorous "martyr" Siyavush, the legendary prince of the Kayanid dynasty in the epic mythology of pre-Islamic Iran. Under neighbouring Christian influences, primarily in Syria and Palestine, Husayn's exploits assumed the proportions of a redemptory sacrifice for the salvation of the faithful. The appellations "Tasu'a" and "Ashura" – the ninth and tenth days of Muharram (the first month of the Islamic calendar) – are curiously found in Aramaic Hebrew as well, like distant echoes of Yom Kippur, the Jewish "Day of Atonement" celebrated on the tenth day of Tishri, the first month of the Jewish calendar, in reflection, supplication for forgiveness of sins, and the hope of salvation. Husayn's acts and those of his companions form the principal subject of the *ta'ziya*, the Shi'i religious dramas born in Iran around the 18th or 19th century. Accompanied by poetry, chanted lamentations and processions, they are often impressive spectacles and certainly unique in the Islamic world. Thus, not only has the Karbala tragedy been not only a powerful sign of community identity; it also brought about a cultural melting pot.

Our discussion of Husayn would not be complete without reference to two women in his entourage. First his sister Zaynab, mentioned earlier, an important cult figure among Shi'i saints, venerated for her exceptional courage and dignity in suffering the violent loss of her loved ones. History tells us that after she was taken captive and brought before the caliph Yazid in Damascus, she was sent under escort to Medina in the company of the other survivors of Karbala. Her alleged tomb in Damascus is a high place of Shi'i pilgrimage.

The second is Shahrbanu, Husayn's wife. According to tradition, she was a daughter of the Iranian king Yazdegerd III, the last Sasanian emperor preceding the Arab conquests. She was the preferred wife of the third imam and the mother of the fourth, through whom she became genetrix of the entire lineage of successive imams. Without any doubt we are dealing here with a legend that probably arose around the year 201/817 amid the pro-Shia Iranian entourage of the Abbasid caliph al-Ma'mun. Nevertheless, this legend has had very real historical and cultural consequences.

In effect, Shahrbanu establishes a link between pre-Islamic Iran and Shi'ism. This is extremely important for the Iranian "national" consciousness. The imams in the line of descent of Shahrbanu thus possess a twofold legitimacy, a double light, in the eyes of Iranian converts: that of 'Ali and Fatima's initiatory Islam and that of the royal glory of ancient Iran. While it is utterly incorrect to claim, as some have done, that Shi'ism is an "Iranianized" form of Islam, it is nevertheless undeniable that quite rapidly – that is, in the very first centuries of Islam – convergences of all sorts came to be established between persecuted Shia and the conquered and frequently humiliated Iranians. Shahrbanu appears to have been one of the main factors – indeed, the symbol par excellence – of a rapprochement that facilitated the Shi'i assimilation and transformation of numerous elements of ancient Iranian religions (Mazdaism, Zoroastrianism, Manichaeism, Zurvanism). Consider, for example, the notion of Cosmic Man, the central importance of secrecy and initiation, and the dualist vision of the universe. Even the name Shahrbanu (literally "Lady of the Land"; i.e. the land of Iran) is the ancient title of Anahita, the goddess of waters and fertility in the ancient Iranian pantheon. For centuries now, women have sought treatment for sterility in Shahrbanu's putative sanctuary on the slopes of Mount Tabarak at Rayy, south of modern-day Tehran. Grandmother Shahrbanu (Bibi Shahrbanu as she is called in Iran since she is the "mother" of the imams who are the true "fathers" of the faithful) thus perpetuates in popular belief the cult of the ancient Mother-Goddess, matron of the Sasanian kings.

4 'Ali Zayn al-'Abidin, son of al-Husayn

Accordingly, the fourth imam, one of the few survivors of Karbala, is said to be the son of Husayn and Shahrbanu. Only days after the massacre, Yazid hurried him off to Medina where he led a life of piety and seclusion, never threatening Umayyad power, never joining any of the countless Shi'i insurrectionary movements fomented in revenge for Karbala. The most significant of these insurrections, one that did pose a serious threat to the caliph's power for a time, was Mukhtar's revolt. Mukhtar was a follower of Imam Muhammad ibn al-Hanafiyya, another of 'Ali's sons (by a wife he took after Fatima's death).[9] The fourth imam was highly esteemed and venerated – even among Sunnis – for his life of renunciation, devotion, prayer and dedication to the transmission of religious knowledge. He held many honorific titles, among them Zayn al-'Abidin (the Ornament of the Pious) and al-Sajjad (the Prostrator). He apparently died of natural causes around 92/711, though Shi'i hagiography claims that he was poisoned by an Umayyad caliph, either Walid or Hisham ibn 'Abd al-Malik. He is buried in the cemetery of Jannat al-Baqi' in Medina. In addition to numerous hadiths reported in the canonical sources, he is credited with a beautiful collection of prayers, the "Book of al-Sajjad" (*al-Sahifa al-Sajjadiyya*), also known as the "Psalms of the House of Muhammad", very popular among the Shia and the focus of numerous commentaries.

Before we turn to the other imams of Twelver Shi'ism, we need to touch briefly on Zayd ibn 'Ali, one of 'Ali Zayn al-'Abidin's numerous children and the eponym of a great Shi'i family, the Zaydis, also known as Fiver Shia.[10] What characterizes Zaydism at its origins, around the middle of the 2nd/8th century, is its violent activism. Both Zayd and his son Yahya were killed in armed insurrections against the last Umayyads. Not long after, under the early Abbasids, two additional Zaydi leaders, descendants of the second imam, al-Nafs al-Zakiyya and his brother Ibrahim, died in similar circumstances. According to the Zaydi theory of the imamate – at least in its earliest expression – each Alid (Shia) is entitled to make a claim on the leadership of the community. The true imam is the one who establishes his credentials with weapons in his hands in rebellion against the unjust government.

Savage repression forced the Zaydis to take refuge in the remote corners of Iraq, the centre of empire. Thus, in the course of the 3rd/9th century, two small Zaydi states emerged: one in the north of Iran, south of the Caspian Sea; the other in the south of Arabia in the Yemen. In the following century, most Zaydi communities began to lose some of their Shi'i character when, on legal questions, they adopted positions that were closer to the orthodox Sunni schools of law. In theology, their position began to reflect the rationalism of the Mu'tazilite school, and their political doctrine of the imamate became decidedly nuanced in a more moderate direction. Gradually the North Iranian Zaydis disappeared, absorbed by other forms of Shi'ism: first, by Isma'ilism (see below) and later by Imamism (Twelver Shi'ism). As for Zaydism in the south, it survived and developed, producing a rich intellectual tradition throughout the medieval period. The last of the Yemeni Zaydi leaders was overthrown in 1962 by a pro-Nasser revolution. Today Yemeni Zaydis are thought to number some five million, roughly half of the country's total population.

5 Muhammad al-Baqir, son of 'Ali Zayn al-'Abidin

The fifth imam, Muhammad ibn Ali, called "al-Baqir" (an abbreviation of *Baqir al-ilm*, the one who splits open knowledge; i.e. who reveals the mysteries of knowledge), and his son Ja'far, the sixth imam, can be considered the true founders of Imami Shi'ism. The principal written doctrines stem from their teachings. From a purely statistical point of view, the number of traditions attributed to these two imams is greater than all others combined, including those of the Prophet Muhammad and Fatima.

Muhammad Baqir, the son of 'Ali Zayn al-'Abidin, born of a daughter of al-Hasan ibn 'Ali, was the grandson of the second and third imams. He was known for his great piety and erudition and the esoteric nature of his teachings. He pursued no political activity whatsoever. When his half-brother Zayd triggered a revolt near the end of his imamate, he did nothing to assist him. According to tradition, his knowledge of future events was such that he knew the outcome would be fatal. Despite his political quiescence, his relations with the Umayyad dynasty were difficult, especially with the Caliph Hisham ibn 'Abd al-Malik.

His teachings embraced several levels. First, on an exoteric plane, he covered the traditional Islamic sciences, particularly canon law. A large number of authorities, many recognized by the Sunnis as well, followed his teachings at this level: Ibn Jurayj, Awza'i and even Abu Hanifa, the eponym of one of orthodox Sunnism's four main legal schools, Hanafism. Next, on an intermediate level, Shi'i religion was taught to his more intimate disciples. But this teaching was still an exoteric form of Shi'ism and was concerned more particularly with theology and exegesis. Some members of his circle, including the celebrated Muhammad ibn al-Tayyar and Zurara ibn A'yan, actually developed their own independent theological thought, clashing at times with their mentor. Finally, at a manifestly esoteric level, he initiated the advanced followers who were closest to him into secret knowledge. Such illustrious figures as Mughira ibn Sa'id, Jabir ibn Yazid al-Ju'fi and Abu Mansur al-'Ijli, presented by the later heresiographic literature as dangerous "deviants and extremists",[11] give us a sense of the adepts at this level. It is perhaps because of this esoteric teaching that even Sufism, bound up as it is with Sunni Islam, would come to rank al-Baqir among its founding figures.

Under the fifth imam, certain signal elements of doctrine were elaborated in pretty much definitive form. These include: 1) the twinned Sacred Alliance/ Sacred Separation (*walaya/bara'a*) concept, handed down respectively to the imams and their adversaries (in effect, most of the Prophet's Companions and specifically the first three caliphs); 2) the obligation of "keeping the secret" (*taqiyya*); 3) the fundamental precepts defining eligibility for the imamate, including descent from Fatima, possession of divinely granted knowledge (*'ilm*), and investiture (*nass*) by the previous imam; 4) equality of the imam's rank with that of the Prophet in the transmission of sacred traditions; and finally 5) the systematic formulation of Shi'i law.

The exact date of Muhammad Baqir's death – as, indeed, of his birth – is disputed. He apparently died of natural causes around 119/737. Shi'i martyrology claims that he was poisoned by an Umayyad caliph, either Hisham al-Walid or Ibrahim ibn al-Walid depending on the narratives and dates accepted for his death. He is buried in the Jannat al-Baqi' cemetery in Medina.

6 Ja'far al-Sadiq, son of Muhammad al-Baqir

Like his father al-Baqir, Ja'far ibn Muhammad, also called "al-Sadiq" (The Truthful), is recognized by Muslims of all traditions as one of the great scholars of his age. He lived in troubled times when power was brutally transferred from the Umayyad to the Abbasid dynasty.[12] During this period of frequent armed insurrection, when many Shia hoped that the family of 'Ali would finally come to power in the person of Ja'far, he showed no political ambition whatsoever and remained carefully aloof from intrigue. This would explain why he was never troubled by the ruling authorities, who certainly had plenty of other problems on their hands. Ja'far took advantage of this situation to consolidate the foundations of the doctrine he represented, which he appears to have sought to systematize more fully than any other imam.

Ja'far is identified with an impressive number of hadith; his teachings covered a wide range of disciplines. Perhaps inspired by a practice recommended by his father, he was the first to require his disciples to methodically transcribe Imami teachings, so forming the first collections of Shi'i tradition. Like his father, he appears to have had different categories of disciples corresponding to different levels of instruction. His disciples of the "exoteric circle" included Abu Hanifa and Malik ibn Anas, founder of Malikism, another major Sunni school of law. In the intermediate circle were to be found such thinkers and theologians as Hisham ibn al-Hakam, Hisham ibn Salim and Muhammad ibn Nu'man. Finally the inner circle seems without doubt to have included Abu al-Khattab, an important figure of early Shi'i esotericism (later accused of "extremist deviation") and the quasi-legendary Jabir ibn Hayyan, the "father" of Islamic alchemy.

Ja'far Sadiq is credited with extensive knowledge, ranging from the traditional Qur'anic disciplines to the occult sciences (alchemy, astrology, the science of letters and other divinatory sciences) as well as law. Indeed, he is regarded as the founder of the Imami Shi'i school of law, also known as Ja'fari law. Again like al-Baqir, he is revered by the Sufis as one of the movement's "founding fathers". Indeed, Sufi authors attribute to him the oldest mystical commentary on the Qur'an.

Ja'far died in 148/765 – according to Shi'i tradition, poisoned by the Abbasid caliph al-Mansur – and was the last imam to be buried in the Jannat al-Baqi' cemetery in Medina. (The Shi'i section of this locus of intense spirituality, that harbours the tombs of several imams, was razed by the Wahhabis in the 19th century.) Many of the works attributed to Imam Ja'far – primarily in the field of the occult sciences – are almost certainly apocryphal.

Ja'far's eldest son, Isma'il, is eponymous with the second great family of Shi'i Muslims, the Isma'ilis, otherwise known as the "Sevener Shia".[13] Many of the more esoterically minded of Ja'far's disciples, who perhaps were also among the most revolutionary on a political level, claimed Isma'il as their imam, doubtless disappointed by Ja'far's unrelenting quietism. According to most sources, Isma'il had died before his father. But some rejected the idea of his death, declaring that he had gone into "occultation" and recognizing in him the anticipated Saviour of the End Time. Others, even more numerous, accepted the imamate of his son Muhammad. Thus was Isma'ilism born – from a historical, spiritual and intellectual perspective, one of the richest currents of thought in Islam. Though it merits a full-scale study in its own right, we must limit ourselves to the following few lines.

Within its many currents and factions, Isma'ilism has preserved an esoteric dimension rooted in the teachings of the imams and in elements of diverse provenance (Iranian, Neoplatonic, Pythagorean, Gnostic and others), all now part of the doctrine.[14] The different expressions of Isma'ilism left their mark throughout the Middle Ages because of their historical importance for the Islamic empire and their impact on the political stage. In the 9th–10th centuries the Carmathian movement, whose political theology combined an egalitarian system with armed struggle against the Sunni Abbasid authorities, blazed rapidly throughout southern Iran, the Persian Gulf region and a large portion of the Arabian Peninsula. The Fatimid Caliphate (the descendants of Fatima), builders of Cairo and Al-Azhar (the oldest university in the world), ruled Egypt and parts of North Africa for more than two centuries (10th to the 12th century); several influential schools of theology, philosophy and law developed during their reign. When al-Hakim, the sixth Fatimid caliph, died in 412/1021, some of his followers saw in him the promised Mahdi and believed he had gone into occultation. They took the name Muwahhidun (Unitarians) but later became better known under the name of Druze.[15] Today there are several hundred thousand Druze in southern Syria, the Lebanon and Israel.

The greatest split within Isma'ili Islam occurred upon the death of the caliph al-Mustansir in 487/1094, when the faithful split into two rival factions, the Musta'lis and the Nizaris (later they subdivided even further). These communities survive to this day. The Musta'lis, numbering at least several hundred thousand, today live mainly in Yemen, East Africa and India (especially in Gujarat, where they are known as Bohras). As for the Nizari Isma'ilis, they conducted an energetic and successful campaign of propaganda in Syria and especially in Iran. It is they the medieval chroniclers of the Crusades call the Assassins. The stronghold of Alamut, their headquarters in northern Iran, ruled for a time by Hasan Sabbah, became a place of legend. The image, as derogatory as it is false, created by Crusaders and Sunni propagandists alike portrayed the Isma'ilis of Alamut as terrorists, hashish addicts and fanatics. This image utterly obscures a movement that while openly political, was also one of immense intellectual richness and included a number of illustrious thinkers, philosophers and mystics. After the Mongol invasion and the fall of Alamut (13th century), the Nizari Isma'ilis went into hiding; their followers dispersed, and many reverted to Twelver Shi'ism or to the Sufi brotherhoods, keeping their doctrinal beliefs a secret. Present-day Isma'ili communities are primarily a product of a Nizari schism. The majority, perhaps several million (no reliable statistics are available), live in India, where they are known as Khoja Isma'ili; they are also found in Central Asia, Eastern Iran and in small secret communities widely dispersed throughout the Near and Middle East, Yemen, East Africa, Europe and North America. Now no longer clandestine, the imams acknowledged by most descendants of the Isma'ilis of Alamut belong to the renowned family – Iranian in origin – of the Aga Khan.

7 *Musa al-Kazim, son of Ja'far al-Sadiq*

Another of Ja'far Sadiq's sons, a full twenty-five years younger than Isma'il, was recognized by several of his father's disciples. His name was Musa ibn Ja'far, called "al-Kazim" (Master of Himself). According to Twelver Shia, his father designated him in infancy to be the next imam. Be that as it may, following the death of Ja'far al-Sadiq, he had to deal with considerable pressure from different schisms among the ranks of the faithful. Celebrated for his piety and his renunciation of the world, he was also renowned for his oratorical and polemical skills. He too adopted a quietist political attitude. Nevertheless, he was soon caught up in anti-Shia repressions that were instigated and sustained by the Abbasid al-Mansur owing to armed revolts led primarily by the Zaydis. Musa al-Kazim was harassed, detained, held under house arrest and imprisoned from 158/775 during the caliphates of al-Mahdi, al-Hadi and Harun al-Rashid (the famous caliph of *The Thousand and One Nights*) until his suspicious death in prison around 183/799. According to Shi'i tradition, but confirmed by other sources as well, Harun had him poisoned. He was interred in Baghdad in the cemetery reserved for the city's Arab aristocrats and known as the Tombs of the Quraysh. The quarter would later come to be known as al-Kazimiya.

Under the fifth and sixth imams, Shi'i doctrine made comprehensive methodological advances, and the community strengthened considerably. Judging by the increase in the amount of donations that Imam Musa Kazim and his agents took in, the number of followers grew significantly. Indeed the increase was such that the caliph Harun al-Rashid expressed his concern about Alid financial networks. With the death of al-Kazim, a peculiar faction of Shi'ism came to light, the Waqifa, literally "Those who stopped"; that is, those who halt the line of imams with the seventh imam and reject transmission of the imamate to his son. True, some Waqifis were religiously motivated and believed that Musa Kazim was the occulted Saviour. It was not the first time that such a belief had surfaced, but no one had ever held that the line of the imams would thus come to an end.

Still, it seems undeniable that others entertained this notion, stirred as they were by purely material considerations. In particular, the financial agents who controlled large sums of wealth entrusted to them by the faithful refused purely and simply all requests to hand over the funds to the successors of al-Kazim. Thus, under the seventh imam, a period marked by sharp growth in the size of the Shi'i community, a new class of influential individuals emerged; namely, the imam's agents who are responsible for the hierarchical organization of the faithful. As we shall see, these agents will assume increasing importance in the daily lives of the faithful. Some will even achieve a large degree of independence in regard to the imam's authority, sometimes going so far as to make themselves his substitutes.

8 'Ali al-Rida, son of Musa al-Kazim

The eighth imam, 'Ali al-Rida, had to face the hostility and the defection of many of the faithful in the crisis that followed the death of his father. Though his uncle, Muhammad ibn Ja'far, and several of his brothers and half-brothers joined many of the Shi'i revolts after the death of the Caliph al-Amin, 'Ali al-Rida abstained.

At Medina he led a life of seclusion, surrounded by his disciples, when suddenly the demands of public life and politics fell upon him. In 201/817, the Abbasid Caliph al-Ma'mun unexpectedly adopted a pro-Alid stance and named al-Rida his official successor. The sources agree that al-Rida was reluctant to accept the nomination and did so only under extreme pressure from the caliph and several of his ministers as well as some of al-Rida's own followers who represented opposing interests. Al-Rida set out for Merv in Central Asia, where the caliph Ma'mun had settled. The caliph's decision to nominate al-Rida provoked violent opposition in Abbasid and Sunni circles in Iraq, and violent revolts broke out against this decision. Sunnis and Shia clashed in the streets of several cities. Ibrahim, son of the former Caliph al-Mahdi, was proclaimed caliph in Baghdad. Apparently, influential members of the Abbasid family promised to support Ma'mun's claim for universal recognition as caliph provided he abandon his pro-Shia policies. After some hesitation, Ma'mun set out for Iraq. During the journey his pro-Shia vizier Fadl ibn Sahl, an Iranian, was assassinated. A few months later, in 203/818, still en route for Iraq, al-Rida died in Tus under suspicious circumstances. The city, later named Mashhad (from Mashhad al-Rida; i.e, the place of Rida's martyrdom) in present-day north-eastern Iran, is now the greatest pilgrimage site in Iranian Shi'ism. These deaths, which were very opportune for the advancement of al-Ma'mun's political career, are laid at his feet – and not only by Shi'i sources, despite the fact that he seems to have nurtured genuine Shi'i sympathies until the end of his life.

Famous for his piety, oratorical skills and theological teachings, al-Rida is attributed with the authorship of two celebrated literary works: *al-Risalat al-dhahabiyya* (the Golden Dissertation), a little medical treatise which Ma'mun had copied in golden ink (hence its title) and which attracted numerous commentaries; and the *Sahifat al-Rida* (Rida's Notebook), a small collection of several hundred doctrinal hadith.

9 Muhammad al-Jawad, son of 'Ali al-Rida

10 'Ali al-Hadi, son of Muhammad al-Jawad

11 Al-Hasan al-Askari, son of 'Ali al-Hadi

These three imams seem to have played a less important role than the others. The first two were underage when they became imam. The third held his position for no more than a few troubled years. Together they occupy a modest place in the canonical traditions.[16] Muhammad ibn 'Ali, among whose wives was a daughter of al-Ma'mun, died in 220/835 while still young; he was buried alongside his grandfather Musa Kazim in the Quraysh cemetery of Baghdad. The two tombs were later brought together in Baghdad's al-Kazimayn (the two Kazims) mausoleum, now a high place of Shi'i pilgrimage.

During the caliphates of Mu'tasim and Wathiq, 'Ali al-Hadi lived quietly in Medina. But under the anti-Shia policies of Mutawakkil and his successors, he was forced to move to the new capital of Samarra, where he died in 254/868 under house arrest in the military encampment of the town.

His son, the eleventh imam, spent most of his life under house arrest in the same encampment. He died there in 260/874, still quite young. Thus the Iraqi town of Samarra holds the tombs of these two imams and, for this reason, is another much-venerated Shi'i holy city. Yet again, Shi'i written accounts present the deaths of these three imams as assassinations ordered by one caliph or another.

Lasting no more than a few decades in total, the lives of these three imams, together with their particular circumstances and the many schisms that erupted with each death, marked the start of a period of deep crisis.

By this time, the fundamental features of a Shi'i hierarchy were firmly in place. The imam's authority and influence, especially in the outlying regions, were so weakened that well-placed individuals higher up in the hierarchy had little difficulty amassing ever more power. The process that first appeared under Musa Kazim's imamate henceforth increases in sweep and scale.

On the eve of the occultation of the last imam – a defining moment in Shi'i history which marks the closure of the historical time of the imams – three main camps wielded influence among the community of the faithful, whose divine Guide seemed to have increasingly withdrawn. First, there were the religious scholars, the doctors of Law who claimed the role of the guardians of doctrinal orthodoxy. Next were the powerful aristocratic families who, accepting to serve the Abbasid rulers, attempted to infiltrate the apparatus of the state. Finally, there were the esoteric factions, gnostic and revolutionary in spirit and organized in more or less secret sects, who claimed to be the true repositories of the imam's hidden teachings. They too attempted to seize control of the Abbasid state. At the outset the lines of separation between the three camps appear to be blurred, but gradually over the course of the following century, the distinction would become clear and would lead to violent opposition.

12 Muhammad al-Mahdi al-Qa'im, son of al-Hasan al-Askari

When the eleventh imam died, Shi'i followers split into more than a dozen factions. Some claimed that al-Hasan al-Askari had passed away without offspring. Others believed that he was the awaited Saviour and had gone into occultation. Still others turned to his brother Ja'far.

But according to tradition, Imam Hasan Askari also had a son whose name was Muhammad. This gradually became a tenet of faith for the Twelver Shia. The Imamis or Twelvers (the followers of the twelve imams), the largest of the Shi'i communities in terms of number, believe that the twelfth imam is the "Messiah", the long-awaited Saviour. He is called *al-Mahdi* (the Guided One), a general term used throughout Islam to name the eschatological redeemer. He is also known as *al-Muntazar* (the One who is awaited), *Sahib al-zaman* (the Master of the Age) and, most importantly, *al-imam al-gha'ib* (the Hidden Imam) or al-Qa'im. This last term has been interpreted in several ways depending on the various meanings of the Arabic root. It can mean the Standing One (in contrast with the other imams who are the "Seated"), The One who will rise up again or reappear, the Resurrector, and so forth.

The classically accepted date of his birth is the 15th Sha'ban 256/870, the date of a great Imami holiday. Again according to tradition, in the year 260/874, when his father died and he was still a little four- or five-year-old boy, Muhammad went into what is known as the Minor Occultation. This lasted nearly seventy lunar years, during which time the "Hidden Imam" communicated with his followers through a succession of four deputies, the only ones to have the honour of consulting with him or knowing his whereabouts. In

329/940–941, on his deathbed, the fourth and final deputy received a signed letter from the twelfth imam announcing that henceforth he would have no representative, that anyone claiming to be his deputy was an impostor, and that he would only manifest himself to all at the End of Time. For Twelver Shia this letter marks the onset of the Major Occultation, which continues to this day and which will last until the final coming of the Qa'im, when the latter will destroy – violently and forever – the forces of Ignorance and Injustice on the earth.

This concept of occultation (*ghayba*), which probably traces its origins to the old Shi'i sect of the Kaysanis, was supported at first by several points. One, of a spiritualist tendency, held that while the Hidden Imam was indeed physically dead, his "spiritual substance" will survive in the world until his final return. Another theory suggested that the imam had indeed died but had secretly left a son who had succeeded him; thus, the lineage of the imam will continue during the occultation from father to son until the last imam finally reveals himself publicly as the Saviour. Both theories were quickly abandoned.

One theory that was kept and steadily became an article of faith was of a "corporist" type: the Hidden Imam is indeed physically alive; moreover, he is miraculously endowed with an exceptionally long life, enabling him to pass through the ages and to reveal himself at the End of Time. This notion of the invisible but physical presence of the Hidden Imam and of his messianic reappearance at the end of the ages would ultimately crystallize much Shi'i devotion. We will return to this major aspect of Shi'ism in our discussion of eschatology.

And so, with the occultation of the Hidden Imam, the lineage of the Shi'i family of the Imamis, henceforth to become the Twelvers – by far the majority branch of Shi'ism – comes to a close.[17] From the 16th century on, Imami Shi'ism became the state religion of Iran, making it the only Shi'i nation in the world. Today Iranian Shia number some sixty million. There are a further sixty million, if not more, dispersed throughout the Indian subcontinent in different regions of India and Pakistan. Twelver Shia also form a majority in countries such as Iraq, Bahrain and Azerbaijan. Twelver communities of varying significance exist in virtually every Sunni-majority country in the Near East and Middle East as well as in Central Asia and Afghanistan, though they frequently conceal their religious identities. How many Shia are there worldwide? Statistics before the Iranian Revolution of 1978/1979 usually posited the figure of 20 per cent, all branches considered, of all Muslims worldwide. This figure was later adjusted to 10 per cent. Was this an attempt to diminish the perceived threat of Shi'ism? Although exact statistics concerning Shi'i populations in Sunni-majority countries do not exist or are unreliable, the calculation is fairly simple: There are at least 160 million Twelver Shia around the world today. In addition, there are several tens of millions of Shia who do not speak their name: the Alawis (Nusayris) in Syria, the Alevis and Bektashis in Turkey and the Ahl-i Haqq Kurds. To these we must add several million more Zaydis and Isma'ilis. In sum, Shia thus represent between 150 and 200 million people, between 15 and 20 per cent of all Muslims.

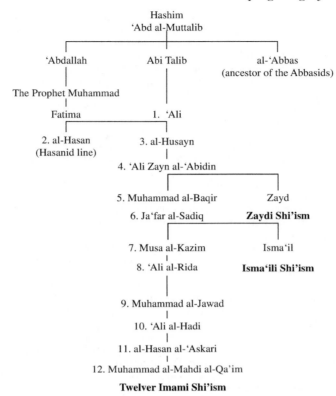

Figure 2.1 A genealogy of the imams and the main divisions of Shi'ism

Notes

1 In the early centuries of Islam, some Shi'i sects professed the imamate of other descendants, non-Fatimid, of 'Ali. These sects were not long-lived and do not require our attention.

2 As the Hijra calendar is lunar, and therefore shorter than the Gregorian solar calendar, the anniversary dates of the Muslim calendar do not correspond to the calendar of the Common Era from one year to the next.

3 They are held to be the "adversaries" of 'Ali, the leaders of the "forces of Ignorance" in their time, the true cause of the deviation and decadence of mainstream Islam. In Shi'i communities, the search for men with these names is fruitless; whereas for the Sunnis, they are the names of the most venerated of the Prophet's Companions.

4 Allusion to Qur'an 20:115.

5 Where his head lies is a matter of diverging opinion: Najaf, Kufa, Karbala, Medina, Cairo?

6 The reader will be familiar with the celebrated ceremony of mourning often marked by spectacular processions, lamentations, self-flagellation, lacerations and mutilation. These expressions of penitence are fairly recent (probably 18th or 19th century), doubtless inspired by the ancient Movement of the Penitents of Kufa

(*al-tawwabun*). Shortly after the Karbala massacre, this movement crystallized the remorse of the Shi'i inhabitants of Kufa for having invited Husayn to become their imam without having the means to support and protect him.

7 Beginning around the 10th/16th century, the mourning of the Karbala martyrs gave rise to a treasure trove of texts – particularly in Persian – constituting the true literary foundations of popular devotion. Continuing the Arabic medieval literary tradition of the Maqatil (assassinations) of the historical figures of Shi'ism, we can identify the elegies of Kashifi (9th–10th centuries/15th –16th centuries), the "Battlefield of the Martyrs" (*Rawdat al-shuhada*, which gave the name *Rawda* to the Karbala ceremonies of mourning), Muhammad Baqir Majlisi's "The Brilliance of Eyes" (*Jala al-'uyun*) (11th/17th century), and Harawi Qazwini's "The Flood of Tears" (*Tufan al-buka'*) as well as Ahmad Naraqi's "The Arsonist of Hearts" (*Muhriq al-qulub*) (13th/19th century).

8 To our knowledge, Imami Shi'ism is the only religious current within Islam that explicitly establishes in its sacred texts such a separation between the temporal and the spiritual. But how can we explain the paradox that one of the least political movements of Islam resulted in the Iranian Islamic Revolution? In the course of our argument, we will have to address this.

9 The followers of Imam Muhammad ibn al-Hanafiyya, the so-called Kaysani Shia, had a short but significant existence. For example, the Kaysanis played a decisive role in the victorious Abbasid revolution and the fall of the Umayyad dynasty. Moreover, certain fundamental Shi'i beliefs are of Kaysani origin; for example, the divine nature of the imam and his superhuman knowledge, the notion of the imam's occultation or of his future coming as the Saviour Messiah.

10 Although this term is convenient, it is not historically accurate. Many Zaydis believe that the imamate is uninterrupted and, therefore, refuse the imamate of 'Ali Zayn al-'Abidin. Although they accept the imamate in the direct line of descent from Hasan and Husayn, they reject the hereditary character of the supreme authority in principle.

11 The case of the "extremists" (*ghulat*) has yet to be clarified historically. The *ghulat* extremists adhered to doctrines that their adversaries qualified as "exaggerated"; that is, "beyond the law" (*ghuluww*). Some look on the *ghulat* as the true founders of Shi'i esotericism. They are often seen in opposition to "moderate" Shia; that is, the imams and their disciples who follow "orthodox" (or what is styled as such by later authors) Shi'i ideas. The main ideas of the extremist currents, denounced by the heresiographers, are the deification of the imam, the unlimited knowledge and power of the imam and his disciples, the transmigration of the soul, and various messianic and millenarian doctrines. These different distinctions remain ambiguous and appear to have died out in any case. All the great figures of "extremism" had been disciples of imams. Moreover, virtually all of the ideas expounded by the *ghulat*, in whatever form, are part of the "official", that is to say "moderate", teaching that can be traced back to the imams and the authority of the hadith. Thus a clear-cut distinction between "extremist" Shia and "moderate" Shia in ancient times seems to be artificial or at least problematic.

12 At the outset Abbasids and Alids found themselves in the same camp, with many Shi'i groups actively taking part in the revolution that resulted in the fall of the Umayyad dynasty. But once in power the Abbasid Shia separated from the Alid Shia, and the violent cycle of insurrection and repression began all over again.

13 As we observed in our discussion of Zaydism above, this formulation, although convenient, is historically inaccurate. Isma'ili imamology, rooted in a theory of periodic cycles of "veiling" and "unveiling", is far more complex. Moreover, for Isma'ilis, the imamate remains uninterrupted.

14 The same may be said of the esoteric currents of Twelver Imamism as well.

15 Gradually the Druze distanced themselves from Isma'ili Shi'ism and from Islam in general. Today they present their beliefs as an independent religion: the Druze religion.

16 Imam Hasan al-Askari is credited with the authorship of an important and lengthy commentary on the first two chapters of the Qur'an. However, the commentary remains incomplete. The authenticity of this work is also disputed.

17 In addition to the twelve main imams, Twelver Shi'ism allows for a number of "secondary" religious figures who are presumed to descend from them. Their tombs are pilgrimage sites dear to the hearts of the faithful.

Bibliography for Part I

With very few exceptions, references are not supplied to the articles in such works as *The Encyclopaedia of Islam, Encyclopaedia Iranica, The Cambridge History of Arabic Literature, The Cambridge History of Iran, Encyclopaedia of Religion,* etc. With regard to individual figures, historical events, themes and technical terms, geographic locations, the titles of works and the like, the reader who wants more information may easily consult these. In our bibliographies, perforce selective, only works in European languages are listed. The reader who is a specialist in Islam or Arabic will find references to written works in one of the languages of Islam in the bibliographies of the titles listed.

M.A. Amir-Moezzi, "Du droit à la théologie: les niveaux de réalité dans le shi'isme duodécimain", *Cahiers du groupe d'études spirituelles compares. L'esprit et la nature* (conference proceedings, Paris11 and 12 May 1996), 5, 1997, pp. 37–63.

M.A. Amir-Moezzi, "Seul l'homme de Dieu est humain: théologie et anthropologie mystique à travers l'exégèse imamite ancienne (Aspects de l'imamologie duodéciamine, IV)", *Arabica*, 45, 1998, pp. 193–214. ["Only the Man of God is Human", English trans. by D. Bachrach in a collection of specialist articles edited by E. Kohlberg, *Shi'ism: The Formation of the Classical Islamic World*, vol. 33, Aldershot, England: Ashgate, 2003, article no. 2.]

M.A. Amir-Moezzi, "Considérations sur l'expression din 'Ali. Aux origines de la foi Shiite", *Zeitschrift der Deutschen Morgenländischen Gesellschaft*, 150/1, 2000, pp. 29–68.

M.A. Amir-Moezzi, "Shahrbanu, Dame du Pays d'Iran et mère des imams: entre l'Iran préislamique et le Shiisme Imarnite", *Jerusalem Studies in Arabic and Islam* (Studies in Honour of Shaul Shaked), 27, 2002, pp. 487–549. [Abridged version, "Shahrbanu, princesse sassanide et épouse de l'imam Husayn. De l'Iran préislamique à l'Islam Shiite", in *Comptes rendus de l'Académie: des inscriptions et belles lettres*, January–March 2002, pp. 255–285.]

M.A. Amir-Moezzi, *La religion discrète. Croyances et pratiques spirituelles dans l'islam shi'ite.* Paris: Vrin, 2006 [*The Spirituality of Shi'i Islam: Beliefs and Practices*, English trans., London: I.B. Tauris, 2011.]

M.A. Amir-Moezzi, *Le Coran silencieux et le Coran parlant. Sources scriptuaires de l'islam entre histoire et ferveur.* Paris: CNRS, 2011. [The Silent Quran and the Speaking Quran, English trans., New York: Columbia University Press, 2015.]

M.A. Amir-Moezzi & Pierre Lory, *Petite histoire de l'islam*, Paris: Librio, 2007.

S.W. Anthony, *The Caliph and the Heretic: Ibn Saba' and the Origins of Shi'ism*, Leiden: Brill, 2012.

C. Van Arendonk, *De Opkomst van het Zaidietische Imamaat in Yemen*, Leiden: Brill, 1919. [*Les Débuts de l'imamat zaidite au Yémen*, French trans. by J. Rykmans, Leiden: Brill, 1960.]

M. Asatryan, *Contrversies in Formative Shi'i Islam. The Ghulat Muslims and Their Beliefs*, London: I.B. Tauris, 2017.

M. Ayoub, *Redemptive Suffering in Islam: A Study of the Devotional Aspects of Ashura in Twelver Shi'ism*, The Hague: Mouton, 1978.

M.M. Bar Asher, "The Qur'anic Commentary Ascribed to Imam Hasan al 'Askari", *Jerusalem Studies in Arabic and Islam*, 24, 2000, pp. 358–379.

T. Bayhom-Daou, "Hisham ibn al-Hakam (d. 179/795) and his Doctrine of the Imam's Knowledge", *Journal of Semitic Studies*, 58, 2003, pp. 71–108.

T. Bayhom-Daou, "The Second-Century Ghulat: Were They Really Gnostic?", *Journal of Arabic and Islamic Studies*, 5, 2003–2004, pp. 13–61.

M.A. Buyukkara, "The Schism of the Party of Musa al-Kazim and the Emergence of the Waqifa", *Arabica*, 47, 2000, pp. 78–99.

A. Cameron, *Abu Dharr al-Ghifari: An Examination of His Image in the Hagiography of Islam*, London: Royal Asiatic Society, 1973.

L. Capezzone, "Abiura dalla Kaysaniyya e conversione all'Imamiyya: il caso di Abu Khalid al-Kabuli", *Rivista degli Studi Orientali* 66, 1992, pp. 1–14.

P. Chelkowski (ed.), *Ta'zieh: Ritual and Drama in Iran*, New York: New York University Press, 1979.

W. Chittick, *The Psalms of Islam* (translation with an introduction and annotation of al-Sahifat al-kamilat al-sajjadiyya by Imam Zayn al-'Abidin 'Ali ibn al-Husayn), London: The Muhammadi Trust, 1988.

D.K. Crow, "The Death of al-Husayn b. 'Ali and Early Shi'i Views of the Imamate", *Alserat* (al-Sirat), 12, 1986, pp. 71–116. [Now available in E. Kohlberg (ed.), *Shi'ism: The Formation of the Classical Islamic World*, vol. 33, Aldershot, England: Ashgate, 2003, article no. 3.]

F. Daftary, *A Short History of the Ismailis: Traditions of a Muslim Community*, Edinburgh: Edinburgh University Press, 1998. [*Les Ismaéliens: histoire et traditions d'une communauté musulmane*, French trans. by Z. Rajan-Badouraly, Paris: Fayard, 2003).

F. Daftary, *A History of Shi'i Islam*, London: I.B. Tauris, 2014.

F. Daftary, & G. Miskinzoda (eds), *The Study of Shi'i Islam: History, Theology and Law*, London: I.B. Tauris, 2014.

M. Dakake, *The Charismatic Community. Shi'i Identity in Early Islam*, Albany, NY: State University of New York Press, 2007.

H. Djaït, "Les Yamanites à Kufa au 1er siècle de l'Hégire", *Journal of the Economic and Social History of the Orient*, 19, 1976, pp. 141–181.

J. van Ess, *Theologie und Gesellschaft im 2. und 3. Jahrhundert Hidschra*, 6 vol., Berlin, New York: De Gruyter, 1991–1997.

T. Fahd, "Ja'far al-Sadiq et la tradition scientifique arabe", in *Le Shi'isme imamite*, (conference proceedings, Strasbourg, 6–9 May 1968), Paris: Presses Universitaires de France, 1970, pp. 131–142.

F. Gabrieli, *Al-Ma'mun e gli Alidi*, Leipzig: Verlag Van Eduard Pfeiffer, 1929.

N. Haider, *The Origins of the Shi'a: Identity, Ritual and Sacred Space in Eighth-Century Kufa*, Cambridge: Cambridge University Press, 2011.

H. Halm, *Die Schia*, Darmstadt: Wissenschaftliche Buchgesellschaft, 1988. [*Shi'ism*, English trans. by J. Watson and M. Hill, Edinburgh: Edinburgh University Press, 2004.]

G. Hawting, "The Tawwabun, Atonement and 'Ashura", *Jerusalem Studies in Arabic and Islam*, 17, 1994, pp. 166–181.

J.M. Hussain, *The Occultation of the Twelfth Imam: A Historical Background*, London: The Muhammadi Trust, 1982.

S.H.M. Jafri, *The Origins and Early Development of Shi'a Islam*, London: Longman, 1979.

Khaled Kheshk, "The Historiography of an Execution: the Killing of Hujr ibn 'Adi", *Journal of Islamic Studies*, 19, 2008, pp. 1–35.

V. Klemm, "Die vier Sufara' des zwölften Imam. Zur formativen Periode der Zwölfer-shi'a", *Die Welt des Orients*, 15, 1984, pp. 126–143 [English trans. by G. Goldbloom, in E. Kohlberg (ed.), Shi'ism: *The Formation of the Classical Islamic World*, vol. 33, Aldershot, England: Ashgate, 2003, article no. 6.]

E. Kohlberg, "From Imamiyya to Ithna-'ashariyya", *Bulletin of the School of Oriental and African Studies*, 39, 1976, pp. 521–534. [Now available in a collection of articles by the author, Belief and Law in Imami Shi ism, Aldershot, England: Variorum, 1991, article no. 14.]

E. Kohlberg, "Some Shi'i views on the antediluvian world", *Studia Islamica*, 52, 1980, pp. 41–66. [Now available in *Belief and Law in Imami Shi'ism*, article no. 16.]

E. Kohlberg, "Some Imami Shi'i views on the Sahaba", *Jerusalem Studies in Arabic and Islam*, 5, 1984, pp. 143–175. [Now available in *Belief and Law in Imami Shi ism*, article no. 9.]

E. Kohlberg, "In Praise of the Few", in *Studies in Islamic and Middle Eastern Texts and Traditions. In Memory of Norman Calder*, ed. G.R. Hawting, J.A. Mojaddedi and A. Samely, Oxford: Oxford University Press, 2000, pp. 149–162.

A.R. Lalani, *Early Shi'i Thought: The Teachings of Imam Muhammad al Baqir*, London: I.B. Tauris, 2000.

H. Laoust, *Les Schismes dans l'Islam*, Paris: Payot, 1965.

H. Laoust, "Comment définir le sunnisme et le chiisme", *Revue des études islamiques*, 47 (1), 1979, pp. 3–17.

W. Madelung, *Der Imam al-Qasim ibn Ibrahim und die Glaubenslehre der Zaiditen*, Berlin: Walter de Gruyter, 1965.

W. Madelung, "New Documents Concerning al-Ma'mun, al-Fadl b. Sahl and 'Ali al Rida", in *Studia Arabica e Islamica: Festschrift for Ihsan Abbas on his Sixtieth Birthday*, ed. W.al-Qadi, Beirut: American University of Beirut, 1981, pp. 333–346.

W. Madelung, *Religious Trends in Early Islamic Iran*, Albany, NY: State University of New York Press, 1988.

W. Madelung, *The Succession to Muhammad: A Study of the Early Caliphate*, Cambridge: Cambridge University Press, 1997.

H. Modarressi, *Crisis and Consolidation in the Formative Period of Shi'ite Islam: Abu Ja'far ibn Qiba al-Razi and his Contribution to Imamite Shi'ite Thought*, Princeton, NY: Darwin Press, 1993.

H. Modarressi, *Tradition and Survival: A Bibliographical Survey of Early Shi'ite Literature*, vol. 1, Oxford: Oneworld, 2003.

M. Moosa, *Extremist Shiites. The Ghulat Sects*, Syracuse, NY: Syracuse University Press, 1987.

T. Nagel, *Rechtleitung und Kalifat. Versuch über eine Grundfrage der islamischen Geschichte*, Bonn: Orientalisches Seminars der Universität, 1975.

Hasan Nawbakhti, *Les Sectes shi'ites*, trans. M.J. Mashkour, Tehran, 2nd edition, 1980.

E.L. Petersen, *Ali and Mu'awiya in Early Arabic Tradition*, Copenhagen: ACLS, 1964.

M. Pierce, *Twelve Infallible Men: The Imams and the Making of Shi'ism*, Cambridge, MA: Harvard University Press, 2016.

W. al-Qadi, "An Early Fatimid Political Document", *Studia Islamica*, 48, 1978, pp. 71–108,

J. Ruska, *Arabische Alchemisten. II-Ja'far al-Sadiq, der sechste Imam*, Heidelberg: Winter, 1924.

B. Scarcia Amoretti, "Gli ashab di 'Ali al-Rida: il caso di Fadl ibn Sahl", *Quaderni di Studi Arabi*, 5–6, 1987–1988, pp. 699–707.

M. Sharon, *Black Banners from the East: The Establishment of the Abbasid State – Incubation of a Revolt*, Jerusalem; Leiden: Magnes Press – The Hebrew University; Brill, 1983.

M. Sharon, "Ahl al-Bayt – People of the House", *Jerusalem Studies in Arabic and Islam*, 8, 1986, pp. 169–184.

D. Sourdel, "La politique religieuse du calife abbaside al-Ma'mun", *Revue des études islamiques*, 30, 1962, pp. 27–48. [Now available in *Belief and Law in Imami Shi'ism*, article no. 17.]

L.N. Takim, *The Heirs of the Prophet: Charisma and Religious Authority in Shi'ite Islam*, Albany, NY: State University of New York Press, 2006.

J.B. Taylor, "Ja'far al-Sadiq, Spiritual Forebear of the Sufis", in *Islamic Culture*, 40, 1966, pp. 97–113.

W. Tucker, *Mahdis and Millenarians: Shi'ite Extremists in Early Muslim Iraq*. Cambridge: Cambridge University Press, 2008.

C. Turner, "'The Tradition of al-Mufaddal' and the Doctrine of the Raj'a: Evidence of Ghuluww in the Eschatology of Twelver Shi'ism?" *Iran*, 44, 2006, pp. 175–196.

L. Veccia Vaglieri, "Il conflitto 'Ali-Mu'awiya e la secessione kharigita riesiminati alla luce di fonte ibadite", *Annali dell'Istituto Universitario Orientale di Napoli*, 4, 1952, pp. 63–95.

L. Veccia Vaglieri, "Sul Nahj al-Balag'ah e sul suo compilatore al-Sharif al-Radi", *Annali dell'Istituto Universitario Orientale di Napoli*, 8, 1958, pp. 3–105.

C. Virolleaud, *Le Théatre persan ou le Drame de Kerbela*, Paris: Adrien-Maisonneuve, 1950.

W.M. Watt, "Shi'ism under the Umayyads", *Journal of the Royal Asiatic Society*, 3–4, 1960, pp. 158–172.

W.M. Watt, "The Rafidites: A preliminary study", *Oriens*, 16, 1963, pp. 110–121.

J. Wellhausen, *Die religiös-politischen Oppositionsparteien im alten Islam*, Berlin: Weidmannsche Buchhandlung, 1901. [The Religio-Political Factions in Early Islam, English trans. by R.C. Ostle and S.M. Walzer, Amsterdam: North-Holland, 1975.]

Part II
The sources and contents of the sacred teachings

3   The foundational sources

The Qur'an and the hadith

Two centuries after the Hijra, the Qur'an and the hadith (literally the deeds and sayings of the Prophet, also called the traditions) had become widely accepted – though not without tension and strife – as cornerstones of Islam. This did not occur peacefully. Today Sunnis and Shia do agree on the importance of these scriptural sources, but their conceptions of each of these sources are divergent.

The official Sunni version of the Qur'an is the text we are familiar with today. According to Muslim tradition, this version was compiled under the third caliph, 'Uthman ibn 'Affan (ruled 24–35/644–656). For orthodox Sunnis, "the Codex of 'Uthman" represents the full and faithful reproduction of the Word of God "sent down" to the Prophet, though the order of its chapters does not follow the actual chronological order of the revelations as Muhammad received them.

The Sunni hadith provide a record of the Prophetic traditions; that is, the words, sayings and deeds ascribed to Muhammad during his lifetime. The length of a hadith can vary quite significantly, though it is usually fairly short. A list of names tracing the chain of transmission back to the Prophet authenticates the hadith. As the Prophet was hailed quite early as the archetype of the true Muslim, his tradition eventually assumed a normative value. This explains why not long after his death every political and religious movement, every legal and theological school, every current of thought was concocting hadith attributed to the Prophet to justify their point of view and/or to refute the opinion of their adversaries. Barely a century after Muhammad's death, tens of thousands of hadith circulated throughout the Islamic empire in every conceivable social milieu and geographical region. As most were patently apocryphal, as everyone was well aware, there was a growing need for some reliable criteria of authenticity.

By the 3rd/9th century, what we know as Sunni orthodoxy had more or less reached its final expression, and criteria for authenticating the hadith were established in accord with its norms. These criteria were based on the credibility of the transmitter in the chain as well as on the nature of the material.

The application of these two criteria occasioned the rejection of many hadith. Those that were accepted were included in collections of "authentic" hadith (*Sahih*).

According to convention, there are six collections of Sunni hadith, the "Six authentic Books". All date from the 3rd/9th century. Their authors are recognized as the supreme authorities of hadith transmission: Bukhari, Muslim, Tirmidhi, Ibn Maja, Abu Dawud and Nasa'i.[1]

The Shia, quite naturally, have a different view of the matter. If we begin our discussion with the hadith, that is because it played an important role in determining the attitude of the Shia towards the Qur'an, particularly in the early period up until the middle of the 4th/10th century.

Shi'i hadith

In comparison with the Sunni hadith, the traditions of the Twelver Shia are far more voluminous, since the speaker, he who offers instruction, is not the Prophet alone but the totality of the Fourteen Impeccable (or Sinless) Ones[2]; that is, Muhammad, his daughter Fatima and the twelve Imams. In this huge body of material, comprising several thousands of pages, the portions devoted to the fifth and, in particular, the sixth Imam, Muhammad al-Baqir and Ja'far al-Sadiq, respectively, are much greater than the others. Moreover, simply because there are twelve of them, the traditions attributable to the imams outnumber those ascribed to the Prophet. Furthermore, the very centrality of the figure of the imam means that every member of the entire group of the Impeccables possesses equal weight on the scales of the spiritual. As a close examination of the compilations of Shi'i hadith reveals, the most important doctrinal teachings are always attributable to one of the twelve imams, for the imam is the messenger of the esoteric and in Shi'ism the hidden is always superior to the manifest. In the final analysis, the Prophet has a fairly modest place in the Shi'i corpus of hadith.

Not surprisingly, Sunni Islam vehemently objects to the Shi'i attitude. Meanwhile Shi'i Islam denies the truth of the Sunni hadith (there are a few traditions – particularly in the field of law – which the two communities do agree to share in common). The reason for the Shi'i rejection of Sunni traditions is simple enough. The critical link in the chain of Sunni transmitters is the group of the Prophet's Companions. The Shia, of course, view them as traitors to Muhammad's cause, and they are accorded no credibility. A Shi'i chain of transmission is only valid if it includes the name of one or more imams as author or transmitter; even a prophetic hadith can only be transmitted by the imams.

The systematic transcription of hadith appears to have started in the first half of the 2nd/8th century under the imamate of Ja'far al-Sadiq, probably on his orders. Gradually this resulted in a compilation of "400 Original Writings" (*'asl*, plural *usul*), collections of hadith – in Arabic, of course – transcribed by disciples from the dictation of one or another of the imams. All that remains of these originals are a few dozen pages of fragments, though these were apparently integrated into the vast compendia at a later date. The oldest of the fragments that have come down to us date from between 250/864 and 350/961. This is the period roughly corresponding to the imamate of the final three or four imams, hence to the beginning of the occultation. Because of this chronology, the touchy question of the authenticity of the hadiths included in the compendia looms more pointedly for the Shia, because the person of the living imam responsible for personally overseeing the contents of the compilation is the requisite and the sufficient guarantor of their truthfulness.[3] It is probably for this reason that in contradistinction to Sunnism where it developed quite early, a Shi'i "science of hadith authentication", charged with determining the criteria to identify authentic traditions (i.e. with distinguishing the "authentic Books" from collections of forgeries), took its definitive shape much later in Shi'ism, around the 7th/13th century.

Clearly, the collections of hadith played a central role in the formulation, consolidation, expansion and perpetuation of doctrines. Their authors and compilers are considered champions of the faith and are hugely respected. In large measure it was due to their efforts in researching, collecting and writing down the hadith that Twelver Shi'ism, weakened after the major crisis under the last four imams and the mass conversions of the faithful to other forms of Shi'ism, slowly began to recover, eventually becoming one of the most powerful religious currents in Islam.

Among the many important compilers of hadith, the following are particularly noteworthy: Abu Ja'far Barqi (d. 274/887 or 280/893), Saffar Qummi (d. 290/902–903), 'Ali ibn Ibrahim Qummi (d. circa. 307/919), Muhammad ibn Mas'ud 'Ayyashi (d. circa 320/932), Muhammad ibn Ya'qub Kulayni (d. 329/940–941), Ibn Abi Zaynab Nu'mani (d. ca. 360/971) and Ibn Babuya (an Iranian name – in Arabic, Ibn Babawayhi; d. 381/991).

It is interesting to note that the great majority of these early Traditionists came from two cities in central Iran: Qumm and Rayy, south of Tehran, both of which became Shia quite early. It should be noted as well that the hadith collections of the two schools of Rayy and Qumm, the oldest systematic proof of Twelver sacred teachings, are in Arabic. The specific feature of this large body of writings lies in its esoteric, initiatory and often magical orientation. The Twelver teachings seem to reproduce a more fully developed version of an early Shi'i tradition from the Iraqi city of Kufa. Textual proof of the exact age and original form of this doctrine is sadly missing. Be that as it may, the Shi'i hadith of the Iranian schools became the principal instrument of the "non-rational esoteric tradition", as it is called today.[4] We referred to this particular tradition in our presentation of the basic doctrinal principles in Part I. We will return to it again in Chapter 4 when we discuss the sacred teachings of the imams. In Part III, we will come across another current, the "rationalist tradition of the Baghdadi jurists and theologians". Its advocates ultimately sidelined – and indeed persecuted – the school of Rayy and Qumm after the middle of the 4th/10th century.

Thus in the minds of the faithful, the hadith represent the utterances of the Fourteen Impeccable Ones and, especially, the teachings of the Twelve Holy Guides. What then do these Guides have to say about the Qur'an?

The Qur'an according to Shi'ism

"Any hadith that does not conform to the Qur'an is a nice lie." This particular tradition attributable to Imam Ja'far defines the elementary criteria for assessing the authenticity of any hadith, and at the same time it emphasizes the fundamental sacredness of the Qur'an. This is significant because much of the material pertaining to Shi'i doctrines found in the collections of the hadith – for example, cosmogonic myths, eschatological beliefs and the notion of the imam – does not have its textual basis in the Qur'an, in any case not in the text of "the vulgate of 'Uthman", the accepted standard version today.

According to tradition, Imam Ja'far said,

> I am a descendant of the Messenger of God [i.e. Muhammad]. I know the Book of God, wherein is the knowledge of how the world was first created and the knowledge of all that will come until the Day of Judgment. Therein is the story of all the events in the heavens and the earth, of paradise and hell, and the news of the past and of the future. I know all of those things as clearly as if I were looking at the palm of my own hand.

But the text of the Qur'an does not include all of this. What is meant by this?

Up until the first half of the 4th/10th century, Shi'i texts report a large number of traditions attributed to the imams, evoking an issue so explosive and of such dire implication that the majority of Shia rejected it almost immediately; namely, that the official text of the Qur'an, known to the faithful as the standard text, is in fact a censored, altered and falsified version of the true Revelation given to the Prophet Muhammad.

It is true that it took time for the so-called vulgate of 'Uthman version to achieve more or less unanimous acceptance, and that did not come about without violence. There is evidence from historiographic, heresiographic and doctrinal sources – quite guarded, to be sure – to suggest that some of Muhammad's Companions, various Kharijite followers or a few Mu'tazilite thinkers cast doubt on the integrity of the official version. But no sect or religious movement has gathered so much systematic and corroborating proof as Shi'ism in its challenge of the official text.

First, there are what might be termed indirect indications. Dispersed within the huge mass of traditions, reported within chapters that often have nothing to do with the subject as though to conceal matters known to be extremely subversive, certain imams resort unequivocally, with reference to the vulgate of 'Uthman, to such terms as "falsification", "alteration" and "modification" to describe what the Enemies of the imams did to the original Qur'an. Moreover, some classical heresiographers[5] have always singled out the idea of a falsified official Qur'an as among the most scandalous and "heretical" of Shi'i beliefs.

Turning now to direct indications, we find them diffused throughout the corpus of the traditions. The seriousness of the matter required discretion. This is why in many traditions the imams advised their disciples to practice "keeping the secret" (*taqiyya*) regarding the problem of the Qur'an's falsification or to recite the official version in the presence of non-Shia. According to these direct signs, after the death of the Prophet Muhammad, the only person possessing a full and complete version of the Revelation was 'Ali, Muhammad's true heir and initiated pupil, his secretary and intimate friend. This unabridged version is nearly three times longer than the official version. Most of the Prophet's Companions, led by Abu Bakr and 'Umar, the first two caliphs, and several influential members of the Quraysh tribe rejected the unabridged text and established a falsified one. The new text, with the most important passages of the original removed, was established and declared official by the third caliph, 'Uthman, who then ordered the destruction of all other versions.

According to the Shi'i hadith, the original Revelation included numerous verses in which 'Ali and the Prophet's descendants – that is, Fatima and the imams – were identified as leaders and role models for the community. Other verses, equally numerous, denounced by name the powerful men of the Quraysh tribe for their betrayal of Muhammad, his Book and his religion. Moreover, the original Revelation was said to contain "everything": the mysteries of the heavens and the earth, the knowledge of all things past, present and future. But all of this was censored in the official version. 'Ali took great pains to conceal the full and complete version, which had been rejected and threatened with destruction. This version was secretly transmitted from imam to imam until the twelfth and final one, who took it with him into his occultation. No one but he knows its exact content, which will not be revealed in full until the Hidden Imam returns at the End of Time. In the meantime, the Muslim faithful must accept the censored, altered version, the "official" version of 'Uthman, even though it derives from the treachery of the Companions. Because of their arrogance and impiety in setting aside 'Ali from the Prophet's inheritance and excising the deepest truths from the Book, they put in motion the decline of the community.

Nearly all the oldest collections of the traditions until the middle of the 4th/10th century included a certain number of Imami writings and sayings with quotations from the "original unabridged Qur'an". These, of course, are not found in the version in use today.[6] Here are a few significant passages from among many (the words and expressions absent from the official version are indicated in italics):

Qur'an 2:225: "To Him belongs all that is in the heavens and in the Earth, *and all that is between the heavens and the Earth or under the Earth, the visible World and the invisible World. He is compassionate and merciful.* Who will intercede with Him except by His leave?"

Qur'an 4:63: "These are the people of whom God knows what is in their hearts, so turn away from them *for the Word of evil and torment is their lot* [here is missing 'exhort them', which is found in the official version]. Address convincing words to them that apply to their own case."

Qur'an 4:65–66: "They will not find any possibility of escape until you will decide *concerning the cause of the divine Friend* [the Imam], and they will yield *completely in obedience to God.* And had We decreed for them: 'Kill yourselves *and submit yourselves completely to the Imam,*' or 'Leave your land *for him,*' they would not have done so except for a few of them. And *if the dissenters* [instead of 'if they'] had done what they were advised, it would have been better for them and helped to strengthen them."

Qur'an 20:115: "And We once confided to Adam *words concerning Muhammad, 'Ali, Fatima, al-Hasan, al-Husayn, and the Imams from their issue*, but he forgot them."

Qur'an 33:71: "And whosoever obeys God and His messenger *in regard to the holy power of 'Ali and the Imams after him* enjoys great felicity".[7]

Qur'an 42:13: "He has decreed for you, *O Family of Muhammad* [i.e. Fatima and the Imams], the same belief He ordained for Noah, and what We revealed to you, *O Muhammad*, and what We ordained for Abraham, Moses, and Jesus: 'Establish the religion *of the Family of Muhammad*, do not be divided about it but stay united.' How Intolerable it seems to those who have set up partners, who associate *other powers with the holy power of 'Ali*, what you invite them to through the holy power of 'Ali. *Verily*, God guides, *O Muhammad*, to this religion those who repent, *the same who accept your call to the holy power of 'Ali* [instead of: God chooses and summons to this religion whomever He wills; He guides those who repent to it]."

While corroborating the premises of critical and philological studies of the history of the compilation of the Qur'an (the establishment of the text over time, the many deletions and rewritings of the early versions, the effect of historical and political events) – not in detail but in broad outline and, to be sure, unwittingly – the attitude of early Shi'ism regarding revelation consists, on the one hand, of endowing its theory of the imamate with Qur'anic foundations and, on the other, of accentuating the limitless impiety and brutality of the "enemies" of Shi'ism. In the eyes of the Shia, harsh diatribes against the Prophet's Companions were justifiable because they had been responsible for shunting 'Ali aside from succeeding Muhammad and for falsifying and censoring the "complete and unabridged Qur'an".[8] Because the Companions "betrayed" 'Ali, the imams blamed them – and the first three caliphs in particular – for the rapid religious and moral decline of the Muslim community which came about right after the Prophet's death. This, at any rate, is how the early corpus of the hadith represented the imams.

The hadith also show them to be distressed by the brutishness and ignorance of the ordinary people, who within decades had abandoned the teachings and instructions of the Prophet and his God. The responsibility for this state of affairs was laid squarely at the feet of the community leaders, who tolerated the falsification of the divine message and imposed it, with trickery and violence, on the majority of Muslims. In the dualistic conception of the world, this represents a mere episode in the universal struggle between the forces of Knowledge and Ignorance. Judaism and Christianity, to name only these two religions, had their holy scriptures falsified after the death of their founders; their members, too, had been isolated and then persecuted by an ignorant majority which had usurped power.

Among the celebrated Traditionists, authors of the early Shi'i hadith which later became classics, Ibn Babuya (d. 381/991) seems to have been the first not merely to have remained silent on these matters but to have adopted a position in accord with Sunni orthodoxy: the official Qur'an of 'Uthman and the Qur'an revealed to Muhammad are one and the same. Anyone who argued otherwise was either a liar or a dangerous deviant. From this moment onward, this attitude would steadily become that of mainstream Twelver Shi'ism. Meanwhile, as we shall see in Part III, two important events took place: the occultation of the last imam (marking the end of the time of the historical imams) and the rise to power of the Shi'i Buyids in Baghdad (between 334/945 and 447/1055) and their capture of the Abbasid caliphate. An important outcome of this for Imami Shi'ism would be the development and consolidation of the "rationalist theological and juridical tradition". The main concern of this movement seems to have been to eliminate, or at least reformulate, the discrepancies that provoked violent conflict with Sunnism in order to prove its consistency with "orthodox" belief. There was no longer any place for belief in the falsification of the vulgate of 'Uthman. Henceforth, orthodoxy and orthopraxis in Islam would be defined and justified by that vulgate, including all rituals, legal precepts, theological doctrine and institutions. Doubting the authenticity of the official Book was tantamount to contesting Islamic orthodoxy. This would not and could not be tolerated by the jurists, who were under Buyid protection, themselves "protectors of the caliphate".

In the end, the main current of Shi'ism abandoned the notion of a "falsified" official version of the Qur'an, which gradually came to be forgotten by most believers. Nevertheless, at different moments in history, there have been authors – and not merely minor ones – who, faithful to the early texts of the traditions, professed this view again from time to time: from Ibn Shahrashub and Tabrisi (6th/12th century) to the great thinkers of the 17th and 18th centuries – Fayd Kashani, Hashim Bahrani, Majlisi, Ni'matallah Jaza'iri, Sharif 'Amili – up to the renowned religious authority of modern times – Mirza Husayn Nuri (d. 1902). Nor should we neglect the controversial work of the 11th/17th century, *Dabestan-e madhaheb*, or the manuscript of the same period from Bankipur, India, which contains the text of two complete suras reportedly belonging to the original unabridged Qur'an: the sura of Two Lights (i.e. Muhammad and 'Ali) and the sura of the *Walaya* (the divine election of 'Ali and his descendants).[9] These authors, almost without exception members of the "traditionalist" school, had to face the opposition – and downright hostility – of their co-religionists, the "Rationalists". In the opinion of the "Traditionalists", the falsification thesis was proved true by the fact that it was hugely present in numerous traditions of the imams and conveyed in the old compilations whose authority and trustworthiness are unanimously accepted. As for the Rationalists, they believed that since the authenticity of the official Qur'an is beyond doubt, the occurrence of this sort of tradition in the corpus of early hadith merely proves that "radical deviant" circles had contaminated the original traditions with "forged" traditions. And so, between the two fundamental sources of Islam, the Qur'an and the hadith, the Rationalists placed their confidence in the Qur'an and the Traditionalists placed theirs in the hadith. This shows just how contentious and divisive this subject has always been among Shi'i scholars, continuing down to the present day.[10]

Notes

1 Six is an approximate number. Sunnis recognize other "authentic" authorities from the early period (Ibn Hanbal, Malik ibn Anas) and after (Baghawi, Ibn Hajar, *et al*).
2 "Impeccable" or "pure" in the sense of "without sin", "faultless".
3 Of course, the historian cannot be content with such criteria arising from religious belief. If the tenth imam accredits the statements of the second imam, for example, this by no means guarantees that the second imam in fact made such pronouncements historically. Frequently, even the textual authenticity attributable to the tenth imam remains for the historian a hypothesis difficult to verify. The important issue is that the faithful believed the hadith to be authentic, and therefore holy, because it was believed to originate with the imam.
4 We avoid the term "irrational" by design as its connotation is too negative. "Non-rational" does not mean something ill-defined, stupid or illogical, but rather something that is not under the control of reason or that is rebellious to rationalization. In the following pages, we will attempt to identify the main elements of this thought with treatment of a universally accepted scientific character in order to remove any ambiguity of meaning. Our purpose is not to rationalize the non-rational – which is impossible – but rather to hold it up and examine it, identifying its components and opposing the strength of a dogma, by definition spiritual, and the fantasies of the "irrational". These distinctions are all the more important because "spiritual non-rationalism" has frequently had to confront the extravagances of religious "irrationalism" as well as the simplifications of scholastic "rationalism".
5 Such important authors as Ash'ari (d. 324/935), Ibn Hazm (d. 456/1054) and Isfara'ini (d. 471/1078–1079).
6 These quotations represent no more than a few lines each time. Much later, in the 11th/17th century, several sources record the text between two short suras.
7 This refers to the pre-existing metaphysical entity of the Pure Beings. Together they represent in absolute terms the Cosmic Imam, the revealed face of God. We will return to this later in our discussion of Shi'i cosmogonic myths.
8 This attitude forms the basis of the notion known as *sabb al-sahaba* (literally, cursing the Companions), which has always scandalized Sunnis. It forms part of a broader notion of hatred or sacred dissociation (*bara'a*) from the forces of Ignorance – the necessary complement of *walaya*, sacred love for the Imam (see Part I). As we have seen, the imams prohibited their followers from manifesting their hatred in open revolt. Hence, *bara'a* must remain internalized until the return of the Hidden Imam, even if this means outward obedience to unjust powers. This is one of the facets in

the struggle which has always opposed the initiation of the ignorant, and "cursing the Companions" is one way for the faithful to sustain their awareness of this.

9 For a discussion of *Walaya*, a central concept of Shi'ism, see Chapter 5.

10 In particular, after the classic heresiological material of the medieval period and the violent diatribes of Ibn Taymiyya in the 14th century, the interest of Sunni intellectuals in the matter waned until the 20th century, at which time the debate ignited again and violently so (at the same time, oddly enough, that attempts were being made to reconcile Shia and Sunnis, during and after several ecumenical meetings in the 1950s). The Sunnis make frequent reference to the work of Mirza Husayn Nuri, mentioned above, when they denounce the Shi'i heresy of the falsification of the Qur'an. Sunni attacks, coming especially from Saudi and Pakistani Wahhabis, redoubled in fury following the Iranian Islamic Revolution in 1979.

4 Shi'i teachings and their levels

It is customary to present Shi'ism as rooted in five principles. The first three –
the "principles of religion" – are shared by Shia and Sunnis alike and are
characteristic of Islam in general. They are: belief in the Oneness of God, belief
in the mission of the prophets, and belief in the existence of reward and punishment in the afterlife. The last two principles are particular to Shi'ism and are
known as the "principles of the school". They are: belief in divine Justice and
belief in the principle of the imamate. This representation of the faith, however,
is somewhat simplistic and anachronistic (it dates from the 17th or 18th century).
It reflects the rationalist tradition of later centuries, which was concerned with
tempering Shi'i doctrine in order to establish its "orthodoxy" and bring it in
line with majority belief. In reality, the fundamental doctrinal sources define the
five principles in a distinctively Shi'i manner. We must take a closer look at this.

Again and again the imams insist, "our teachings are demanding and difficult
to uphold; they are secret: a secret about a secret wrapped in a secret". Ja'far
al-Sadiq reportedly said, "Our teachings include the exoteric, the esoteric and
the esoteric of the esoteric". The truth of this emerges when the corpus of Shi'i
hadith is examined in detail. What we find are different levels of teachings and
doctrines, which are difficult for an "ordinary" Muslim to accept or, indeed, to
understand. No doubt followers were organized in groups according to levels
of knowledge and degrees of initiation. All the same, the doctrines, from the
general to the most specific, are said to be in agreement with the Qur'an. In
fact Shi'ism goes so far as to present itself as a complex hermeneutic of the
Holy Book (this in turn explains the central role of exegesis in Shi'ism).
Because of this, we will return to this point at some length. For the moment,
we will examine several particularly representative topics and their levels of
meaning in order to clarify the traditions just cited and to present the teaching
briefly in its various facets.

Canon law

Legal material occupies a large place in the different hadith compendia. At first
glance, the overall appearance of Shi'i law is quite similar to Sunni canon law.
And indeed, the foundations of private law, penal law and the law of duties are

virtually the same. In formal aspects as well, resemblances are numerous, such as in the organization of chapters (e.g. ritual, which is placed at the beginning, is followed by transactions regarding inheritances); likewise in the titles of sub-chapters and the organization of subject matter. If we take the example of many important institutions for which there is no Qur'anic legal framework, we might expect the jurists to have developed very different legal formulations for the different communities (all the more so since the collections of traditions that fill in the gaps in the Qur'an are rarely identical from one end to the other). Yet there are countless similarities: examples include the revival of dead land, breastfeeding and the pre-emption of property. Because of this it might be said that in general, Shi'i law is not fundamentally any more different from Sunni law than the four Sunni legal schools are from each other. However, there are three specific cases which are particularly noteworthy for the degree of divergence and intensity of disagreement that they have engendered between Shia and Sunnis.

- **Temporary marriage (usually called *mut'a* or *sigha*).** This differs from permanent marriage in that a husband has no obligation to provide any form of support to a wife; nor does temporary marriage involve any form of inheritance between the two partners (though the parties may reach an agreement to the contrary in both instances); and, finally, the marriage contract must stipulate that the union is restricted to a specific time frame. The man is obliged to pay a dower, and any children born of the union will be legitimate. Sunnis hold temporary marriage to be scandalous, a form of prostitution, and have tried for centuries to ban it, but with difficulty since both the Qur'an and the hadith are not precise on the topic. The Shia themselves consider *mut'a* a lower order form of marriage, certainly inferior to ordinary permanent marriage.
- **Repudiation (*talaq*).** Divorce has its legitimacy in the Qur'an and is observed by both Sunnis and Shia. Nevertheless, Shia have organized their form of divorce so rigorously that Shia and Sunni practices have nothing in common. For Shia, in contrast to Sunnis (with the qualified exception of the Malikis), a husband may not divorce a wife during confinement after childbirth, during her menstrual period or if sexual intercourse has occurred since menstruation. Moreover, the divorce procedure, which is uncompli-cated in Sunni law (the husband pronounces three successive repudiations and the divorce is final), is strictly regulated in Shi'i law. Finally, declarations of divorce made indirectly by oath, wager or swearing, which are authorized in Sunni law, are forbidden by Shi'i law. This explains why divorce is rare among the Shia compared with Sunni practice.
- **The laws of inheritance.** The Qur'an established twelve fixed entitlement shares. But what happens to the shares if something remains after they are distributed or if no one is entitled to the inheritance? In Sunni law, the beneficiaries are the closest male relatives of the deceased. In Shi'i law, female and male relatives of the same kinship have the same entitlements.

Could it be otherwise in a system based on the absolute authority of the imams who are descendants of the Prophet through his daughter Fatima?

Finally there are some more discreet specific issues submerged in the teeming mass of legal traditions. The relevant texts are not assembled in any particular chapter, probably to escape the scrutiny of the curious reader who merely leafs through the books, as do most anti-Shia polemicists. Such "esoteric" law deals primarily with the legal status of non-Shi'i Muslims and specifically with their impurity, the invalidity of their faith, the illegitimacy of their birth and their ancestry. Here are a few examples.

A distinction is made between the "moderate" Sunnis, those who do not express open hostility towards the imams and the Shia, and the violent activist opponents of the imams and their followers (called *nasibi* Sunnis). Both are considered infidels, but at least the former can be dealt with as Muslims during this lifetime; God will punish them for their infidelity in the afterlife. Since expressions of hate for the Prophet's family are considered to be a flagrant sign of illegitimate birth, *nasibi* Sunnis are regarded as offspring of adulterous relations and, therefore, illegitimate. Now the first three caliphs, and the Umayyads and the Abbasids after them, rank among the *nasibi*. They are outwardly and inwardly impure. Water they have touched may not be used in ritual or profane purification. A *nasibi*'s sworn statement has no legal value. The Shia are not allowed to assist poor *nasibi*s, nor to eat the flesh of an animal sacrificed by them. They are not permitted to intermarry with them, nor to pray under their leadership. Although a Shia male may take a "moderate" Sunni woman for wife, a Shi'i female – especially one who has been initiated in the secret teachings of the imams (*al-'arifa*) – may only take a Shi'i husband. Naturally, in life-threatening circumstances, the Shi'i believer is allowed to exercise "tactical dissimulation"[1]; in other words, he is permitted to conceal his doctrinal beliefs and ignore the established rules.

This "esoteric law" reveals a strong religious identity and a sense of belonging, as well as a sectarian attitude accompanied by a constant concern for physical and spiritual purity. When the members of the community, believing themselves to be the "Elected", interact with individuals of other religious beliefs (particularly non-Shi'i Muslims), they display a strong anxiety over contamination. In many respects, in their specific details, such attitudes recall certain aspects of Judaism and, still more, Zoroastrianism.[2]

Cosmogony and anthropogony

Shi'i narratives of the origin of the universe and mankind are rooted in several myths. On this topic too the hadith are numerous and eclectic, but also unsystematic and contradictory. The reconstruction of a creation narrative in what might be its original unity involves assembling the pieces of a puzzle which have been widely dispersed, at times quite deliberately and arbitrarily. The fact that there can be several levels in the myths only further complicates the researcher's task.

At the exoteric level, the Shia share the same cosmogonic narratives with one or the other of several Muslim traditions. These narratives include: the Creation ex nihilo; the First Created Things (whether Qur'anic elements – the Pen, the Preserved Tablet, the Throne or the Chair, or the four Elements of ancient tradition); the seven Days of creation, the seven heavens and seven earths; the creation of angels and demons; the creation of the pillars of the universe (the cosmic Cock standing on the Rock balanced on the back of the Whale in the Ocean of Darkness, etc.); the creation of the regions, the various inhabitants, the ages and cycles of the universe; the creation of Adamic man and the non-human creatures inhabiting the earth, etc. These various narratives can be found in Muslim cosmographic works, the oldest of which are contemporary with the earliest Shi'i hadith compendia (3rd–4th/9th–10th centuries). With many elements in common with biblical and Midrashic literature, the origins of these narratives are generally ancient Near Eastern and, especially, Mesopotamian sources.

The esoteric cosmogony and anthropogeny are detailed in Shi'i narratives and have no equivalent in the Sunni tradition. In fact we are faced with several separate yet interrelated and overlapping myths.[3]

First, there is the creation of the worlds and their inhabitants. In the beginning, there was only God-Light. Thousands of years before the creation of the material world, God brought forth from his Light, on the one hand, the First World, called the Mother of the Book,[4] and on the other, the "inhabitant" of this world, the unique dual Light of Muhammad (symbol of the manifest aspect of being) and 'Ali (symbol of the hidden and secret aspect of being). This is the luminous, pre-existential entity of the supreme Prophet and Imam united in one being: Cosmic Man or the Cosmic Imam. This primordial being is frequently identified with the Five of the Mantle (Muhammad, 'Ali, Fatima, Hasan and Husayn), whose names derive from the divine Names, or with the ensemble of the Fourteen Impeccable Beings (Muhammad, Fatima, and the twelve imams).[5]

Next, another world is created: the First World of Particles or Shadows, also called the World of the Covenant. Here the luminous entities of the Impeccable Ones, as yet unformed, take on the form of human silhouettes composed of particles. These "silhouettes of light" begin to gravitate around the divine Throne, testifying to God's Oneness and praising His Glory. The next creation – also as particles – are the "pure beings"; they are the pre-existential forms of the angels, prophets and imams to come, and of the "believers" (*mu'min*), the future initiates of all times.[6] Next comes the Pact, the primordial Covenant (one of the appellations of this world) that God concludes with these "pure beings". This comprises four solemn oaths of fidelity: to God, to the prophetic mission of Muhammad, to the sacred Cause of the imams (*walaya*, cf. Chapter 3), and to the advent of the Mahdi at the End of Time.

As in every initiation rite, the pledging of an oath provides access to initiation. It is at this moment that the primordial initiation occurs: the luminous forms of the Impeccable Ones (the Masters of Initiation) transmit the secrets of God's

Oneness and Glory to the pre-existing shadows of the "pure beings" (the initiated disciples).[7] It is important to note that the "believers" (i.e. the "Shia") are attributed the same weight in the scales of the sacred as the angels, prophets, and imams. All four together comprise the forces of knowledge.

Then, the Second World of Particles or of Shadows is created. Its inhabitants are the particles (or shadows) of the future descendants of Adam created from earth and water. Things are now less and less intangible, more and more material. The beings emerging from the Clay are divided into the "People of the Right" and the "People of the Left", a division we will return to.

Finally, the sensible world and Adam, the father of humanity, come into being. In Adam – in his "loins", as the texts put it – God placed the unique dual Light of Muhammad and 'Ali: the Light of the Alliance (*walaya*) between God and his creatures in its twofold exoteric and esoteric aspects: the vehicle of initiated knowledge and spiritual power. This light is transmitted to the descendants of Adam in two ways: through the teaching of sacred knowledge and through the seminal fluids of the initiates. Thus the Light of knowledge commences its long journey through the generations of mankind, meandering through time and space – through humanity's sacred History – until it reaches its predestined agents par excellence, Muhammad, 'Ali and Fatima, "the Confluence of the Two Lights", thence to be transmitted to the other imams. The imams in turn pass it down to their spiritual heirs, the initiates, and to their physical descendants, the *sayyids*. [8]

This explains why the Shi'i tradition accepts two different genealogies for the Prophet and the twelve imams. On the one hand, there is the natural physical genealogy corresponding to the lineage provided by Sunni sources (an approximate correspondence, given the many changes to names over time). This includes the Arab ancestors going back to Ishmael, son of Abraham and "father of the Arabs". The lineage stretches back to Adam and includes many important biblical figures and prophets: Abraham, Sarug, Noah, Methuselah, Enoch and others.

Then there is the spiritual genealogy that connects Muhammad and the imams to Adam. This particular line includes the initiated ones, among them various prophets and saints. In addition to some of the names already mentioned, there are Moses, Joshua, David, Solomon, Joseph and Jesus, whose teachings are passed down to Muhammad – via the apostle Simeon, St. John the Evangelist and others not always easy to identify – and after him to the imams.[9]

But there are also other creation myths. Human beings, Adam's descendants, can be divided into two opposing groups: the beings of light and knowledge (the imams and their faithful throughout all time), and the beings of darkness and ignorance (the perennial adversaries of the initiates). From the very beginning of creation, these two groups have their origins in two different worlds and emerge from two distinct "prime matters". The first are created from the paradisal *'Illiyyin*, the second from the hellish *Sijjin*.[10] This radical dualism, and the uncompromising determinism with which it is charged, is attenuated by other hadith. One such tradition claims that after separately kneading the Clay for the virtuous and that for the evildoers, God mixed them together, making it possible to switch from one group to the other. The "mixing of the Clays" forms the basis of the Shi'i theology relating to determinism and free will: "neither the one nor the other but something between the two".

In the same vein, we find a renowned and lengthy hadith referring to the Armies of cosmic Intelligence and cosmic Ignorance. This much commented hadith states that at the dawn of creation, the first being that God created – drawn from the right side of the Throne and made of divine Light – was cosmic Intelligence (*al-'aql*). Its chief characteristic is its proximity and obedience to God. Next, He created cosmic Ignorance (*al-jahl*), dark and arrogant. Then, God provided these opposing forces with seventy-five armies each; the Armies of Intelligence were endowed with as many virtues and moral qualities as the Armies of Ignorance were invested with vices and faults. Thus, Good, the lieutenant of Intelligence, stands opposite Evil, the lieutenant of Ignorance; moderation opposes excess; forgiveness opposes revenge; courage opposes cowardice, and so on. These virtues and vices are presented as universal forces, symbols of a cosmic struggle, which began with the creation of the world and, like a red line, traverse the entire history of creation. This struggle will not end until the final victory of the Mahdi over the forces of Evil at the End of Time. There is an obvious parallel between, on the one hand, the Armies of Intelligence – the Immaculate Beings and the "pure creatures" on the Right – and, on the other, the Armies of Ignorance, the People of hell on the Left. Furthermore, the myth not only serves to "explain" the unfolding of the history of mankind; it also establishes the foundations of Shi'i morality. It deals with the origins of exterior and inner events. In fact, in the final chapter of the narrative, it is announced that the faithful follower can attain the ranks of the prophets and the imams if he absorbs all the Armies of Intelligence within himself and purifies himself of the Armies of Ignorance.

In conclusion we need to stress that the two cosmogonic and anthropogenic myths and the traditions that portray them – the myth of the worlds and their inhabitants, the myth of the two opposing categories of creatures – correspond to the fundamental principles of Shi'i doctrine: on the one hand, the conception of a dual world and of unbroken initiation; and on the other, the vision of a dualistic world and of perpetual struggle.

Eschatology

The chapter on the End of the world and the destination of man necessarily deals with matters that are predominantly esoteric in nature. There are, nevertheless, some issues that the texts develop more freely than others, and again there appear to be two levels of teaching. On the one hand, there is an outward, universal, collective eschatology said to work in the historical time of humanity, intended to create upheaval; on the other, there is an inner personal eschatology, which overwhelms the very being of the believer.

The sources provide ample material in regard to the first, whereas the second is only occasionally, and subtly, alluded to. In both though, the Mahdi – the living imam in occultation, the Saviour to come – plays a decisive role. In fact, it might even be said that Shi'i eschatology is so dominated by "the Imam of Time", his occultation, his manifestation at the End of Time, his final struggle with the forces of Evil or the circumstances of the world at the time of his return that the classic Islamic narratives – the description of events on the Day of Resurrection and the Last Judgment; the existence of the Chosen in paradise; the lot of the Damned in hell – pale by comparison and account for very little, at least quantitatively, within the vast immensity of the eschatological literature.

The collective dimension

In the hadith material, there is the occasional reference to the approaching End Time and the re-establishing of the Mahdi's justice (perhaps in anticipation of the collapse of the Umayyad or Abbasid dynasties?); however, the exact moment of his rising is not certain, a fact that soon becomes a tenet of faith. Indeed, it is expressly forbidden to "hasten" or "fix the time", and the faithful are bidden to patiently await the "joyful liberation". The coming of the Hidden Imam is the most frequent topic of the predictions ascribed to the Fourteen Impeccable Beings (such predictions deal primarily with the "precursory signs" of the anticipated return). In the rich and sometimes chaotic profusion of the traditions, there are several recurring "signs" that may be divided into two categories:

1   Universal and general signs announcing the rising include the invasion of the earth by Evil; the almost total crushing of the forces of knowledge by the forces of Ignorance; a loss of the sense of the sacred; the destruction of all bonds between man and God and between man and his fellow man; the overthrow of all human values. From this comes the expression: "the Mahdi [or the 'Qa'im'] will rise at the End of Time and fill the earth with justice, just as prior to his coming it overflowed with oppression and injustice ['darkness']".

2   Numerous special signs of the Mahdi's return; there are five that recur: 1) the coming of al-Sufyani at the head of an army composed of the "enemies" of the imams[11]; he is joined by al-Dajjal (the Impostor), the Islamic Anti-Christ; 2) the coming of al-Yamani (the Yemeni), who will oppose al-Sufyani and preach support for the Mahdi; 3) the Cry – a cry from heaven of supernatural origin calling all men to join the army of the Saviour; 4) the engulfing of an army (sometimes called the army of al-Sufyani) in the desert (sometimes situated between Mecca and Medina); 5) the assassination of the Qa'im's messenger, called al-Nafs al-Zakiyya (the Pure Soul), in Mecca.

Then the Qa'im will manifest himself in the splendour of his wondrous youth. He is the last in line, a direct lineal descendant of the imams. He possesses the sacred relics of the earlier prophets, a direct inheritance from father to son. He also possesses the complete and unaltered version of the Holy Scriptures from the past. The Mahdi returns to fight and root out all Evil and to prepare the world for the Last Judgment. Though this is the principal reason for his return, there are others as well. The Mahdi combats Evil for an "historic" reason: to avenge the saints who fell victim to injustice in their communities, especially the Imam Husayn. Indeed, to re-establish order and justice, one of the most fundamental aspects of the Saviour's mission entails avenging the murder of al-Husayn so that majority Islam may be purged of the most odious crime ever committed. By the same token, according to the Shi'i doctrine of *al-raj'a* ("the return to life"), the murdered saints together with their assassins will come back to life so that the former can wreak revenge on the latter. The Mahdi's return also has what might be termed a religious motivation: he will return in order to restore the lost sense of the sacred by re-establishing all religions – in effect, Islam, Christianity and Judaism – in their original fullness and purity. He will hand over to the faithful of each community their Holy Scriptures in their original, unaltered versions, as they were before the so-called "guardians of orthodoxy" of each community falsified them. And finally, there is a spiritual motivation for the final Deliverance: what the Qa'im will set right in the religions will be not just the exoteric doctrines, but the esoteric spiritual teachings as well. This universal initiation will eliminate all distance between the hidden and the manifest, bringing wisdom to all mankind and enabling each individual to reclaim his "inner imam".

To be sure, the Saviour will not fulfil his mission unassisted. First, other saints will return from the past in his service: Muhammad, certain imams, certain biblical prophets (depending on different sources) and, above all, Jesus Christ, who is presented everywhere as the principal Companion of the Qa'im.

As in the case of many religious traditions, Shi'i eschatology is a warrior eschatology. The Mahdi stands at the head of an army in his struggle against the forces of darkness. This army has different kinds of soldiers: angels (in particular, the 313 angels at the Prophet's side during the Battle of Badr[12]); the terrifying heavenly being known as the Fear (*al-Ru'b*), marching at the head of an army[13]; and finally the Companions of the Qa'im called the initiated believers (*mu'minun*), who have supernatural powers.[14]

Swollen by the oppressed masses and the legions of volunteers dedicated to the sacred Cause, the Qa'im's army will emerge victorious. The "Enemy", Ignorance, and its corollary, Injustice, will be eliminated from the face of the earth forever. Justice will prevail and humankind will be revivified by the Light of knowledge. What will come after? The Mahdi will prepare the world for the resurrection and the Last Judgment when the Impeccable Beings will intercede before God for the salvation of their faithful. According to some traditions, the Mahdi will reign for a specified number of years (7, 9, 19 or more), and then all humanity will perish shortly before the Last Judgment. Other hadith claim that following the Qa'im's death, the government of the world will continue under the rule of the initiated saints until the Day of Resurrection.

The personal dimension

From a devotional perspective, the greatest joys of the Shi'i believer are witnessing the return of the Saviour of Time and becoming a soldier in his army. But, of course, not all believers will be able to witness the End Time, and it is perhaps for this reason that the traditions attributed to the imams repeatedly stress that belief in the invisible presence and the final advent of the Saviour is equal to being among his Companions.

This ray of hope, intended no doubt (initially at least) for those believers who felt disappointment and frustration at the endless wait for the Saviour's return, introduces a personal dimension into the eschatology. Belief in the Hidden Imam is a tenet of faith that concerns all followers and even ranks among the "tests" set the Shi'i believer. As one of the challenges of the difficult period of occultation, it enables a distinction to be made between "true Shia" and "Shia in name alone". Here too, however, the teachings of the imams appear to embrace different levels for different categories of disciples. Some traditions in fact seem to go beyond a direct invitation to believe unequivocally in the existence of the awaited Imam and suggest that certain more advanced believers can aspire to know "the place where the Hidden Imam can be found"; in other words, that they have the possibility of coming into contact with him and even perhaps of seeing him in person.

There is a hadith attributed to Ja'far al-Sadiq which says:

> the Qa'im will make two occultations, one of short duration, the other long. During the first, only some of the elect among the Shia will know the place where he is. But for the second, only the elect among his faithful friends will know the place.

The expression "the elect among the Shia" refers to the "representatives" of the Hidden Imam during the Minor Occultation. As noted, tradition affirms that only they have had the privilege of knowing the imam's "location" and of seeing him. "The elect among his faithful friends" probably refers to disciples with sufficient initiation to attain direct contact with the twelfth Imam during the Major Occultation. Ja'far al-Sadiq continues,

> The Lord of this Cause [the Hidden Imam] will know two occultations. One will be so long that some Shia followers will claim he is dead, others that he has been killed, and others still that he has vanished forever. Only a few among his followers will remain committed to his Cause, but no one even among his faithful followers will know the place of his abode, except the special deputy who attends to his Cause.

Shi'i believers very quickly came up against a contradiction. On the one hand, the Hidden Imam announced in his final letter to his last deputy that he would no longer be visible until the End Times and that any person claiming the contrary must be considered an impostor. On the other hand, official Shi'i texts record – indeed from the very start of the Major Occultation – the testimony of numerous individuals who claim to have encountered the Hidden Imam. But the contradiction was resolved almost as quickly as it arose. Theologians, Traditionists and jurists agreed that what the imam's final letter declared impossible was neither the meeting with the imam nor the sighting of him as such but, rather, the use of the sighting to claim special status as the imam's "deputy" – as in the case of the four deputies during the Minor Occultation. What was forbidden was to acquire the sure religious authority that the Hidden Imam's delegation would confer by claiming the privilege of having met him. Barring this, nothing disallowed the gratification occasioned by a sighting of the imam of the Time; moreover, such a sighting offered yet further proof of his *actual* existence. The elect happy enough to have had this signal privilege was tacitly expected to remain humble and discreet.

Encounters with the Hidden Imam are of several sorts. The majority of narratives relating such meetings refer to the humanitarian aspect of the figure of the Hidden Imam, his exceptional compassion towards righteous men (usually Shi'i believers, but not always) and his concern for their welfare (his mission being, according to the expression, "to minister to the weak and hearken to the needy"). In these narratives, the imam of the Time is cast as a loving father with a tender heart for the sufferings of the righteous. In times of great danger and distress, or in moments of agony and trial, the Hidden Imam manifests himself to the victim, providing comfort and delight.

Other narratives highlight aspects of a more initiatory nature. Again the imam makes a providential, almost supernatural appearance, instructing his protégé in prayer, assisting him in the resolution of a theological or spiritual matter, imparting secret knowledge. In this type of encounter, the will of the believer is not a factor. However, for some authors, primarily mystics, the meeting with the Hidden Imam may indeed be prompted by the desire and will of the believer, though there are no guarantees of success since in the final analysis it is the imam who decides to manifest himself or not. Moral attitudes, ascetic practices, prayers, purification and spiritual exercises are recommended so that the believer is prepared and worthy of the vision.

More than any others, Sufi and traditional mystics meditated and commented on these narratives, theorizing the vision of the Saviour of Time and defining its eschatological scope for the individual believer.[15] When these narratives, which fill entire books, are compared with what tradition holds to be the last autograph epistle of the Hidden Imam (in which – to repeat – it is said that he will not be seen again until the End of Time), we find that their authors set out, albeit in different forms, rather considerable elaborations which may be summarized in the following syllogism: "The Hidden Imam, the Imam of the Resurrection, will reappear only at the End of Time; but certain individuals have seen the Hidden Imam; therefore, these individuals have reached the End of Time". The death in question, in the conclusion of the syllogism, must clearly be taken in its initiatory sense: the vision of the Resurrector (one of the multiple meanings of the word "*qa'im*") signals the death of the ego and the resurrection of the believer; that is, his spiritual rebirth.

Furthermore, an encounter can occur in the external world with the "physical" person of the imam of the Time or in the inner world at the level of the "heart" with the imam as light. This second point, touching as it does on the initiatory, merits further discussion.

In the oldest surviving Shi'i texts, traditions refer allusively to an initiatory practice that later would become one of the most secret of all Muslim mystical practices in general and of Shi'ism in particular. It is referred to as the vision "by" or "in" the heart: *al-ru'ya bi l-qalb* (the particle *bi* can mean either "by" or "in"). The practice involves focusing one's concentration on the heart with the aim of encountering and meditating on the "inner imam" as the Light–Form in order to receive his "teaching". This initiation by the inner guide results in the acquisition of transformative knowledge and supernormal powers.[16] A famous tradition attributed to 'Ali – the full manifestation of the Cosmic Imam – says, "He who knows me as Light knows God, and he who knows God knows me as Light". It is the discovery of the light of this Imam that some mystics have equated with the Hidden Imam as the living Imam of our Times; and this light represents a sign of spiritual rebirth due to initiation by the "Master of the Heart".

It has been said again and again that Shi'i eschatology reflects the frustrated hopes of an often severely oppressed minority. While this may be so, it is not the whole story. In fact, the Shi'i attitude, retributory as it is, centred very early on the figure of the "awaited" Imam and on the hope of his final manifestation. But eschatology cannot be reduced to the political dimension alone. Like some of its predecessor religions, including certain Iranian religions or certain Judeo-Christian Gnostic movements, Shi'ism fundamentally represents a mythical approach combined with an initiatory orientation. Such a doctrine always appears to depend upon a triptych in which each term achieves its full meaning only in relation to the other two; namely, the triptych of the origin, the present and the last things. In other words, a cosmic anthropogeny characterized by the pure origins of creation and the onslaught of Evil; a cosmology where the "real" drama in which the eruption of the original events simultaneously sets the scene for the Ultimate End; and, lastly, an eschatology characterized by salvation gained through suffering which effects the return to the sacred Origin.

Within this context, the collective dimension of Shi'i eschatology, so strongly marked by the war against Evil, recalls the cosmic battle between the Armies of Intelligence and the Armies of Ignorance. This battle, with its starting point at the beginning of creation, is waged throughout history, since it recurs from one age to the next in the struggle pitting the imams and their initiates of every period against the dark forces of Evil. The Mahdi's final destruction of these forces will return the world to its original state, when it was peopled solely by the forces of Intelligence before the creation of the forces of Ignorance.

With regard to the individual dimension, initiation and knowledge play the key roles. Initiation, which began at the dawn of creation, determines the spirituality of all humanity and is renewed in every age by the teaching of the imams. The faithful believer who achieves knowledge by means of the Imam of Light in his heart in fact re-actualizes that primordial initiation, in the World of Particles, in which his pre-existing self had been initiated into the divine secrets through the luminous form of the Impeccables.

Theology and imamology

The notion of a dual world and the dialectic of the manifest and hidden in relation to God are proofs that theology and imamology are indivisible, because the Imam in his metaphysical aspect represents the revealed Face of God. This explains why Shi'i theology is basically mystical and theosophical in nature. It is explicitly critical of a purely speculative theology. In the teachings attributable to the imams in the corpus of the hadith, theology is never called *kalam* (literally "speech"), a term which refers to rational scholastic theology. Such theology is in fact rejected as leading to confusion and perdition. Moreover, the methodological tools used in a rationalizing "discourse" about God are forbidden, including analogical reasoning (*qiyas*), the reasoned opinion of the theologian (*ra'y*) and the effort of independent reasoning applied to matters of faith (*ijtihad*).[17] In the hadith compendia, theology is simply referred to as "the science of divine Unity" or, more accurately, "the science of [affirming God's] Oneness" (*'ilm al-tawhid*). This unity cannot be comprehended, but it can be assimilated spiritually by scrupulously observing the teachings of the Masters of Initiation, the imams. The knowledge of God's mysteries can be neither discursive nor determined by rational or dialectical categories; rather, it is initiatory since the purpose of such knowledge is solely to provide intellectual references along the spiritual path.

Still, even here there are examples of what might be called "exoteric theology". References to purely Shi'i doctrines are very rare, indeed virtually absent. The theoretical formulations that are found are similar in expression to those of several other Islamic schools of theology. This is true for the proofs of God's existence or of the wisdom and justice that govern the universe; the exoteric explanations of the divine Names and Attributes; the distinction of Essence and Attributes; the various qualifications of the divine Essence and those of the Names and the Attributes; classical debates on predestination and free will, etc. All of this seems intended for a category of uninitiated, non-Shi'i disciples. In order to attain the genuinely Shi'i dimension of these theological teachings, that which is intended for the closest adherents, it is necessary to go further and explore "esoteric theology", concomitant with imamology. This is attested to in the following words spoken by different imams: "We [the Imams] are the most beautiful Names of God"; "It is through our existence that it is possible to adore God"; "We are the Hand of God, the Face of God, the Tongue of God, the Eye of God". This requires closer examination.

As we have noted, the figure of the imam dominates all Shi'i belief. It pervades and determines the doctrines so thoroughly that one would be justified in arguing that Shi'ism is an imamology. Even so, among the many doctrines there is one, perhaps the most significant, which is specifically concerned with the figure of the imam. Who is the imam? What are his specific traits? What representations of the imam do the sacred Shi'i texts create in the religious consciousness of his followers?

Three definitions can be found. They reflect the three levels of reality that the imam incarnates. They provide yet another example of what the sixth Imam, Ja'far al-Sadiq, said about Shi'i doctrine; namely, that it always contains three layers: the exoteric, the esoteric and the esoteric of the esoteric.

The imam as religious scholar

At the first level, the imam is the undisputed master of religious affairs in the strict sense. He teaches exoteric aspects of law, exegesis, theology, cosmology and other disciplines to all kinds of students, including Shia (the initiated and uninitiated alike) and non-Shia. Even more than the fact that they descend directly from the Prophet, it is as religious scholars that the imams are held in great esteem in the Sunni tradition, and especially as jurists and Traditionists. And for good reason: the imam's exoteric teaching contains no specifically Shi'i features and so can be heard and accepted by non-Shia without offending them.

The imam as Master of Initiation and as thaumaturge

This is the figure of the imam revealed through teaching reserved exclusively for the Shia. The esoteric aspects of the doctrines, including the technical terminology, culminate in a description – and hence, in a definition of sorts – of the imam which far exceeds the boundaries established by Sunni "orthodoxy". It is at this esoteric level that the texts affirm that the conception and birth of the imam are miraculous, that he is endowed with supernatural abilities from childhood and, most importantly, that he is imam because he fulfils two functions: he is an initiatory guide and thaumaturge par excellence. In other words, the imam possesses the knowledge of initiation (*'ilm*) as well as its fruits; that is, supernormal powers (*a'ajib*).

There are many sources attesting to the imam's sacred knowledge in regard to the mysteries of God, man and the universe. First, there are the heavenly sources. Like the prophets, the imam receives inspiration and revelation from celestial beings. He is *muhaddath*, "a person to whom the angels speak", including Gabriel, the messenger of the Revelation, and the celestial being *al-Ruh* (the Spirit). Thus, heaven descends to the imam. But the imam is also capable of ascending to heaven in order to renew and increase his knowledge. Every Friday night, for example, he journeys to the Throne of God to perform a "pilgrimage" in the company of the spirits of the prophets and saints, from which he returns laden with knowledge. The initiatory knowledge also has its occult sources, such as the supernatural forces that "leave a mark on the heart" or "pierce the eardrum". The imam also has the power to visualize a "column of light" in which he can see the answers to his questions. He can use manticism and different types of divination, or he can communicate with the spirits of the dead, notably with those of the prophets and the imams of the past.

There are also written sources for the knowledge. These include the holy books of earlier religions as well as the Qur'an; all such books, of course, in their complete and unfalsified versions. There are also a number of secret books containing special knowledge transmitted from imam to imam: The "All-Encompassing Page" (*al-Sahifa al-Jami'a*), containing knowledge of what is licit and illicit; *al-Jafr*, comprising various sacred Scriptures from earlier prophets, knowledge of the past, present and future, and knowledge of Good Fortune and Misfortune; Fatima's Book, 'Ali's Book, the Book of the Initiated Ones and their genealogy, volumes containing a register of the Righteous Ones and the Evildoers and the Book of the rulers of the earth. Finally, there are the oral sources – that is, the teaching transmitted by the previous imam – extending back to 'Ali who received initiation from the Prophet himself. This transmitted knowledge and the explicit designation of the imam by his predecessor (*nass*) constitute together the two decisive principles of the imamate.

As far as the transmission of knowledge from master to student is concerned, the hadith affirm that the primary mode is "hereditary". It represents the main component of the Light of *walaya* transmitted from generation to generation through semen and through initiation. Other "magical" modes of transmission are listed in teachings attributed to the imams; for example, the teacher places his hand on his disciple's chest and transmits his knowledge directly to him, or the disciple places his hand on the teacher's chest to receive knowledge. Body fluids can serve as "spiritual vehicles" and transmit knowledge. Other than seminal fluids, one finds references to sweat and especially saliva, which the master inserts into the body of his student through the pores of his skin, through his eyes or through his mouth.[18] Knowledge is transmitted to the disciples as well. True, the ancient hadith compendia refer almost exclusively to the imam's knowledge received from a preceding imam and transmitted to the next. The disciples are virtually absent in this literature. But this is doubtless out of discretion and the discipline of the mysteries. In the same corpus there are, however, descriptions in at least two passages of students receiving the secret knowledge from the imams: Salman al-Farisi receiving initiation from 'Ali, and al-Fudayl al-Nahdi receiving initiation from the fifth Imam, Muhammad al-Baqir. These cases are rare and virtually "hidden", dispersed as they are in the traditions.

The supernormal powers of the imam flow principally from his initiatory knowledge. Moreover, most of these powers are presented as sciences: the science of the past, present and future; the science of events in heaven and earth; the science of good and ill fortune (i.e. the knowledge of individual destinies); the science of the inner workings of the mind and of souls; the science of reading thoughts, knowledge of languages (including the languages of animals and supernatural beings); and the occult sciences (astrology, alchemy, the divinatory arts, particularly the science of letters), etc.

The imams can revive the dead, cure illnesses, rejuvenate the elderly, walk on water, travel and transport others (their disciples) supernaturally, mount the clouds and ascend into heaven, and see and hear at great distances. Finally, the imams possess a number of "objects of power", which seem to be their exclusive property. There is, first, the Supreme Name of God, a magic formula in Syriac or Hebrew with tremendous powers.[19] Then there are relics with magical powers inherited from earlier prophets: Adam's tunic; Solomon's seal; Moses' Ark of the Covenant and the Ten Commandments; Muhammad's Invincible Weapon. These "objects of power", received at the last by the twelfth Imam, were taken with him into his occultation and will appear again only after he returns at the End of Time.

The imam as the revealed Face of God

At this point, we come again to esoteric theology. This is the esoteric of the esoteric (*batin al-batin*), the innermost level of the imam's reality that lies at the heart of the deepest secret of Shi'i doctrine. It was taught only to the most trusted followers, the initiated Shia. By definition, the earthly imam is the tangible manifestation of the ontological metaphysical Imam, who himself is the "vehicle" of the divine Names and Attributes; that is, the locus of revelation of what can be known about God.

This is the Secret of Secrets, since it clearly defines a notion, considered highly subversive, of the possible deification of Man. Thus, by a theophanic "play of mirrors", the earthly imam reflects the revealed God. Diffused throughout the traditions and submerged in their sheer mass, there are countless daring assertions that evoke the historical imam as the means by which the Cosmic Imam appears to address the faithful to reveal the secret of the Man-God to them.

Imam Ja'far is quoted as saying

> God has made us [the Imams] His eyes among His worshippers, His speaking Tongue among His creatures, His compassionate and merciful Hand held out to His servants, His Countenance by which we turn towards Him, His Threshold which guides us to Him, His Treasure in heaven and on earth. ... Through our adoration God is worshipped. Without us there is no adoration of God.

These final phrases are veiled in deliberate ambiguity.

In the words of another hadith, also attributed to the same sixth Imam,

> We manifest light in darkness. We are the frequented Shrine where he who enters finds safety [allusion to Qur'an 52:4]. We are the Magnificence and the Grandeur of God. We are beyond all description. Through us, eyes are illumined, ears hear and hearts fill with faith.

"We are the First and the Last", says a hadith from al-Hasan, the second Imam.

> We are the Commanders. We are the Light. The Light of the spiritual beings proceeds from us. We enlighten by the Light of God; we awaken by His Spirit. In us, His dwelling place [i.e. the Spirit of God]; towards us, His soothing spring. The first among the imams is identical to the last and the last is identical to the first.

The fourth Imam 'Ali Zayn al-'Abidin is quoted as saying, "It is we who have prepared the highest heaven; how shall we not scale it? We are the bearers of God's Throne and we are upon the Throne. The Throne and the Seat belong to us."

Another celebrated hadith declares that the Prophet himself revealed the secret of 'Ali's reality: 'Ali, the supreme symbol of the archetypal Imam.

> 'Ali is the most radiant Imam, the longest of God's spears, the widest of His Gates. Let him who seeks God enter by this Gate. Without 'Ali, there is no distinction between right and wrong, between the believer and the unbeliever. Without 'Ali, God cannot be worshipped. No Curtain hides God from him, no Veil between him and God. What am I saying? 'Ali himself is Curtain and Veil.

To conclude, we quote from one of the many sermons attributed to 'Ali. In a series of affirmations (some several pages long), whose repeated emphases in rhyming prose are said to have cast his listeners into a trance, 'Ali boldly declares his identity with God (the words in italics are the divine Names in the Qur'an):

> I am the Treasurer of Knowledge; I am the Secret of the Invisible; I am the Secret of Secrets; I am the Face of God; I am *the First*, I am *the Last*; I am *the Hidden*, I am *the Manifest*; I am the created, I am *the Creator*; I am *the Compassionate*, I am *the Merciful*; I am the Paymaster of men on the Day of Retribution; I am the Supreme Judge; I possess the incisive Word; My insight penetrates the Way of the Book; I possess the knowledge of destinies and misfortunes and the knowledge of Judgments; I am the Perfection of Religion; I am God's Gift to all creatures.

As a doctrine centred on the concept of divine Friendship or Alliance (*walaya*), Shi'ism casts itself as the secret of Muhammad's religion. The earthly imam is the guardian and transmitter of this secret, while the Cosmic Imam is the subject matter itself. The imam, as absolute archetype of the initiated follower and as divine Guide, makes the deification of man the ultimate horizon of Shi'i spirituality.

Notes

1 This is another meaning of the word *taqiyya*, which we have encountered above, in the sense of "to keep the secret", the discipline of divine mystery, the fact of hiding secret doctrine from the unworthy.

2   We are indebted to three articles for these reflections on Shi'i law. Concerning exoteric law, we refer the reader to Y. Linant de Bellefonds, "Le droit imamite". On esoteric law, cf. E. Kohlberg, "Non-Imami Muslims in Imami fiqh" and "The Position of the *walad zina* in Imami Shi'ism". Full bibliographical references may be found at the end of Part II.

3   As we have noted, the source material is extensive, scattered and imprecise. The narratives we describe in this section reflect our cataloguing of recurrent data available from the oldest original sources.

4   *Umm al-kitab*; this enigmatic expression is used three times in the Qur'an (3:7, 13:39 and 43:4). Shi'ism frequently establishes parallels between the notions of the "world" and the "book". Each world is a book written by God; the seeker of knowledge is invited to unlock and comprehend this world. Likewise, each true book may be taken as a world to be explored.

5   We are dealing here with metaphysical archetypes of saints who are not yet incarnate in human form (the taking of human form comes later, as the reader will see). The identity of names, which are symbols of the identity of fundamental realities, underscores the divine nature of the holy figures of Shi'ism.

6   The notion of "believer" refers, in its technical meaning, to the "Shia" of all religions; that is, the one initiated into the esotericism of the religion. This is different from the Muslim, the one in "submission" only to the exoteric; that is, the letter of the religion (see Part I).

7   We find in the teaching of this primordial initiation the usual Muslim prayer formula: "there is no god but God" (*la ilaha illa Illah*), "Glory be to God" (*subhana Illah*), "God is Great" (*allahu akbar*), "There is neither Power nor Ability save by God" (*la hawl wa-la quwwa illa bi-llah*), "Praise be to God" (*al-hamdu li-llah*). These expressions, repeated daily and often mechanically by the faithful, recall the mantras of Indian tradition, very powerful formulae conveying deep spiritual, iniatory and even magical secrets. This explains the central importance of all forms of prayer in the various devotional practices of Shi'ism. The material concerned with prayer in Shi'ism is very large.

8   This explains the infinite respect the Shia hold for genuine and alleged *sayyids*. Among the clerics, those who claim to be *sayyid* wear a green or black turban, depending on their lineage and hierarchical rank. Concerning *walaya* and its Light, see Chapter 5.

9   This spiritual genealogy is sternly rejected by the Sunnis since it establishes next to the archangel Gabriel, who is the Prophet's instrument of revelation, additional sources of knowledge and inspiration. The dual genealogy of Muhammad and the imams recalls the dual ancestry of Jesus, which was both "natural" and "royal" (cf. Luke 3:23–28 and Matthew 1:1–17).

10 Both terms are from the Qur'an (83:18–21 and 83:7–9, respectively), where they are presented somewhat obscurely as the "Book of the Virtuous" and the "Book of the Evildoers". Both are "covered with inscriptions". Once again the Shia understand these "books" to be worlds, "places" of creation.

11 The name refers to Abu Sufyan, who was the ancestor of the first Umayyad caliphs.

12 It is usual to find parallels between the final combat of the Mahdi and the Battle of Badr. Badr marks the first victory of the Prophet over the unbelievers. The name symbolizes the beginning of the reign of Islam. Mahdi's battle signals the final victory of the initiated against their "enemies". Whilst Badr universally established the exoteric religion, the Mahdi's revolution will universally inaugurate the esoteric religion.

13 This Shi'i notion is comparable with the Old Testament idea of *emat Yahweh* (terror of God) in Exodus 23:27: "I will send my fear before you, putting to flight all the people to whom you come" (see also Job 9:34 and 13:21).

14 Also called *jaysh* or company (in the military sense), these initiate warriors of the Qa'im are 313 in number, the same number as the Badr fighters. It is interesting to

note the numerical value of the word *jaysh* (company, militia: J + Y + Sh = 3 + 10 + 300) is 313. Numerology, the science of letters, is greatly prized in Shi'ism.

15 We have in mind here the teachers of the Twelver Shia Sufi orders such as the Ni'matullahiyya, Dhahabiyya, Khaksariyya and the mystico-theological sect of the Shaykhiyya (for more on these orders, see Part III, Chapter 9, p. 128).

16 This practice, even in its technical details, recalls the yogic practice of concentrating on the subtle centre of the heart (*anahata chakra*) in order to discover the self (*atman*), the true master, in the form of a miniscule particle of light. It is also reminiscent of "omphaloscopy" (contemplation of the centre of the body) practiced by the Hesychastic monks of Mount Athos, the goal of which is to attain the light of Jesus Christ in one's heart.

17 Later, following the rationalising turning point of Shi'ism in the 4th/10th century, the jurist-theologians of the rationalist movement would reinstate these notions, thereby preparing the way for the doctors of Law to assume ever greater power. We will come back to this in Part III.

18 Regarding saliva, there is an ancient ritual practice, known in Arabic as *tahnik*, in which whoever wishes to transmit his spiritual qualities, his blessing or his knowledge (he can be a spiritual master but also a parent or grandparent) puts his tongue or his saliva into the mouth of the recipient (disciple or child). The practice is still in use today in certain Arab tribes and among Sufis.

19 According to various traditions, the first Imam, 'Ali, revealed the Supreme Name of God to Salman al-Farisi, one of his favourite disciples.

5 *Walaya*: The nucleus of faith

We must now turn our attention to *walaya*, an essential concept in Shi'i Islam. The sources repeatedly define *walaya* as the esoteric component, the secret dimension, of prophecy (*al-walaya batin al-nubuwwa*). Shi'ism is frequently called "the religion of *walaya*", and the Shia willingly call themselves the "people of *walaya*".[1] It is the only concept to figure on both sides of the list of "corresponding" pairs and "opposing" pairs listed at the beginning of the present work in order to provide a schematic representation of Shi'ism's dual and dualistic vision of the world. *Walaya* is thus the very essence of the Shi'i believer's faith whether he is an ordinary believer or a member of the elite.

Walaya, in its Shi'i technical sense, has two principal meanings: one relates to the imam, the other to his faithful follower.

1   *Walaya* refers to the sacred function of the imams and in this sense is the equivalent of the imamate; that is, the temporal and spiritual guidance of the faithful. The term might also be translated as "power", even "sacred power", since it is bestowed on the imams by divine election. If the imam is called to lead the community after the death of the Prophet, it is because the imamate/*walaya* constitutes the indispensable complement of prophecy. The Prophet (*nabi, rasul*) brings the letter of Revelation to the majority of the faithful, while the imam/*wali* [2] initiates a select minority of followers into the spirit of the divine Word. According to a saying attributed to the Prophet, "There is one among you who fights for the hidden spiritual meaning of the Qur'an (*ta'wil*), just as I fought for the letter of its revelation (*tanzil*). That person is 'Ali."

2   *Walaya* also refers to the essential nature of the imam, his ontological status; that is, his reality as a theophany of the revealed God. Another hadith quotes the Prophet as saying to 'Ali, There is something in you that resembles Jesus, son of Mary. If I did not fear that certain members of my community might speak of Jesus as the Christians do, I would reveal something about you that would cause people to gather the dust at your feet in order to receive a blessing.

This "something" is nothing less than the theophanic secret of *walaya*.

In a conversation with Imam Ja'far, one of his students enquired whether on the Day of Judgment the initiated followers would be able to see the Face of God. The Imam replied that they had already seen God at the dawn of creation when they made a pledge of allegiance to Him. After a long moment of reflection, Ja'far continued: "The initiates already perceive God in this world, well before the Day of Resurrection. Don't you see him now, at this very moment, standing before you [i.e. through my person]?" The astonished student asked if he might be allowed to report this conversation. The imam replied, "No, because a denier ignorant of the true meaning of these words will use them against us and accuse us of being assimilationists and infidels." Here Ja'far as Guide refers to himself as the seat of the highest form of *walaya*. In this sense, and in accordance with the different meanings of the root WLY, the concept can be translated as "Friendship" (with God), "Alliance" (with God), "Proximity" (to God). All three express the highest degree of "holiness".

The second semantic level of meaning of *walaya* relates specifically to the imam's followers. In this sense it means the love, fidelity, devotion, loyalty and submission that the disciple owes to his initiatory master. Again, these various meanings are included in the root WLY.[3] In the lapidary words attributed to Ja'far, "*Walaya* is love". Ja'far also said, "In the name of God, if a rock loves us, God will resuscitate it in our presence. Is religion anything else but love?" "Everything has a foundation. The foundation of Islam is love for us."

Now because Shi'i doctrine is deeply affected by a dualistic conception of the world and its history, love for the imam cannot be separated from hate for his enemies. Thus, *walaya* (sacred love for the Guide of all knowledge) is inseparable from its opposite, *bara'a* (sacred disassociation from the forces of ignorance). A hadith attributed to several imams affirms, "The love of God is only attainable through the love of His friends and hate for His enemies". The Prophet is quoted as saying,

> In the name of the One who sent me as the messenger, and who elected me from among all His creatures, if a person worships God for a thousand years, it will not be pleasing to Him, O 'Ali, if he does not at the same time uphold your *walaya* and the *walaya* of the imams of your issue. And your *walaya* will be acceptable only if it includes *bara'a* towards your enemies and the enemies of the Imams of your lineage.

Here, in this sense, *walaya* – love, affection, submission – is directed either towards the historical imam or, through him, towards the metaphysical Imam who is the Face of God. The first instance is what forms the basis of the cult of the imams, particularly in popular Shi'ism. The second is more common among philosophers, theosophists and mystics.

Now it is easier to grasp how Shi'i religious consciousness, in its several aspects, could discern different levels of interpretation in Muhammad's famous statement in his address at Ghadir Khumm, which the Shia call "the prophetic hadith of *walaya*". According to the the Shia, it was at Ghadir Khumm that Muhammad clearly stated 'Ali's temporal and spiritual caliphate: "May he who takes me as his object of *walaya* now take 'Ali as the object of his *walaya*. Oh God, love him who loves 'Ali and be the enemy of him who is against him".[4]

For the Shia, therefore, *walaya* in its technical acceptation has several distinct meanings that are still complementary and interdependent: the imamate, the love of the imam, and the theology of the Cosmic Imam as divine theophany. Now if all these notions are combined in a single term, it is because there is an inseparable link between them in the mind of the Shi'i believer. The mission of the historical imam is to provide initiation into the religion of the love of the Face of God who is the Cosmic Imam.

In any discussion of the fundamentals of *walaya*, it is important to keep these different semantic layers in mind, as Shia themselves do when the fundamental importance of the notion is emphasized. For example, according to the hadith, the "original, unaltered" Qur'an made explicit and conscious reference to *walaya*, and for good reason, because it epitomizes the true meaning and central tenet of all religion. The passages of the Qur'an, which provide proof of the divine election of 'Ali and the imams descended from him, are said to have been expurgated by their enemies. Here are several examples of these passages (the words and expressions missing from the standard version are in italics):

Qur'an 4:167–170: "Those who are unjust [instead of: those who disbelieve and are unjust] *with respect to the rights of the Prophet's family*, God will not forgive them, nor guide them to a path/ except to the path of Hell, in which they will abide eternally. For God this is easy./ O Men, the Messenger brings you the truth from your Lord *concerning 'Ali's walaya*; have faith in it, that is better for you and if you deny *'Ali's walaya*, [then know that] to God belongs what is in heaven and on Earth."[5]

Qur'an 17:89: "We have given people in this Qur'an every kind of example, but most people refuse stubbornly to believe *in the walaya of 'Ali*."[6]

Qur'an 33:71: "And whosoever obeys God and His messenger *concerning the walaya of 'Ali and the walaya of the imams following him* enjoys great felicity."

Qur'an 41:27: "We will let those who have rejected *the walaya of the Prince of the initiates* ['Ali] taste a severe retribution *in this world below*. And We will requite them for the evil that they have committed."

Qur'an 67:29: "O people of deniers, *though I gave you the message of my Lord concerning the walaya of 'Ali and the walaya of the imams following after him*, you will come to know who is disastrously astray."[7]

Likewise, not only does *walaya* rank among the Pillars of Islam; it is in fact considered *the* central pillar.[8] Various hadith dating back to the imams emphasize this:

Islam is based on five things: ritual prayer, almsgiving, fasting, the pilgrimage to Mecca and *walaya*. And it is to the latter in particular that people have been called.

The principles of faith are as follows: the testimony that there is no God but God and Muhammad is His messenger; the belief that the Prophet received from God the five daily prayers; almsgiving; fasting during Ramadan; pilgrimage to Mecca; *walaya* for the divine Friend [the Imam] who resides among us; dissociation from our enemy; and, finally, consorting with the 'true ones' [perhaps a reference to the initiated?].

God imposed five duties on Muhammad's community: prayer, almsgiving, fasting, the pilgrimage to Mecca and our *walaya*. Regarding the first four, there are certain exceptional circumstances which may be invoked and which exonerate from obligation [e.g. illness, financial difficulty, menstruation]; but *walaya* may never be relinquished.

Walaya determines the validity of the other pillars and whether they are pleasing to God:

> If a servant worships the Lord for a hundred years in Mecca; if he devotes his days to fasting and his nights to prayer even into old age; he will receive no reward [from God] if he remains ignorant of our *walaya*.

This is because without *walaya*, without love for the divine Man, the ultimate goal of the spiritual path manifested in the model of the earthly imam, there is no true faith. According to a hadith attributed to the Prophet: "He who recognizes the *walaya* of the Imams is a believer; he who does not is an infidel." This, moreover, is why the Shi'i profession of faith includes three statements: "I bear witness that there is no god but God; I bear witness that Muhammad is the Messenger of God; I bear witness that 'Ali is the *wali* of God."[9]

Generally speaking, *walaya* lies at the very heart of all the revelations and of all the prophetic missions. It comprises the esoteric aspect of prophecy. Without *walaya*, there is no religion. Without the spirit, the letter is dead, an empty shell, lifeless remains. Imam Ja'far is quoted as saying,

> God has made our *walaya*, we the members of the prophetic Abode, the pivot around which the Qur'an revolves, around which all the holy Books of the past revolve. The clear suras of the Qur'an turn around *walaya*; the Scriptures are filled with *walaya*; through it faith is acknowledged.[10]

Hence, to deny *walaya* is to deny divine revelation. The reason is simple enough: the *walaya* of the Impeccable Ones – the theophanic Guides who are living exemplars of divine Man – is the ultimate goal of existence. The eleventh imam, Imam al-Hasan al-Askari, said, "The *walaya* of Muhammad and the imams of his lineage is the ultimate goal and the supreme objective. God created creatures and sent out his messengers solely to call all men to this *walaya*."[11]

Notes

1 We ask for the reader's patience as we withhold a translation of *walaya* (also rendered *wilaya*) for the moment. Throughout this chapter, we will demonstrate the semantic complexity of the concept and the absurdity of fixing it in a single translation.

2 *Wali* (plural *awliya'*) from the same root WLY, signifies the person possessing *walaya* – by and large, Friendship or divine Alliance. In Muslim mysticism the term is usually translated as "saint".

3 "Al Matawila" (probably the irregular plural of *mutawalli*; in French, *métouali*), is used to refer to certain Shia of the Lebanon and Syria. If this is the case, the expression stems from the same root WLY and means "the people who perform *walaya* with respect to the imams".

4 The term *mawla*, derived from the same root WLY, is translated here as "object of *walaya*" in accordance with the Shi'i understanding of the word.

5 In such texts, "Ali" refers to the original historical imam as well as to the highest symbol of the Cosmic Imam.

6 A reminder that in Shi'i terminology the expression "the majority" (or as here "most people") refers to either non-Shia or uninitiated Shia. The expression "a minority" in contrast refers to initiated Shia.

7 See p. 50, verse 42:13 in which "*the holy power of 'Ali*" means *walaya*. We have also stressed that certain very late works quote the full text of the "sura of the *Walaya*", which is of course missing from the standard 'Uthman version of the Qur'an (see p. 47ff).

8 Although the foundations of Islam were shaky at the outset, it is now accepted that there are five core principles of Islam: the testimony of faith (there is no god but God and Muhammad is His Prophet); obligatory daily prayers; almsgiving to the needy; self-purification through fasting during Ramadan; the pilgrimage to Mecca. The hadith we quote from show that the principles had yet to be established in their final form.

9 *Wali*, the Friend or Companion of God, the possessor of *walaya*. These phrases are an integral part of ritual prayer, especially of the call to prayer, and introduce *walaya* into Shi'i ritual.

10 Here again the Family of the prophetic Abode, referring to the Fourteen Pure Ones, are understood as perfect "vehicles" of the Cosmic Imam.

11 As discussed above, *walaya* is seen by mystics in particular as conveying an "organic" reality in the form of a light within the individual. The "light of *walaya*" – the vehicle of redeeming knowledge and spiritual powers – is transmitted by semen and by initiation. It transforms itself from a potential state to an active one only after one has exerted effort along the spiritual path towards self-perfection.

6 Symbolic interpretation (*ta'wil*)

Esotericism in general

If there is a single practice that characterizes Shi'ism, it is symbolic interpretation. This mode of understanding applies above all to the Qur'an. Educated Shia developed it as a method, a means of access, to every reality freighted with mystery, whether in the realm of language or in the various real worlds. Interpretation is the preferred method, leading to a truth that other ways of knowing cannot even approach. For Shia, it presupposes a symbolic vision of things that comes from an immediate grasp of each of them, from a spontaneous apprehension of each word. This thing or that word becomes a means of mediation which leads to another level of reality and then is itself transformed into the apparent face of a hidden reality. To interpret is to know because to know is to interpret.

Every reality has an outer and an inner aspect, a visible appearance and a disclosed meaning, an exoteric and an esoteric. All genuine knowledge cannot elude a principle that might be called generalized esotericism. Interpretation enables the Shi'i believer to see a sign of God in each thing and to find in each verse (or sign) of the Revelation an essential hidden meaning – essential just because it is hidden. A truth that superficial representations based on the senses or deductive and demonstrative understanding are unable to convey to the common run of humanity

This mode of comprehension corresponds to a mode of being, to a subject's attitude in relation to his own personal history and to the sacred History of mankind. It is not simply a method of deciphering, which leaves the interpreter indifferent and unchanged. On the contrary, the Shi'i believer is expected to understand the hidden meaning of the Qur'an and of the creation in order to alter and transform himself and purify his existence so as to conform to the ideal model of the imam. Interpretation makes it possible to acquire the knowledge suitable for enduring the wait for final ends – for God's promised retribution and the moral demeanour to prepare for it; and it opens the way to the salvation that one has the right to hope for. Finally, symbolic interpretation animates the mysticism of Shi'ism, inseparable from its conception of the perfect man, a microcosm encompassing the macrocosmin its wholeness, and of the imam, the Man of God who manifests in himself the entirety of the divine attributes.

The Arabic technical term for this type of interpretation is *al-ta'wil*, which is also the word used in Persian-language texts. Literally, this verbal noun, formed from the root *'wl*, means "to cause to return", "to lead back to", "to trace back to". It comes to denote the interpretation of the inner and esoteric meaning of the Qur'an because it designates the hermeneutic of visions, which itself can take the form of a vision. Often *ta'wil* appears as a narrative or story but also as a picture or as a structural arrangement of an inner space. *Ta'wil* makes visible nocturnally what is invisible diurnally. In the vernacular, it refers to the digressions and gibberish of an unbridled imagination. In learned usage, *ta'wil* involves a synthesis of hermeneutical activity and imagination inspired by truth.

From the same root *'wl*, several important words are formed; for example, *al-'awwal* (plural *al-awa'il*) meaning the beginning. Thus exegesis is a return to the beginning, to what was first, prior or earlier. The overall attitude it presupposes is a focusing of the mind on an originary principle of meaning. *Ta'wil* is an archaeological exploration of meaning accomplished by sifting through the successive layers of the soil of revelation, going back to the divine act – foundational and originary – to the hidden truth, shrouded and primordial.

We are, of course, discussing Shi'i *ta'wil*. It is important to remember that symbolic interpretation is a common method of Sufis and philosophers as well. In fact, virtually every form of reasoning involving non-literal meaning resorts to symbolic interpretation of some kind. In its widest sense, *ta'wil* refers to different forms of interpretation. Shi'i authors go to considerable lengths to identify and disqualify the forms they consider incorrect; for example, when the interpreter presumes to express a personal opinion or judgment based solely on his own authority, or when he shows too much fondness for obscure Qur'anic verses, which then sound over-passionate because they cannot be made to square with a general interpretation of the Book, including even the verses that are clear. In order to produce an authorized *ta'wil*, it is necessary to follow in the steps of "the teachers of the spiritual path", to possess a keen spiritual intelligence and to submit to the traditional teachings of the imams.

We must also mention the meaning of *ta'wil* in reference to interpretation of the *shari'a* or religious law. In this sense, *ta'wil* refers to the explanation of laws and is synonymous with *tafsir*. (*Tafsir* explains the Qur'an on three levels: its literal meaning, its historical meaning and its legal meaning.) We will not dwell on this type of interpretation here.

Various synonyms can be found for *ta'wil* that shed additional light. There are frequent references to "unveiling" (*al-kashf*), emphasizing the notion of laying bare a hidden (veiled) meaning. Stronger still is the expression "secret" or "secrets" (*al-sirr*; plural *al-asrar*) in reference to the presumed hierarchy of worlds, each bearing a veiled meaning, to the degrees of knowledge that correspond to different degrees of supra-sensory reality culminating in the ultimate "secret" or "mystery"; viz. that of the divine Real in its primordial revelation, the divine Throne, the angelic world and all the prophetic and imamological phenomena that can be known.

Ta'wil and messianic hope

As early as the 2nd century Hijra (8th century CE), Shi'i exegesis seems to have played a pre-eminent role in the doctrinal production of the followers of the imams. This was particularly intense in so-called "extremist" circles and can be explained as follows. Groups of the learned who were actively participating on behalf of the Prophet's descendants and contributing to clandestine propaganda in support of an Alid successor agitated from a messianic position. They experienced the present as though it were a period of occultation of divine truth and authentic justice. Now, this was a time of Qur'anic rule of law, which under the reigning caliphate had deteriorated into a mere tool of state ideology at the behest of a social connection that was basically incapable of re-establishing the order and harmony God had willed. In short, the law had reduced God's revelation to its literal sense.

This was why those learned men rejected any accommodation of *shari'a* law within illegitimate state power, offering in its place the coming reign of another revelation – the revelation of the hidden meaning of the Qur'an and of the truth (*haqiqa*) which bears within itself the world to come, the just world, the world of the resurrection, and the Man who will inaugurate it, the supreme imam, or even the one the Shia call the new and awaited prophet after Muhammad, a "resurrector" who will not bring a new law but who will abolish all the legalistic religions or legal systems in order that the pure, spiritual element of monotheism may reign supreme.

On a deeper level, the requirement to find a hidden meaning concealed in the Qur'an – one situated in a realm of signification radically different from that in which the law is central – brought with it a kind of meticulous understanding, an original definition, of that very Qur'anic law. According to this form of understanding, *shari'a* was less an abstract, impersonal, external law than a *way*, a path, in the original sense of the word *shari'a*. Therefore the truth of the Sacred Book could not be just the path but had to be the purpose and destination of the journey, a final goal whose spiritual nature was laid bare beneath the symbols of a legalistic religion. Not a law reduced to the apparent meaning of exoteric rules and commands, but the fulfilment of this law. Therefore the World-to-Come demanded deciphering. And this perfect world could not fail to be the secret of divine providence. But this secret had to be present in the eternal model of the Book, the "Mother of the Book", the Book "in heaven". Hence, the purpose of Qur'anic interpretation was to subvert passive obedience to the letter of the Qur'an so as to bring to life the meanings of the eternal Book, replete with future promises.

Furthermore, exoteric law was bound up in – and contemporary with – all the lapses, failings and errors of the times. At best, in a more positive sense, exoteric law was the embodiment of the spiritual truth revealed to

Muhammad, the last temporal prophecy, eternal in its essence. But like all transient physical reality, it threatened to kill the very spirit it encompassed. In order to free the spirit from mortality and the deceptions of the law – or at least to set it free from blind obedience to the law – it was necessary to search in the corpus of the law for the secrets (*batin*) that outward appearances (*zahir*) conceal. This required an interpretation of the body of *shari'a* in terms of attacking the husk to disclose the fruit within. It is possible to recognize in this effort an echo of Manichaeism and certain forms of Gnosticism.

In such a messianic outlook, *ta'wil* becomes indispensable. Only interpretation could shed light on the tensions and oppositions between the two poles of the Holy Book: on the one hand, *shari'a* law (the body of legal prescriptions) and, on the other, *haqiqa* (religion consonant with the everlasting archetype of the Holy Book existing "in heaven" and revealed to the descendants of the holy imams). Thus *shari'alhaqiqa* functions as if it were synonymous with opposing pairs: oppression/liberation and darkness/light. *Haqiqa*, the truth of the divine Word and the effective reality of all creatures (real essence and essential reality), can only come to light and triumph in this world through the deeds of the providential Man, the supreme Revealer at the end of historical time. In anxious expectation of this time it was possible to foresee and to prepare for this coming by circulating the hidden meaning of the Qur'an (*sirr al-qur'an*) in restricted circles, notably among the elite of the faithful. The pair "visible meaning/ hidden meaning" became synonymous with two pairs: legalistic religion/inner (or true) religion; and oppressive caliphate/Cause of the Imam.

This is how certain convictions within Shi'i circles came to be established: the common, the ignorant ones, who cling to overt meanings (*zahir*) are supporters of the exoteric religion; in contrast, the adherents of the inner meaning (*batin*) are the true followers of the imam's teachings – they alone know the path leading to truth (*haqiqa*). Thus men can be divided into three categories: genuine scholars, those who are initiated by these scholars in the esoteric in genuine messianic expectation and, finally, the ignorant ones. Exegetic practice is based on the certainty that the Qur'an is the most esoteric of holy books.

Though this radical view found its expression primarily in the movements of Isma'ili Shi'ism, it was influential in Twelver Shi'ism as well (the reader will recall our foregoing discussion of the quietist political attitude of Twelver Shi'ism). The withdrawal from politics recommended by the messianic writings and sayings of the imams – and accepted by the Twelver Shia – does not dispel the constant tension that exists in the Shi'i mind between *zahir* and *batin*. This tension was rethought in terms of a harmony and balance between the hidden and the visible, between an inner religion and an "outer" legalistic religion. A messianic intention by no means disappears; but as every earthly effort appears vain and illegitimate, because it runs counter to the hidden meaning of the revelation, the focus turns inward.

Twelver *ta'wil* seems haunted by one concern: the concern to strike a balance between the visible aspects of the Qur'anic verses and the hidden meaning revealed by the imam. Why is this so? If the hidden meaning of the verses destroys the overt meaning, if truth makes *shari'a* and cult religion pointless, ipso facto inner religion will become the outward religion and would threaten to turn into the dominant authority and exert temporal power. *Haqiqa* would be converted into a new and arbitrary *shari'a*. In order to protect the proper nature of the inner religion, it must remain inward. This is why *ta'wil* ceases to be the inversion of overt meanings and remains what it should never cease to be, secret spiritual knowledge.

Interpretation remains the path to the true meaning of prophecy. It rejects slavish obedience to the law; indeed "corporal" obedience becomes entirely secondary. But interpretation refuses a role in any revolt against the order imposed by the commandments. *Ta'wil* sees itself on a set of scales poised between two errors. On one side is "corporalism" or pure literalism, which associates divine truth with creaturely realities, reduces it to corporeal practices (*tashbih*) and to agnosticism, which strips God of all the garb that revelation accords Him – attributes, deeds, acts of will (*ta'til*). The radical Gnosticism of those who deny the hidden truth of its physical aspect can only lead, according to Twelvers, to what they most wish to avoid: a fundamental agnosticism. It is therefore necessary to interpret the letter in order to find the spirit hidden in the letter, the spirit that breathes life into the body of the Qur'anic revelation.

Allegory or symbolism?

Ta'wil is an interpretation that aims at an ever deeper level of meaning. Some scholars argue that there are seven degrees of hidden meaning, that a finite number of letters, words and verses within the Qur'an is not incompatible with an infinite number of hidden meanings. Likewise *ta'wil* is also an *uplifting* towards ever higher levels of reality. This is why it is an exact translation of the term *exegesis*. It is a *symbolic* exegesis because the very mode of interpretation converts what is presented to the mind and what needs to be understood into a special kind of sign, into a symbol. Why refer to symbol rather than to allegory? The question is worth asking. Shi'i exegesis of the Qur'anic verses seems often to follow the practices of the great earlier exegetes of sacred scripture in both Judaism and Christianity – what has been characterized as allegorical exegesis. This practice involves substituting a hidden meaning for a visible one; the referent is a spiritual reality that is foreign to the phenomenal world implied by the apparent meaning.

Shi'i *ta'wil* is quite close to the biblical exegesis of Philo of Alexandria. There is, for example, the same tendency towards syncretism. Both are persuaded that the truth, by its very nature, is hidden; that it is cloaked in figures that need to be explained in order to discover it. Again there is the same distinction between the ignorant believer and the initiated elite. Like Philo, Shi'i exegetes substitute a realm of supra-sensible intelligible realities for the realm of sensible physical realities. Like Philo, they know that this approach is forbidden to the wicked and to the enemies of the truth of the spiritual law. Both Philo and Shi'i exegesis associate literalists with the impious, who live by the body alone and are incapable of passing beyond physical realities to rise to a higher spiritual plane. Like Philo, Twelver Shia stress that exegetic practice does not absolve one from the demands of exoteric commands, from religion and its ritual practices or from the obligation to live in peace in civil society. Finally, both make a careful distinction between symbolic exegesis and all pagan mythology. Is *ta'wil* then an allegorical exegesis?

For an answer to this question, we turn to the Isma'ili exegesis of certain practices of traditional Muslim religion. For example, purification (*tahara*) means, according to *ta'wil*, "to purify oneself from the adherents of literal religion"; in other words, to return to the science of the imam. The hidden meaning of collective prayer is a conjunction with the secret knowledge dispensed by the imam, culminating in a "perpetual prayer" which conjoins with the mystical knowledge of the imam. The hidden meaning of fasting is the "discipline of the arcane" (*taqiyya*), the safeguarding of the esoteric teachings, their removal beyond the reach of enemies (allegedly malevolent Sunni Muslims). Such interpretations can seem arbitrary or founded on fanciful etymologies and random decisions. It is indeed an accusation that other Muslims frequently level at the Shia.

Other cases analogous to these examples make it obvious that we are dealing with an *allegorist* attitude, which aims to unleash the real meaning of a term from its apparent sense in order to uncouple one kind of obligation – held to be essential, liberating and genuine – from another – thought to be archaic, futile or illusory. It is like a light that tears apart the veil of an outdated law. But in the whole vast field of Shi'i *ta'wil* – especially among Twelver authors – the steps involved in interpretation are far more complex. First, because they continue to preserve the letter of the texts under the focus of hermeneutic investigation. The literal meanings of the Qur'anic verses are not rejected; they are preserved and thoroughly explored and appraised. In fact the literal sense, because it is raised to a new plane with a different horizon, is intensified and set within a context in which it can actually possess a truth. In the specific case of Isma'ili exegesis, the intent is clear: it is purely and simply a matter of substituting a spiritual truth for the rule of the *shari'a*. This is not what we most frequently find among the Twelvers. Radical allegorism corresponds to a radical Messianic passion, while symbolism, which brings the letter and the spirit into harmony, corresponds to a hope that has been tempered.

An example of this is found in an exegesis of the fifth verse of sura 28, *al-Qasas*, "the Story": "And We want to grant our favour to those who are oppressed in the land, and to make them guides, inheritors". The apparent sense of the verse bears on the "children of Israel", whereas the hidden meaning refers to the family of the Prophet Muhammad. The guides of whom the verse speaks are meant to lead men in accord with justice and righteousness, not in accord with injustice. But the sons of Israel who came after Moses were not just; only Moses and Aaron were worthy of the role of guide (imam). This historical exegesis inspires a comparison, following a hadith attributed to the fourth Imam, 'Ali ibn Husayn: The People of the House – the family of the Prophet – are the oppressed and the guides whom the revealed text speaks of, and their "Shia" with them, just like Moses and Aaron "and their Shia". Thus the Pharaoh's historical oppression of the Jews finds its equivalent in the oppression suffered by the true friends of God; that is, the prophetic family of Muhammad. The *ta'wil* of the verse draws a historical line that diverges markedly from the ordinary historical narrative of peoples and nations. It is a "transhistorical" history of oppression and justice in which the peoples of the Book – the communities of Israel and Ishmael – are set on the same plane.

It is to save this literal meaning from the triviality of a profane interpretation that exegesis converts it into the symbol of a deeper or a higher reality. The point is not to destroy the letter of the Qur'an by substituting another text for it, but rather to create the opportunity for it to make sense – to make infinite sense – by using a hierarchy of meanings, raising the word in question by stages of truth far removed from the immediate stage of naïve signification. This is why it is preferable to speak of *symbolic* exegesis, thereby preserving the distinction between symbol and allegory, as Henry Corbin so often recommended.

Here is another example: The *Fatiha*, the Qur'an's opening sura, announces that God is "King of the Day of Judgment". Imam 'Ali offers this *ta'wil*. He says that it is a matter of understanding the attestation of divine sovereignty on this particular day, the day when all mankind will be judged, as a personal invitation to each believer to "make a personal accounting of himself". The imam thus interprets the final stocktaking of good and bad deeds as one that each individual must undertake now in the present, without waiting for the end of the world, and do so in a daily examination of conscience. How have I spent my day? Have I helped my fellow brother to ease his pain? Have I shown concern for his family and his affairs? The lesson of the *ta'wil* is a moral one; it preserves the letter of the Qur'anic verse and locates its active significance in the realm of the soul, in the relationship that God establishes in the soul between itself and itself. The verse has a symbolic meaning which is the duty that one has in regard to one's self and to the followers of the true faith. Divine sovereignty is no longer the dominion of a prince over his subjects; it is the guidance of an interior master over the moral concern of a disciple. There is nothing here that suggests simple allegory. In summary, if by allegory we understand, broadly speaking, a signifier which requires the removal of extraneous layers of meaning in order to make sense, or if the intention of the author is to show the vanity of the letter, then *ta'wil* is indeed allegorical. But if we understand allegory to be a sign, which is not useful to meaning, if the author's intention is to preserve both the literal meaning and the usefulness of the signs, it is better to speak of symbol.

The Book and its interpretations

The quintessential object of exegesis is the Holy Book. This has to be understood in its broadest sense whereby the divine Book is revealed in the order and time frame of its successive prophetic revelations in the *Suhuf of* Abraham, in the Torah, the Psalms, in the Christian Gospels and, finally, in the Qur'an. Each of these revelations requires and receives a *ta'wil*. In the view of some, Jesus figures as having advanced a spiritual exegesis of Mosaic law, even while providing his own copy of the divine Book. The Qur'an[1] embodies the entirety of these prophecies and all the hidden meanings that lie within them. As such, it manifests the full scope of divine commands but above all, and most especially, the totality of God's secrets, in so far as they can be manifested. Excluding the unfathomable secret of God's essence, all else is revealed in the Book, and everything warrants interpretation. But if everything is spoken, if God's Verb and Imperative are manifested there in full, then the task of interpretation can only be infinite and inexhaustible. Here we touch on a fine existential point: the Shi'i believer himself is grounded in the temporality, as it is lived, of the history of prophecy.

There is in fact a close connection between the Twelver Shi'i conception of the historical time of the prophecy and the dictates of *ta'wil*. The symbolic interpretation of the Book expresses and gives form to the Shi'i philosophy of history. As we have seen, Shi'ism, like Islam in general, receives the doctrine of the "Seal of the Prophecy" fulfilled in the person and mission of Muhammad. But it is based on a belief in the specific calling of the imams, which will only be accomplished in full at the End of Time. Thus the history of prophetic truth is not yet closed; it is perpetuated in and through the performance of *walaya*.

Of course the chronological time of the imams, like that of the prophets, corresponds to the pre-eternal order of the Pure Ones, and in this sense it is anchored in the closed circle of Muhammad, Fatima and the twelve imams. But the teachings are given in historical time, at least until the occultation of the twelfth imam. This occultation closes the time of revelation of the authorized traditions, but it does not close the time of *ta'wil*. On the contrary, each exegesis has its own future; each must assume a special inner form in the heart of each believer and let its particular spiritual message unfurl there. The transmission of the exegesis produces in each believer an understanding of the Book which becomes an understanding of self, a gradual understanding of the interpreted truth and, at least in its mystical fulfilment, an understanding of God's decree, submission to God and freedom in God.

The Shia are not the only ones to engage in Qur'anic exegesis. As soon as the Qur'anic canon came into being it became absolutely clear that the Book required a science of interpretation. The composition of the Book itself; the order of each of its 114 verses; the connections between them; the authorized readings attributed traditionally to the seven "readers" in the 2nd century Hijra (8th century CE) – these different aspects attest to a work of interpretation in the actual compilation of the standard version of the Qur'an itself.

Even if the Qur'an is the Word of God in the eyes of the believer, that same believer is not dispensed from the effort of understanding its accepted and forbidden readings. If we add to this the protestations of the Shia against the scholars who established the text of the Qur'an under 'Uthman – for the Sunnis, the third caliph – and the suras or verses, which the Shia believe to have been scandalously excluded from the holy text, it follows that the Book is open to interpretation from its very inception and that it is in fact one with its own interpretation. Even those who believe that the text must be taken literally and who reject all manner of spiritual exegesis, nevertheless join in the interpretative fight and thereby adopt one hermeneutic decision among others.

The Qur'an is never really independent of its accompanying commentaries. The authors of commentaries do not actually feel they have any freedom of choice, nor do they consider themselves the direct individual sources of their exegesis, notwithstanding specific self-styled doctrinal insights or polemic signatures. The art of commentary is not that of a personal work by an independent person guided by his own criteria. The author as we know him, since the beginning of the modern age in the West, is an unknown figure in the world of *tafsir*, or elucidation of the Qur'an.

Traditionally, throughout all Islam, the composer of a commentary must defer to a higher authority (viz. the Qur'an itself) for a justification of his exegesis. The commentator distinguishes between "clear" and "obscure" verses and explains the one by the other. He recognizes the authority of the Prophet and bows to the authentic traditions reported in the hadith literature. If he is a Sunni Muslim, he welcomes the consensus of the community with regard to the accepted meaning of this verse or that. Finally he may choose to resort to reason, though not to *his* own reason. *Reason* is a faculty of the intellect, which strives to be as impersonal and universal as the rules of logic and the truths they yield. Reason is divine, deposited in the human mind and awakened by the Light of divine intelligence; or even more simply, actualized by study. It is not a free-wheeling Cartesian exploration.

Reason makes it possible to move away from the obvious sense of a verse if this sense contradicts the more general facts of revelation, as reason itself admits them, because revelation examined closely by reason alone gives divine reality its due. So it is with those verses in which God presents Himself as having bodily features – upright on His Throne, His feet resting on a pedestal, possessing hands, etc. To avoid the trap of anthropomorphism, which contradicts God's transcendent reality and unfathomable Oneness, reason dictates a figurative interpretation of such verses. But this rationalist decision never achieves unanimity; it remains restricted by the limits of revelation. In the Qur'anic commentary (*tafsir*) of the great Sunni authors, to quote Guy Monnot's trenchant expression: "the apparent sense is the real sense, unless there is reason to deny it".

This reminder of some of the bases of the Sunni mentality should help us to clarify the very special intention of Shi'i *ta'wil*. In fact, in Shi'i exegesis, the visible meaning is never really the true meaning unless there is a reason to recognize it. The Holy Book is a revelation; it results from an act by which God sends down the contents of His Word in the envelope of a discourse accessible to the Prophet (*tanzil*). In this figure – the descent from above – we are to understand that the word has been "made simple" for man, but also that it has suffered if not a degradation, then at least a darkening, a concealment of its original brilliance. Regardless, if the literal sense is not the true sense, the letter itself is not rejected.

Let us return to the example of the "anthropomorphic" verses of the Qur'an. We have observed that a "rationalist" reader of these verses interprets them metaphorically. The Shi'i exegete takes a different approach. He acknowledges the anthropomorphic features such as the Throne, the Hands of God, His speech, etc. But he shows their hidden meaning: in fact, these physical aspects do not concern God, or rather the transcendent and impenetrable essence of God; rather, they are the Attributes of God, *such as He reveals Himself in man* – that is, in the perfect man who is the imam. The truth of the letter is saved in that it is resituated in its true meaning.

The purpose of symbolic exegesis (*ta'wil*) is to reverse the descending arc of truth, redirecting it upward again, back towards its divine source. In a certain sense it repairs the effect of the descent by restoring the revelation to its fullness, by closing the perfect circle in a descending and an ascending arc.

The pair of terms descent/ascent finds its corresponding complement in the pair Prophet/imam. The Prophet is the receptacle and the subject of the descending literal revelation. The imam is the receptacle and the subject of the signification ascending back towards its source in the divine Word. The Prophet has authority over the letter; the imam has authority over the spirit. Of course, the Prophet potentially possesses the spiritual light of revelation's meaning; he resumes within himself the two arcs of prophecy and *walaya* since the book he brings, and which he transmits, infallibly contains his letter and his spirit. But it is the imam's purpose to effect the letter's ascent back to the spirit or, to put it more rigorously, the ascent of the apparent sense of the verses to their hidden meaning.

The sacred text has an apparent aspect (*zahir*) – its literal expression – and a hidden meaning (*batin*) – its inner, esoteric meaning. Let there be no misunderstanding: When we refer to Shi'i esotericism, it is not to a bunch of doctrines such as those found among the spiritualists or in this or that sectarian phenomenon led by some illuminated figure or other. On the contrary, the reference is to a body of interpretations held together by a specific authority, by specific rules, and which never stray into the presumed prophecy of the realm of phantasmagoria.

On the contrary, if the entire Qur'an should be seen as having an apparent face and a hidden face, the hidden aspect is the meaning of the apparent; and it must help make the apparent face worthy of itself and allow it to appear in its truth. Paradoxically, Shi'i esotericism is a vibrant tribute to the apparent, to the apparition of God in His Word. It is faithful to the apparent in that it restores it to its full power. It expresses all the possible meanings of what God says about Himself: "I am the apparent and I am the hidden", apparent as hidden, hidden as apparent. In a celebrated sermon, Imam 'Ali offered a daring exegesis of this definition that God provides of Himself. In self-reference, 'Ali said: The profound oneness of the apparent and the hidden is the Imam himself who says of himself. "I am the First and the Last; I am the Apparent and the Hidden".[2]

Exegetic reading, directed by the teachings of the imams, as we shall see, begins with the letter, then takes the direction of one or several hidden meanings. In this interpretative movement, the letter curbs the exegete in his journey towards the spirit. To take an example, it is impossible to describe paradise or hell in any other way than the Qur'anic verses do. They are the starting point; there is no other. When a Shi'i philosopher interprets paradise in Platonic terms, deciphering the symbols of the intelligible world, he remains faithful to the Qur'an's exact literal descriptions. But in fact, this movement, which starts with the letter, already contains another movement within itself, whose meaning and direction are reversed. It is from symbolic exegesis that the apparent side of the verse must be represented; it is from the spiritual meaning that the literal sense must be heard. Exegesis subverts the literalist attitude, which is subjected to the passive, slavish acceptation of the letter, by revealing the sense of the letter, by starting from meaning in order to revert back to the interpreted letter, clarified at last and which now assumes its full meaning. So the esoteric directs the exoteric – the apparent – because it determines its truth.

Exegesis starts from the Imam and comes back to him

In spite of its many forms, exegesis does possess some constants. The most important is that the subject and object of interpretation are one and the same reality: the imam. The imam is the subject of *ta'wil* in two ways: it is he who receives the esoteric truth within his own person, and he is subject *to* this truth; it is he who teaches and enunciates the truth to his chosen disciples, and he becomes the subject matter *of* the truth. In his relationship with God, he is enlightened by eternal divine assistance (*al-ta'yid*); this assistance reveals the unmediated hidden truth to him. In his relationship with the faithful, he is the living subject of a teaching, a spiritual pedagogy (*al-ta'lim*) in which each *ta'wil* finds its confirmation. But the imam is also the object of *ta'wil*, that very thing of which he speaks to us; and he is its final cause, that toward which his exegesis tends. In the end, all the secrets of the Qur'an converge on the person of the Imam in his cosmic, metaphysical reality, a reality manifested by all imams from 'Ali ibn Abi Talib to the twelfth Imam, the Resurrector. And so exegesis leads back to its own starting point. It is a circle that begins with the imam who teaches and comes back to the imam who is taught.

This is what the Shi'i exegesis of the Qur'an means, even in the formal aspects of its utterances. Even when an author quotes various secondary sources or refers to a mystic, philosopher or earlier commentator, he always submits his sources to the ultimate authority of a tradition of the imams. The hadith is confirmed by various reliable witnesses in a chain of transmission analogous to the chain used in prophetic traditions. It can be traced back to a given imam, who in turn refers back to the ultimate source, the first imam, and naturally to one of the Prophet's own hadith that confirms the authority of the imam. The following hadith is as an example: "Since men know when 'Ali was named 'the Prince of believers', they will not deny his pre-eminence. The Prince of believers and Adam were named in between [the creation of] the spirit and [the creation of] the physical body."

The imam's commentary gives the *ta'wil*; it is his interpretation that will be quoted, discussed and further interpreted by the exegete in his references to it. Now these early exegetic interpretations taught by the imam show, directly and indirectly, that the hidden meaning of the Qur'anic verses to which they apply is none other than the spiritual reality of the imamate or that of the family of the Prophet.

A few more examples will illustrate this. In the second verse of the second sura, "The Cow" (*al-baqara*), the text says: "This is the Book!" The *ta'wil* maintains that the Book is Imam 'Ali, the Prince of believers; that those "who believe in the mystery" (as the verse that follows states) are those who believe in the resurrection, the return of the Resurrector (the last imam) and the "return" of all things to God through the office of the Resurrector. Thus the hidden meaning of the Book is explicitly the messianic role of the imam, the "Speaking Qur'an".

In the second sura, verse 31 reads: "He taught Adam all the names, then He presented them to the Angels and He said: 'Tell Me the names of these things if you are truthful'". The apparent sense of this verse is uncomplicated. It refers to the names of the creatures that God teaches Adam. But the hidden meaning as taught by Imam Husayn is much different. According to the imam, when God created Adam, he taught him the names of all creation, and as these were presented to the angels, He introduced five "silhouettes" or "spectral forms" (*ashbah*): Muhammad, 'Ali, Fatima, Hasan and Husayn (the Five of the Mantle). God placed them in the "loins" of Adam. Their lights radiated over the horizon, crossing the heavens, penetrating the veils that protect divinity, reaching all the way to paradise and the Throne of God.

In verse 34, the Qur'an reveals that God ordered the angels to prostrate themselves before Adam. Imam Husayn's exegesis explains why. God made Adam into a receptacle able to hold the light of the five spectral forms embodying all the realities of the worlds. This is why all angels, except Satan, consented to bow down to him. Satan's gesture signalled his hostility to the prophetic family and inaugurated the long line of those who oppose the prophecy and the *walaya*. The other angels humbled themselves before Adam, pledging obedience to the everlasting reality of the "People of the Prophet's Household".

These extraordinary scenarios are expanded further with a hadith attributed to the fourth imam, 'Ali ibn al-Husayn, who refers to an earlier teaching of his grandfather Imam 'Ali. It is a thoroughly mystical teaching, representing a dialogue between Adam and God. Adam sees the light shining in his "loins" and asks God what it is. God explains in a sort of *ta'wil* that the light is that of the five light forms, which from his Throne, He has caused to come down to Adam. Adam asks for a more detailed explanation, and God instructs him to turn his gaze towards the Throne. As Adam meditates, he observes the light of the five persons ascending to the Throne. He recognizes that the light shining in his own loins is the reflection of the five lights, like forms appearing in a mirror. He asks God what these five forms are and God explains how He took from His own Name the names of Muhammad, Fatima, 'Ali, Husan and Husayn. Using analogy and etymology, God explains how each of the names expresses a divine Name: the Praiseworthy for Muhammad, the Elevated for 'Ali, the Creator for Fatima, the Benevolent for Hasan and Husayn. God concludes His *ta'wil* with a celebration of Hasan and Husayn as the finest among the youth in paradise, and He reveals that the five people of light are the intercessors between Himself and His creation and that through them will come all reward and punishment.

Qur'an 7:180 confirms this interpretation: "to God belong the beautiful names, so call Him by them". The teachings of the imams explain this as follows: God is only named by the beautiful names by His servants, through the knowledge they have of us [the imams]. Knowledge of the People of the Prophet's House is the true path of naming God because the names of Muhammad, Fatima, 'Ali, Hasan and Husayn derive from divine Names according to a mystical practice of etymology, and the reality of the imams turns out to be the theophanic locus of these divine Names.

We lack space here to provide a fuller idea of the far-reaching consequences of such *ta'wil*. Suffice it to say that starting from meditation, the believer can pursue several paths: an exegesis of the divine Names, an examination of Adam's role, or a venture down more complicated paths in mystical anthropology. In any case, we can see that the esoteric of the Qur'an, which is the subject of exegesis, presents itself as an utterance whose secret leads back to the divine Word; because it is God who, in accord with this exegesis, has made Himself the first spiritual instructor of man and, so to speak, the absolute model for the imam's function.

The Qur'an provides many historical narratives: the lives and acts of the prophets, the events initiated by divine will, the tribulations of the righteous – in short, a sacred History of humanity since Adam, punctuated by the rhythm of the prophecies. With each twist and turn of the narrative, the Shi'i *ta'wil* attributes a hidden meaning to these facts, that rebounds back to the spiritual reality of the imamate. Hence the verse, "We shaded you with clouds, and sent down to you manna and quails: 'Eat from the goodness of the provisions We have provided you'" (Qur'an 2:57). The *ta'wil* taught by the imam claims the authority of a hadith attributed to Muhammad which interprets the manna and quails as follows: they are the proof (*hujja*), supplying knowledge of divine Reality and of the discipline of the mystery, safeguarding the true faithful (the Shia) from the wickedness of men. And this proof is the imam himself.

Each gift of God has the esoteric meaning of the everlasting reality of the *walaya* of the Imam. Take the example of "God's unction" (Qur'an 2:138). His unction is none other than faith, the distinctive mark of the believer. But in a deeper sense this unction is *walaya*, and God consecrates His faithful through this unction at the moment of the Pact with Adam before all time, when mankind accepts God's authority through the unction composed of the reality of the imam.

Symbolic exegesis can sometimes seem tedious as it relentlessly lays bare the one single meaning hidden under the countless Qur'anic symbols: the twelve Imams. But in doing this, it hardly differs from Christian exegesis of Old Testament prophetic texts or from Origen's exegesis, which identifies Christ's presence under a mass of symbols.

Here is an example of this overarching symbolism:

> We are the prayer that is mentioned in the Book of God. We are the fasting, we are the pilgrimage, we are the sacred month [Ramadan], we are the holy land, we are the house of God [the Ka'ba], we are the direction of prayer [*qibla*], and we are the Face of God. God has said: "Wherever you turn, there is God's Face" (Qur'an 2:115). We are the signs [or the verses of the Qur'an] and we are the exegetic explanations. Our enemies are listed in the Book of God. They are crime, forbidden acts, injustice, wine, games of chance, graven images, rites of divination, idols, painted images, rebellion against God, death, murder, and sickness.

Obscure verses provide an ideal platform for highly developed, progressive exegesis. Here is an unusual example: "Between the two there is a curtain and on *al-A'raf* there are men who know each other by signs; and they shall cry out to the hosts of Paradise, 'Peace be upon you!' but they cannot enter it though they desire" (Qur'an 7:46). In his translation of the Qur'an, J. Berque translates *al-A'raf* as "projection", "salient". The term is enigmatic. Here in abstract is a Shi'i *ta'wil* of the verse. It can be compared with many others – in particular, one by Tabari that is quoted by R. Blachère in a lengthy footnote accompanying his translation of the Qur'an. "Between the two" means "between the inhabitants of the Garden and the inhabitants of the Fire". This becomes clear in the context of Qur'an 57:13: "a barrier will be set up between them which has a gate". The hidden meaning is divine mercy, whereas the apparent sense is punishment.

A celebrated Shi'i commentator, Abu 'Ali al-Tabrisi (or Tabarsi), explains the quote "on *al-A'raf* are men". He uses a hadith by the sixth Imam, Ja'far al-Sadiq. His interpretation is like a painting that conveys a scene imbued with strong moral and aesthetic overtones that are deeply moving. According to the Imam, *al-A'raf* refers to the dunes situated between the Garden and the Fire. Each prophet, surrounded by his Companions, makes a halt at these dunes. He does so because there are men in his group who are weak and who have acted wrongly. Like a military leader with exhausted troops on a long march, he brings his group to a halt. Those who have done right proceed into the Garden, while the man of God stays behind with those who have done wrong and addresses them: "look at your brothers who have gone before you into Paradise!" And the unfortunate lot standing outside the Garden call out to their brothers: "Peace be upon you". The Qur'anic text states, "They did not enter, though their desire was intense". Here is the meaning: though they implore God, through the intercession of the Prophet and the Imam, the guilty will not enter the Garden. They look on the inhabitants of the Fire and cry out: "Oh God, do not cast us among the wicked people!"

In this exegesis, on the strength of its scenography, it is suggested that the man of God – the intercessor, the guide – does not enter the Garden but remains outside with the weak, just as a general does not abandon his rearguard, the ill and the laggards. He points to the Promised Land – paradise – but remains on the dune, in the desert of life, between the Fire and the Garden. This is the compassion of the imam who mitigates the severity of God's decree.

The key to the mystery of predestination itself is the knowledge or denial of the imam. To explain the knowledge that men have of each one of the signs, Muhammad al-Baqir, the fifth imam, explains that these men and their signs are the family of the Prophet. The only ones who will enter the Garden are those who know the Family; the ones who deny them will enter the Fire. Thus the exegesis of the verse sounds a solemn note. The individuals standing on *al-A'raf* are the Five of the Holy Mantle: Muhammad, Fatima, 'Ali, Hasan and Husayn, as well as Khadija, the first wife of the Prophet and mother of Fatima. It is they who cry out: Where are those who love us? Where are our Shia? The cry is no longer that of the unfortunate ones standing outside the Garden, but a summons to those who love and whom the supreme lovers address, the prophetic family – a summons to their friends to assemble. The Five approach their faithful. They know them by their names and the names of their fathers. They take them by the hand and help them along the path leading to the Garden.

And here is the final threshold of this group of exegeses; the one that leads us to the understanding that *al-A'raf* represents the imams themselves. In his reply to a question from one of his followers, 'Ali provides the proof:

> We stand here on the *A'raf* and we know our helpers (*ansar*) by their distinctive signs. And we are the *A'raf* and no one knows God except by the same way that He knows us. We are the *A'raf* whom God will make known on the Day of Resurrection on the path of men. No one enters the Garden whom we do not know and who does not know us, and no one enters the Fire except him who denies us and whom we deny. If God wills, He makes Himself known to His servants. But He makes us His gate, His way, His path and His Face, which is offered by Him. Those who turn away from our *walaya* and prefer something other than us are transgressors because they abandon the way.

Now it is possible for the exegesis to connect the mysterious term *A'raf* with the word that expresses perfect knowledge, *al-ma'rifa*, which is total spiritual knowledge. The imams are the *A'raf* because they possess and they teach knowledge as their right.

The exegesis of correspondences

Shi'i interpretation of symbols is not confined to the Qur'an. It applies to all forms of reality according to a general principle of correspondence – or concurrence – that governs things. We know that this idea directed the methods of interpretation and mystical knowledge in late antiquity and applied to astral theologies as well as to Stoic traditions and Neoplatonism. It also lies at the heart of different Jewish mystical traditions. In Western Christianity it saw widespread application in the Renaissance when the teachings of Plato and Plotinus conjoined with hermetism and Jewish Cabala.

Between the 14th and the 18th centuries, we observe the emergence of a similar conviction among Shi'i intellectuals. It was especially strong in what the Shi'i philosophers and commentators of the Qur'an called wisdom, *al-'irfan*; that is, supreme knowledge. In order to grasp the meaning of this, we must return to two Qur'anic verses whose *ta'wil* will provide a basis for this "science of correspondences", also called "the science of the Scale": "Say, 'If the sea were ink to pen the words of my Lord, it would dry up before the words of my Lord run out even if We were to fill it with the same quantity of ink again'" (Qur'an 18:109); "And if all the trees of the Earth were made into pens, and the ocean fed by seven more oceans were to supply the ink, the words of God would not exhaust them. God is Powerful and Wise" (Qur'an 31:27).

With some help from the work of Ibn 'Arabi, "acclimatized" to the Shi'i world as he was by Haydar Amuli among others, it is possible to understand these two verses thus: The verses would be meaningless if they alluded to the words of God as they appear in the Qur'an, the Torah or the Gospel. The literal sense does seem to point to these holy books. But, then, how is it possible to speak of inexhaustible ink or writing without end? Isn't the writing of these scriptures complete? Doesn't it come to an end with a finite number of letters, words and verses? No, in fact, because the meaning of these verses is the one revealed by spiritual exegesis, which links them to yet another verse: "We will show them Our signs on the horizons and within their souls, until it becomes clear in their own eyes that therein is the truth" (Qur'an 41:53).

In this respect even the idea of the "Book of God" goes beyond the letter of the revealed holy books. It is not restricted to them. The expression "the horizons" refers to the entire universe, which encompasses a hierarchy of different worlds. The expression "their soul" refers to the man-in-full who is perceived as a universe in and of himself. The universe is a book, the "book of horizons"; man is a book, "the book of souls". And these two books correspond to each other as the macrocosm corresponds to the microcosm. As for the revealed Book, the Qur'an, it achieves the synthesis between the book of the universe and the book of man.

No doubt this structural relationship between the Book, the universe and man already existed in the metaphysical speculations of earliest Shi'ism since It authorizes mystical astrology, numerology, the hierarchic ordering of the esoteric being according to the degrees of the world of nature, the world of the soul, the world of intelligence, the establishing of correspondences between the degrees of the Shi'i esoteric hierarchy and the realities of these worlds, the symbolic correlation between the world of prophecy and the imamate on the one hand, and of cosmology, on the other. This relationship takes a new and systematic form with the Twelver Shia. Above all it asserts itself as a doctrine of universal writing by the divine Pen. God writes His Book with the pen of intelligence, and His Book is the universe, it is man and it is the Qur'an. All three books are bound up in a precise correspondence with each other. To interpret is to reveal the hidden meaning in the one as well as in the others. It is a single and unique universe of meaning spreading across the three registers in perfect correspondence, in "concurrence".

The Book of the Qur'an is a collection of verses which brings together "utterances" or ordered words, and the atomic elements of the Book are, in the end, its letters. It is the same for the universe, whose primary elements, whose inseparable units are the letters which when compounded are the "words" (or "verbs") of the World. These "verbs" of the World – like the "verbs" of Man which are composed of "letters" (the basic indivisible elements of his mind) – are eternal essences which arise from the divine act of creation, expressing the divine world of the names through which God reveals Himself. Earlier we saw that these divine Names are the roots of the names of the Prophet and the imams. It will not surprise us to learn that together the book of the universe, the book of man and the book of the Qur'an express – in mutual correspondence and at their respective levels – the eternal Muhammedan reality, the metaphysical reality of the Fourteen Impeccable Beings.

In passing, it is worth making one more point in regard to the infinitude of the universe and man. The atomic compounds (letters) forming the universe and the microcosm (man) are infinite in number; their combinations are likewise inexhaustible. Whereas exoteric cosmology establishes a finite number of celestial spheres and, since the time of Avicenna, the ninth heaven is the threshold of physical realities rising in tiers to the moon and thence to the sublunar world, in contrast, the *ta'wil* of the universe reveals an infinite universe. The esoteric aspect of the finite universe is an infinite universe. The same can be said of the perfect man, the man in his total realization, who is the sum of all worlds that make up the universe by virtue of a play of exact correspondences. Just as the material realm of nature leads back to the realm of the heavenly souls, which leads back to the realm of spirits, which in turn leads back to the realm of intelligences, so it is with the perfect Man whose three main stages of development – natural, psychological and intellectual – represent three forms of divine "writing", and they provide the configuration of three inner realms. As the psychological unfolds in the realm of the soul and the realm of spirits, we come upon the very structure of the universe. It goes without saying that the same structure is found in the Qur'an, whose letters, "verbs" and verses form the totality of all the meanings of the other two realms.

A mystical commentary devoted to the "Light Verse" (Qur'an 24:35) by Mulla Sadra illustrates this "total" exegesis quite well:

> Know that every existent taken one by one, which is a part of this universe, is a place of manifestation for a particular divine Name. As the universe consists of various genera – species and individuals, substances and accidents

(the accidents are quantity, quality, the "when", the "where", place, relation, action, passion and possession), so too among the divine Names there are names of genera, names of species, names of substance, names of accident, quantity, quality, etc. And it is likewise a model of the perfect man, who is the locus of manifestation of gathering together everything that exists in the world of divine Names and that exists in the places of manifestation of the horizons [of this world]. Just as the divine Names, because of their distinct meanings, are fully contained, in synthesis, within the meaning of the name *Allah*, so too the essential realities of their sites of manifestation, which are the parts of the macrocosm – the world of horizons – are gathered together in the place of manifestation of the name *Allah*, which is the perfect man. In one sense, this perfect man is the microcosm; in another he is the entire world, or rather the greatest world! This second perspective is one where he is seen in his ability to envelope by his knowledge – an ability which surges from the depths of God's mine of knowledge – the knowledge God has of all creatures, of their principles and causes, of their forms and finalities, just as the Prince of Believers, the Imam of mystical scholars, the Leader of all true believers in God's One-ness [Ali b. Abi Talib] declared: "You are the clear book which elucidates the secret through its verses but you claim that you are a tiny body and yet within yourself the hugest universe is enfolded".

A form of structural thinking, *ta'wil* is a general hermeneutic of the existing being. Here are a few more examples that, we hope, will provide deeper insight into the exegetic project of the Shia. We make no claim to being exhaustive here.

The Shaykhi school interpreted the Divine Throne as a harmony of the divine Scriptures. The Throne of God displays four lights: white, yellow, green and red. The white light is in correspondence with the world of *Jabarut*, the realm of pure intelligible lights; the yellow is the upper *Malakut*, the realm of spirits; the green corresponds to lower *Malakut*, the realm of souls; the red represents the physical realm of nature. This interplay of correspondences reveals the concurrence of the structure of the realms as constituting the book of the universe and the lights of the Divine Throne.

There is also a second interplay of correspondences: both structures – the structure of the world and the structure of the lights – correspond to the higher realm of the angels. White is the archangel Seraphiel; yellow is Michael; green is Azrael; and red corresponds to Gabriel. Similarly this same structure, according to *ta'wil*, corresponds to the structure of the imamate. White corresponds to the twelfth Imam; green to the second; yellow to the first; and red to the third.

The unity of structure is clear. It expresses the complex interconnections between the Manifest (*zahir*) and the Hidden (*batin*). The activator is the appearance of the colour red, which is its perceptible mode of appearance. We know that the essence of colour is light. The *ta'wil* of the appearance of colour is the world of nature, the first degree of the book of the universe. This *ta'wil* refers to a *batin*, a hidden meaning: the fourth Pillar of the throne of *walaya*, Husayn, the third Imam. He is the fourth pillar because he comes after Muhammad, 'Ali and Hasan. Returning to the book of the universe and to the symbolic exegesis of the world of nature and physical bodies, we disclose its esoteric side: Gabriel, the archangelical giver of form to the world. And if we continue on to the exegesis of the effective reality of the imamate – the *walaya* – as expressed in the person of Husayn, we find the inner imam, who lives in the heart of man and in the secret of the intellect, which is the highest degree of the book of man, the "book of soul" itself.

One would be right in thinking that this exegesis of correspondences had little chance of success against the growing authority of jurisprudence and the figure of the jurist. The rationalism of the doctors of the Law could hardly be expected to accommodate such a *ta'wil* unreservedly. And yet life decided otherwise. The renaissance of Iran under the Safavids, a new golden age of philosophy, witnessed a strong revival of *ta'wil*. Renowned philosophers such as Mulla Sadra Shirazi, Qadi Sa'id Qummi and the masters of the Shaykhi order were also adept in the exegesis of correspondences. They frequently extended the application of the full range of the knowledge of it at their disposal, with the aim of achieving, through *ta'wil*, a figure of the absolute knowledge of the revealed God and His creations.

In addition to the interpretation of Qur'anic commentaries, exegesis of the traditions of the imams assumes a central place in the work of these scholars, and this still forms a significant part of their philosophical work. Shi'i philosophy sees itself as exegetic philosophy. We will return to this. For the moment, here is a further example of this philosophical exegesis – or hermeneutic philosophy – from the writings of Mulla Sadra.

Let us begin with the interpretation of the words "in the name of God" (*bismillah*). Sadra offers an early exegesis of these words in his commentary on the Qur'an. He returns to it later in his *Exegesis* of the collection of traditions by Kulayni, the *Usul al-Kafi*. The *original ta'wil* is found in a statement by the Imam Ja'far al-Sadiq: the letters "*BiSM*" (in the name of) – *ba, sin, mim* – stand respectively for the beauty of God (*ba = baha'*), the majesty of God (*sin = sana'*) and the glory of God (*mim = majd*). Mulla Sadra produces his own *ta'wil* starting from the imam's original *ta'wil*. He states explicitly that the imam's revelation is one that mere human intellect is quite incapable of. He understands his own knowledge as an exegesis directed by an original, normative exegesis. The invocation "in the name of" expresses three major Attributes of God. Sadra generalizes the implicit meaning. God is the divinity of all things, which is the same as saying that God is loved, that He is the Beloved One par excellence. The hidden meaning of the Divine, which permeates the Names and Attributes of God, is love. This establishes a correspondence between the whole of the imams' revelations and all the conceptions of Sufism – particularly those of Ibn 'Arabi, Ghazali and Hallaj. It is an immense correlation in which the philosophy, inner religion and mystical poetry of Islam achieve subtle consonance. It is a decision in favour of spiritual Islam against the claims of literal Islam.

Crowning his exegesis is Sadra's explanation of how God's Attributes are distributed according to a hierarchy. Sadra says that the attributes of every existent are, in fact, a function of its act of existing. Corporeal attributes refer to the world of bodies, to nature; psychological attributes correspond to the world of the soul; intellectual attributes refer to the world of intelligence; the "divine" attributes correspond to the world of the Divine. He describes the progress of an ascension step by step, of a process of becoming that the creature must undertake, of a journey towards God which passes through three levels of existence. Here the *ta'wil* borrows its vocabulary from Neoplatonism, which it puts into correspondence with Shi'i exegesis and with the universes of the Qur'an, man and the world. It reconnects with the perception of a "substantial motion" which moves all creation from God and towards God.

It is this metaphysical movement that the "unveiling" suggests in an exegesis of the Qur'anic verse "Guide us to the straight path" (Qur'an 1:6). Here is a translation:

> Know that knowledge is the essential reality of the way and the straightness of the path; the walk down this path and any straying from it arise from Qur'anic knowledge which is the dominion of the contemplatives and the interpreters and not other Muslims. With one exception: that the only faith and the only submission are faith and submission in divine mystery, and not merely an opinion wrought in the light of certainty. Verily, without interpretation there is no knowledge. […] Know that the path would not be a path if it were not one along which we can travel. This means that all creatures turn their faces toward God, following a conversion ingrained in their nature, in a movement that is natural to each one towards the Causer of causes [God]. In this movement divergence and digression are inconceivable, in what makes them what they truly are, in light of what God has determined for each one of them; God "holds by the tuft": it is written, "there is not a creature that he does not hold by the tuft. Verily, my Lord is on a straight path" (Qur'an 11:56). There is nothing in all creation, which is not a living thing that moves. He is therefore a mount. And the Lord holds every mount by its tuft. […] Thus every living being is created to walk on the path of righteousness without straying. As for the creature called "man", he moves because free will exists, which in him is different from nature; and the rival power of imagination exists which allows him to see deviance and error, punishment and ignorance. His voluntary movements are what cause him to hesitate between closeness to God and estrangement from God; they bear for him either happiness or ill fortune in the next world. Therefore he needs someone to guide him and to remind him of the eternal obligation, and to keep him firmly on the straight path.

Ultimately the *ta'wil* leads back to the figure of the eternal Imam. It is not satisfied with interpreting the verses of the Qur'an as if their ultimate meaning is the physical person of the imam. This would be facile allegorism and slavish adherence to a temporal principle of authority. By taking the metaphysical reality of the imamate as the central focus of exegesis, Shi'ism means to open up the meaning of the verses to the infinite whole of cosmic and supernatural realities, embracing all things from the origin of the existent until its final return to God. This is why the *ta'wil* reveals a moral teaching, taking its inspiration from a metaphysical exploration of existence, freedom and nature. To conclude, Shi'i exegesis constantly confirms what it claims to be: a meditation on spiritual guidance, on the inner man and his destiny.

Notes

1 At least in its original version (see p. 48ff).
2 See p. 69.

Bibliography for Part II

M.A. Amir-Moezzi, "Al-Saffar al-Qummi (m. 290/902–3) et son Kitab basa'ir al-darajat", *Journal asiatique*, 280, 1992, pp. 221–250.

M.A. Amir-Moezzi, *Le Guide divin dans le shi 'isme originel: aux sources de l'ésotérisme en Islam*, Paris; Lagrasse: Verdier, 1992. [*The Divine Guide in Early Shi'ism. The Sources of Esotericism in Islam*, English trans. by D. Straight, New York: State University of New York Press, 1994.]

M.A. Amir-Moezzi, "Aspects de l'imamologie duodécimaine I: remarques sur la divinité de l'Imam", *Studia Iranica*, 25, 1996, pp. 193–216.

M.A. Amir-Moezzi, "Contribution à la typologie des rencontres avec l'imam caché (Aspects de l'imamologie duodécimaine II)", *Journal asiatique*, 284(1), 1996, pp. 109–135.

M.A. Amir-Moezzi (ed.), *Le Voyage initiatique en terre d'islam. Ascensions célestes et itinéraires spirituels*, Bibliothèque de l'Ecole des hautes études, vol. 103, Louvain; Paris: Peeters, 1996.

M.A. Amir-Moezzi, "La vision par le coeur dans le shi'isme imamite", *Connaissance des Religions. Lumières sur la Voie du cœur* (special issue), 57–59, 1999, pp. 146–169.

M.A. Amir-Moezzi, "Fin du Temps et Retour à l'Origine (Aspects de l'imamologie duodécimaine VI)", *Revue des mondes musulmans et de la Méditerranée. Mahdisme et millénarisme en Islam* (special issue, ed. M.Garcia-Arenal), 91–94, 2000, pp. 53–72.

M.A. Amir-Moezzi, "Savoir c'est Pouvoir. Exégèses et implications du miracle dans l'imamisme ancien (Aspects de l'imamologie duodécimaine V)", in *Miracle et karama: hagiographies médiévales comparées*, ed. D.Aigle, Bibliothèque de l'École des hautes études, vol. 109, Turnhout: Brepols, 2000, pp. 251–286.

M.A. Amir-Moezzi, "Notes à propos de la walaya imamite (Aspects de l'imamologie duodécimaine X)", *Journal of the American Oriental Society*, 122(4), 2002, pp. 722–741. [Also published in *Mystique musulmane: parcours en compagnie d'un chercheur*, ed. G. Gobillot & Roger Deladrière, Paris: Cariscript, 2002.]

M.A. Amir-Moezzi, *La religion discrète. Croyances et pratiques spirituelles dans l'islam shi'ite*, Paris: Vrin, 2006. [*The Spirituality of Shi'i Islam: Beliefs and Practices*, English translation, London: I.B. Tauris, 2011.]

M.A. Amir-Moezzi, *Le Coran silencieux et le Coran parlant: Sources scriptuaires de l'Islam entre histoire et ferveur*, Paris: CNRS, 2011.

M.A. Amir-Moezzi, "Cosmogony and Cosmology, V, in Twelver Shi'ism", *Encyclopaedia Iranica*.

M.A. Amir-Moezzi, "Eschatology, III, in Imami Shi'ism", *Encyclopaedia Iranica*.

H. Ansari, *L'imamt et l'Occultation selon l'imamisme. Etude bibliographique et histoire des textes*, Leiden: Brill, 2017.

S.W. Anthony, *The Caliph and the Heretic: Ibn Saba' and the Origins of Shi'ism*, Leiden: Brill, 2012.

S.A. Arjomand, "The Consolation of Theology: Absence of the Imam and Transition from Chiliasm to Law in Shi'ism", *The Journal of Religion*, 76, 1996, pp. 548–571.

S.A. Arjomand, "Imam Absconditus and the Beginnings of a Theology of Occultation: Imami Shi'ism Circa 280–290 AH/900 AD", *Journal of the American Oriental Society*, 117, 1997, pp. 1–12.

M.M. Bar-Asher, "Variant Readings and Additions of the Imami-Shi'a to the Quran", *Israel Oriental Studies*, 13, 1993, pp. 39–74.

M.M. Bar-Asher, *Scripture and Exegeis in Early Imami Shiism*, Leiden: Brill, 1999.

T. Bayhom-Daou, "Hisham ibn al-Hakam (d. 179/795) and his Doctrine of the Imam's Knowledge", *Journal of Semitic Studies*, 58, 2003, pp. 71–108.

T. Bayhom-Daou, "The Second-Century Ghulat: Were They Really Gnostic?", *Journal of Arabic and Islamic Studies*, 5, 2003–2004, pp. 13–61.

R. Brunner, *Die Schia und die Koranfälschung*, Würzburg: Ergon, 2001.

M.A. Buyukkara, "The Schism of the Party of Musa al-Kazim and the Emergence of the Waqifa", *Arabica*, 47, 2000, pp. 78–99.

A. Cameron, *Abu Dharr al-Ghifari: An Examination of His Image in the Hagiography of Islam*, London: Royal Asiatic Society, 1973.

L. Capezzone, "Un miracolo di 'Ali ibn Abi Talib", *Rivista degli Studi Orientale*, 71, 1997, In memoria di Francesco Gabrieli (1904–1990), suppl. no. 2, pp. 99–112.

H. Corbin, *En Islam iranien: aspects spirituels et philosophiques*, 1st ed., Paris: Gallimard, 1971–1972.

H. Corbin, *Corps spirituel et terre céleste: de l'Iran mazdéen à l'Iran shi'ite*, 2nd revised ed., Paris: Buchet Chastel, 1979. [Spiritual Body and Celestial Earth, from Mazdean Iran to Shi'ite Iran, English translation by N. Pearson, Princeton, NJ: Princeton University Press, 1977.]

H. Djaït, "Les Yamanites à Kufa au 1er siècle de l'Hégire", *Journal of the Economic and Social History of the Orient*, 19, 1976, pp. 141–181.

J. Eliash, "The Shiite Quran: A Reconsideration of Goldziher's Interpretation", *Arabica*, 16, 1969, pp. 15–24.

W. Ende, "The Flagellations of Muharram and the Shi'ite Ulama", *Der Islam*, 55, 1978, pp. 19–36.

W. Ende, "Ehe auf Zeit (mut`a) in der innerislamischen Diskussion der Gegenwart", *Die Welt des Islams*, 20, 1980, pp. 32–45.

J. van Ess, *Theologie und Gesellschaft im 2. und 3. Jahrhundert Hedschra*, 6 vol., Berlin, New York: De Gruyter, 1991–1997.

A. Falaturi, "Die Zwölferschia aus der Sicht eines Shiiten. Problem ihrer Untersuchung", in *Festschrift Werner Caskel*, ed. E. Gräf, Leiden: Brill, 1968, pp. 62–95.

I. Friedlander, "The Heterodoxies of the Shiites in the Presentation of Ibn Hazm", *Journal of the American Oriental Society*, 28, 1907, pp. 1–80, and 29, 1908, pp. 1–183.

I. Goldziher, "Beitrage zur Literaturgeschichte der Shi'a und der sunnitischen Polemik", *Sitzungsberichte der kaiserlichen Akademie der Wissenschaften*, 78, 1874, pp. 439–524.

[Republished in a collection of the author's articles prepared by J. de Somogyi, Gesammelte Schriften, Hildesheim: Olms, 1967–1973, vol. I, pp. 261–246.]

A. Gribetz, *Strange Bedfellows: mutat al-nisd' wa mutat al-ha. A Study Based on Sunni and Shi i Sources of Tafsir, Hadith and Fiqh,* Berlin: Schwarz, 1994.

H. Halm, *Die islamische Gnosis. Die extreme Schia und die Alawiten,* Zurich; Munich: Artemis, 1982.

G. Hawting, "The Tawwabun, Atonement and 'Ashura", *Jerusalem Studies in Arabic and Islam,* 17, 1994, pp. 166–181.

M.G.S. Hodgson, "How Did the Early Shi'a Become Sectarian?", *Journal of the American Oriental Society,* 75, 1955, pp. 1–13. [Now available in E. Kohlberg (ed.), Shi'ism: *The Formation of the Classical Islamic World,* vol. 33, Aldershot, England: Ashgate, 2003, article no. 1.]

C. Jambet, "L'islam shi'ite et l'interprétation des symboles", in the author's collection of articles *Le Caché et l Apparent,* Paris: Herne, 2003.

C. Jambet, *Mort et résurrection en islam. L'au-delà selon Mulla Sadra,* Paris: Albin Michel, 2008.

C. Jambet, "'L'essence de Dieu est toute chose'. Identité et différence selon Sadr al-Din Shirazi (Mulla Sadra)", in *Le Shi'isme im amate quarante ans après. Hommage à Etan Kohlberg,* ed. M.A.Amir-Moezzi, M.M.Bar-Asher & S. Hopkins, Turnhout: Brepols, 2009. C. Jambet, *Qu'est-ce que la philosophie islamique?*Paris: Gallimard, 2011.

Khaled Keshk, "The Historiography of an Execution: The Killing of Íujr ibn ÝAdi", *Journal of Islamic Studies,* 19, 2008, pp. 1–35.

E. Kohlberg, "Some Notes on the Imamite Attitude to the Qur'an", in *Islamic Philosophy and the Classical Tradition. Essays Presented by his Friends and Pupils to Richard Walzer on his Seventieth Birthday,* Ed. S.M. Stem*et al.,* Oxford: Cassirer, 1972, pp. 209–224.

E. Kohlberg, "The Term 'Muhaddath' in Twelver Shi'ism", in *Studia Orientalia memoriae D.H. Baneth dedicata,* Jerusalem: Magnes Press, Hebrew University, 1979, pp. 39–47. [Now in *Belief and Law in Imami Shi'ism,* article no. 5.]

E. Kohlberg, "Shi'i Hadith", in *The Cambridge History of Arabic Literature. I: Arabic Literature to the End of the Umayyad Period,* Ed. A.F.L. Beeston*et al.,* Cambridge: Cambridge University Press, 1983, pp. 299–307.

E. Kohlberg, "Non-Imami Muslims in Imami fiqh", *Jeruslam Studies in Arabic and Islam,* 6, 1985, pp. 99–105. [Now in *Belief and Law in Imami Shi'ism,* article no. 10.]

E. Kohlberg, "The Position of the walad zina in Imami Shi'ism", *Bulletin of the School of Oriental and African Studies,* 48, 1985, pp. 237–266. [Now in *Belief and Law in Imami Shi'ism,* article no. 11.]

E. Kohlberg, "Bara'a in Shi'i doctrine", *Jerusalem Studies in Arabic and Islam,* 7, 1986, pp. 139–175.

E. Kohlberg, "*Al-usul al-arba 'umi'a*", *Jerusalem Studies in Arabic and Islam,* 10, 1987, pp. 128–166. [Now available in a collection of articles by the author, Belief and Law in Imami Shi ism, Aldershot, England: Variorum, 1991, article no. 7.]

E. Kohlberg, "Imam and Community in the Pre-Ghayba Period", in *Authority and Political Culture in Shi'ism,* Ed. S.A. Arjomand, Albany, NY: State University of New York, 1988, pp. 25–53. [Now in *Belief and Law in Imami Shi'ism,* article no. 13.]

E. Kohlberg, "Authoritative Scriptures in Early Imami Shi'ism", in *Les Retours aux Écritures: fondamentalismes présents et passés,* ed. E.Patlagean & A.Le Boulluec, Bibliothèque de l'École des hautes études, vol. 99, Louvain; Paris: Peeters, 1993, pp. 295–311.

E. Kohlberg, "Taqiyya in Shi'i Theology and Religion", in *Secrecy and Concealment: Studies in the History of Mediterranean and Near Eastern Religions*, Ed. H.G. Kippenberg and G.G.Strournsa, Leiden: Brill, 1995, pp. 345–380.

E. Kohlberg (ed.), *Shi'ism. The Formation of the Classical Islamic World*, vol. 33, Aldershot, England: Ashgate, 2003.

E. Kohlberg, "Vision and the Imams", in *Autour du regard Mélanges Gimaret*, Ed. E. Chaumont *et al.*, Louvain: Peeters, 2003, pp. 125–157.

E. Kohlberg & M.A. Amir-Moezzi, *Revelation and Falsification: The Kitab al-qira'at of Ahmad ibn Muhammad al-Sayyari*. Leiden; Boston: Brill, 2009.

T. Lawson, "Notes for the Study of a 'Shi'i Qur'an", *Journal of Semitic Studies*, 36, 1991, pp. 279–295.

Y. Linant de Bellefonds, "Le droit imamite", in *Le Shi'isme imamite*, (conference proceedings, Strasbourg, 6–9 May 1968), Paris: Brepols, 1970, pp. 183–200.

J. Loebenstein, "Miracles in Shi'i Thought. A Case Study of the Miracles Attributed to Imam Ja'far al-Sadiq", *Arabica*, 50(2), 2003, pp. 199–244.

H. Löschner, *Die dogmatischen Grundlagen des shi'itischen Rechts*, Erlangen; Nuremberg; Cologne, 1971.

W. Madelung, "The Shiite and Kharijite Contribution to Pre-Ash'arite Kalam", in *Islamic Philosophical Theology*, Ed. P.Morewedge, Albany, NY: State University of New York Press, 1979, pp. 120–139. [Now in *Religious Schools and Sects in Medieval Islam*, London: Variorum, 1985, article no. 8.]

W. Madelung, "Imamism and Mu'tazilite Theology", in *Le Shi'isme imamite*, actes du colloque de Strasbourg (6–9 May 1968), Paris, 1970, pp. 13–29. [Now in a collection of the author's articles, *Religious Schools and Sects in Medieval Islam*, London: Variorum, 1985, article no. 7.]

W. Madelung, "'Abdallah b. 'Abbas and Shi'ite Law", in *Law, Christianity and Modernism in Islamic Society*, Ed. U. Vermeulen and J.M.F. Van Reeth, Louvain: Peeters, 1998, pp. 13–25.

M. Massi Dakake, *The Charismatic Community: Shi'ite Identity in Early Islam*. Albany, NY: State University of New York Press, 2007.

H. Modarressi, *An Introduction to Shi'i Law: A Bibliographical Study*, London: Ithaca Press, 1984.

H. Modarressi, "Early Debates on the Integrity of the Qur'an", *Studia Islamica*, 77, 1993, pp. 5–39.

S.H. Nasr & M. Aminrazavi with the assistance of M.R. Jozi, *An Anthology of Philosophy in Persia. Vol. 3: Philosophical Theology in the Middle Ages and Beyond from Mu'tazili and Ash'ari to Shi'i Texts*. London: I.B. Tauris, 2010.

A.J. Newman, *The Formative Period of Twelver Shi'ism: Hadith as Discourse between Qum and Baghdad*, Richmond: Curzon, 2000.

W. al-Qadi, "An Early Fatimid Political Document", *Studia Islamica*, 48, 1978, pp. 71–108.

W. al-Qadi, "The Development of the Term Ghulat in Muslim Literature with Special Reference to the Kaysaniyya", in *Akten des VII. Kongresses für Arabistik und Islamwissenschaft*, Ed. A.Dietrich, Göttingen: Vandenhoeck & Ruprecht, 1976, pp. 295–319. [Now available in E. Kohlberg (ed.), *Shi'ism: The Formation of the Classical Islamic World*, vol. 33, Aldershot, England: Ashgate, 2003, article no. 8.]

A. Quérry, *Droit musulman. Recueil de lois concernant les musulmans Schyites*, 2 vols, Paris: Imprimerie Nationale, 1871–1872.

U. Rubin, "Prophets and Progenitors in Early Shi'a Tradition", *Jerusalem Studies in Arabic and Islam*, 1, 1979, pp. 41–65.

A.A. Sachedina, *Islamic Messianism: The Idea of the Mahdi in Twelver Shi'ism*, Albany, NY: State University of New York Press, 1981.

Mulla Sadra Shirazi, *Le verset de la lumière: Commentaire*, Ed. M.Khajavi, French trans. & notes by Christian Jambet, Paris: Les Belles Lettres, 2009.

P. Sander, *Le Shi'isme imamite* (conference proceedings, Strasbourg, 6–9 May 1968), Paris: Presses universitaires de France, 1970.

P. Sander, *Zwischen Charisma und Ratio. Entwicklungen in der frühen imamitischen Theologie*, Berlin: Schwarz, 1994.

P. Sander, "Koran oder Imam? Die Auffassung von Koran im Rahmen der imami- tischen Glaubenslehren", *Arabica*, 47(3–4), 2000, pp. 420–440.

W. Tucker, *Mahdis and Millenarians: Shiite Extremists in Early Muslim Iraq*, Cambridge: Cambridge Uiversity Press, 2008.

C. Turner, "The 'Tradition of al-Mufaddal' and the Doctrine of the Raj'a: Evidence of Ghuluww in the Eschatology of Twelver Shiism?", *Iran*, 44, 2006, pp. 175–196.

G. Vajda, "De quelques emprunts d'origine juive dans le hadith shi'ite", in *Studies in Judaism and Islam Presented to Shelomo Dov Goitein*, Ed. Sh. Morag et al., Jerusalem: Magnes Press, Hebrew University, 1981, pp. 45–53.

Part III

The historical evolution of Shi'ism

7 The roots of political Shi'ism

How does it happen that a religious movement whose own sacred texts present it as initiatory, esoteric, mystical and quietist can give birth to a political ideology advocating the concentration of political power in the hands of the doctors of the Law? How did it lead to the ideology of Khomeinism and the Iranian Islamic Revolution, viz. the doctrine of the "leadership of the supreme jurist" (*walayat al-faqih*)[1]? The political victory of this doctrine in 1979 is the outcome of a long, complex process that we must now examine as it played a paramount role in the evolution of Shi'ism. For the sake of brevity and clarity, we will discuss only a few historical "moments" which constitute crucial turning points in this evolution.

The Buyid dynasty and the Baghdad school

The first and no doubt most significant turning point in Shi'i history is the 4th/10th century. This glorious period, although plagued by constant political conflict, was the age of Islamic Renaissance and Humanism, a golden age of Islamic culture and civilization. An extraordinary flourishing of the arts and sciences, thought and literature took place. It was the age of the "Persian Interlude", between the period of Arab domination – beginning with the rise of Islam – and the arrival of the Central Asian Turks in the following century. In regard to the issues that we will discuss, the period displays three important features.

First, the 4th/10th century has been called the "Shi'i century" of Islam. Buyid princes, either Zaydi or Twelver Shia, ruled over Baghdad, the capital of the empire. For over a century Abbasid caliphs were mere puppets in their hands. At the same time the Hamdanids dominated regions of northern Iraq and Syria, and a Zaydi state ruled in Yemen. Egypt and large portions of North Africa were under the rule of an Isma'ili Fatimid dynasty. Southern Iran, the Persian Gulf, Bahrain and a large part of Arabia were controlled by Qarmatians, an esoteric Sevener Shi'i sect with the same doctrinal origins as the Isma'ilis. In short, some of the most important regions in the lands of Islam were under Shi'i government.

Second, the 4th/10th century is a "rationalizing" turning point in Islam. A century earlier a monumental enterprise was undertaken to translate the works of the Greeks and the Alexandrians into Arabic. Over time, in a virtual beehive of activity, schools of translation made available literally hundreds of texts by the most celebrated thinkers and scientists of Hellenistic culture. Naturally it took time for scholars to absorb and adapt the new ideas and concepts to the changed setting. By the 4th/10th century, this appears to have been more or less achieved. Among their many valuable discoveries, Islamic scholars were deeply impressed with Aristotelian dialectics, reasoned argument and logic, and its various intellectual tools that the ancients had devised. Above all, the jurists and theologians of different schools discovered useful methods and resources that could be used to overcome their adversaries in polemic debate and argument. The term *'aql* – in the new sense of "reason" as opposed to the older notion of "intellegence" – became the dominant notion of the century. Not only was it seized on by philosophers, rationalizing theologians and free thinkers in their struggle against the traditionalist defenders of a recently established "orthodoxy"; it also found favour among many of the new orthodox thinkers, who regarded Islam as the "rational religion" par excellence.

Third, and lastly, for the Twelver Shia, this century saw the end of the time of the historical imams. The twelfth and last imam, the Hidden Imam, disappeared permanently in 329/940–941, perhaps four or five years before the arrival of the Buyids in Baghdad. His disappearance inaugurated the period of "Major Occultation". Henceforth, the Shia lacked a "physical" leader. Because their doctrine was comprehensively dominated by the figure of the imam and his authority, his disappearance created a truly awkward situation.

In fact, living in a politically unstable and socially hostile environment, faced with a vacuum created by the absence of the charismatic figure of the imam, who descended directly from Muhammad (and who was also respected by the Sunni Muslims), it is hardly surprising that the majority of Twelver Shia felt themselves in very uncomfortable circumstances. (This was the case for Buyid princes and for all other Shia who moved in their power circles.) As we observed earlier, many texts can be traced to the imams specifically forbidding the faithful from involvement in direct political activity.[2] Scholars and thinkers alike were also discomfited for they found themselves, in this century of triumphant reason and established orthodoxy, heirs to a body of sacred texts strongly marked by esoteric, mystical and even magical features and, indeed, by "unorthodox" beliefs (the divine nature of the imam, the "falsification" of the Qur'an and hostility to the Companions of Muhammad); in other words, highly "non-rational" notions and doctrines viewed, ever more violently, as deviant and heretical.

It was in this time of crisis that a "rationalist" tendency led by brilliant jurist-theologians became ever more firmly established – a tendency that distanced itself increasingly from the old esoteric and non-rationalistic tradition. As we have seen, from the time of the last three or four imams, three influential groups existed within the Shi'i community: the doctors of the Law, the jurist-theologians, who were often part of the upper strata of the hierarchy but who lived for the most part far from the abode of the imams; powerful aristocratic families, who moved in elite power circles and attempted to bring the Abbasid state under their control; and, finally, the leaders of esoteric and revolutionary groups, likewise involved in the struggle for power but achieving their ends either by armed messianic revolt or by infiltration of the state apparatus.

In the 4th/10th century, the first two of these groups were successful in uniting against the third and in eliminating it almost entirely. They did not hesitate to appeal to the Abbasids for assistance in suppressing the revolutionaries. The Abbasids found these inter-Shia struggles quite convenient, as illustrated by the trial and execution of the great mystic al-Hallaj. He was an initiate in several "extremist" Shi'i sects and a friend of various illustrious advocates of esoteric-revolutionary Shi'ism (al-Hallaj gave his name to the Hallajiyyah Shi'i order). By eliminating Hallaj, the Shi'i doctors of Law from Baghdad and Qumm, under the leadership of Abu Sahl al-Nawbakhti – an influential member of the Nawbakhti family – succeeded in eradicating the influence of their esoteric co-religionists in both the Shi'i community and in the state apparatus.

A further illustration of this is found in the role played by an illustrious member of the Nawbakhti family, Husayn b. Rawh, in the trial and execution of Shalmaghani, a celebrated Hallaji Shia. (Later tradition presents Ibn Rawh as the "third representative" of the Hidden Imam during the Minor Occultation.) Hallaj had been executed in 309/921 and Shalmaghani in 322/933. The removal of these "revolutionary" esoteric followers signalled the victory of the great families and their allies, the Islamic jurists. Combined with deepening infiltration of both groups within the Abbasid power structures, these eliminations undoubtedly contributed to the rise to power of the non-revolutionary Shi'i Buyids in 334/945.

Many of the Twelver Shi'i faithful, of the esoteric and Gnostic persuasion, allied themselves with the Qarmatian and Isma'ili movements under the influence of their propagandists. Those who stayed were increasingly marginalized. The Buyids came from a large aristocratic family in northern Iran. In no time they put an end to the influence of the other great Shi'i families. Consequently, only the doctors of the Law remained to fill the power vacuum created by the occultation. Under the prevailing circumstances, numerous compromises and doctrinal redefinitions and reformulations were necessary to ensure the survival of Twelver Shi'ism as an organized religion. During the Buyid period, the principal aim of the doctors of the Law seems to have been to adapt Shi'ism to the demands of rationalism; to refine – indeed to sweeten – any doctrine deemed deviant so as to avoid clashing with orthodoxy, but also to provide justification for power-sharing with the Buyids and, ultimately, with the Abbasids.

But first, Shi'i doctrine had to achieve a compromise with rationalization. The process is discernible through a shift in meaning of the word *'aql*. *'Aql*, as it appears in the earliest hadith texts (i.e. in the original traditions with their non-rational esoteric orientation), refers to cosmic Intelligence; its analogue is the Imam (we highlighted this in our earlier discussion of cosmogonic mythology). Cosmic Intelligence, the leader of an Army of the Righteous, has its counterpart in man as the "inner imam of each person". It embraces an apperception of both – it is important to stress – the rational and non-rational realms. *'Aql* is an ability to apprehend the Divine and comprehend the metaphysical; it is the ultimate spiritual "organ". It is intelligence of the sacred and sacred intelligence; it is the "inner proof" of God, as the Imam is His "outer proof". The imams constantly present sacred intelligence as the best possible means for understanding their teachings, as the axis around which their religion spins, the foundation of their doctrine. It is what enables the faithful to place their belief not only in rational phenomena but also in all that rebels against rationalization in the esoteric and spiritual realms

Important changes begin to occur with the "rationalistic" turning point within Islam when Aristotelian logical reasoning also frequently comes to be translated as *'aql*. This new meaning gradually replaces the old. The jurist-theologians of the Buyid period, seeking to distance themselves from the earlier tradition, took advantage of this double sense in order to criticize the older hadith collections. In their conception, what the imams put forward as the central element of their religion is indeed *'aql*; that is, logical reasoning in the new sense of the word. Many of the early hadith compilers had included traditions that were absurd from the standpoint of reason. It followed therefore that such hadith could not be authentic. And so, as had happened in Sunni circles a century earlier, a new science of hadith criticism took root and flourished in Shi'i circles, the aim of which was to identify the criteria for authenticating or invalidating traditions.

It was in the name of reason that the founder of the rationalist school, Shaykh al-Mufid (d. 413/1022), devoted a critical commentary to the "Profession of Faith" by his master, Ibn Babuya (d. 381/991). His disciple, al-Sharif al-Murtada (d. 436/1044), who had parallel training as a Mu'tazilite rationalist theologian, went so far as to ask his co-religionists to censor entire passages of al-Kulayni's *Kafi*, one of the most celebrated of the early hadith collections, and he did so under the aegis of those same criteria of logical reasoning and dialectical speculation. Aided by the dual signification of the term while ignoring its semantic shift, the rationalist jurist-theologians of the Baghdad school managed to censor the imams while claiming to work in the name of that *'aql* whose merits they so vaunted. Over time they began to ignore a number of esoteric, initiatory and mystical traditions, concerned primarily with imamology, and they addressed the particulars of Shi'ism with a view to narrowing the gap with orthodoxy and providing the rationalist current greater access to the corridors of power without encountering any serious obstacles. Quite often such hadith were deemed heresies and attributed to "heretical extremists" or "exaggerators" (*ghalin*, plural *ghulat*) by these rationalistic scholars.

As we have noted, Shi'ism has two important sources of scripture, the Qur'an and the hadith, the latter interpreting and illuminating the former. According to the original tendency, any tradition in agreement with these two sources and reported by an imam is credible. Any other system of criteria is rejected. Moreover, these same two sources form the sole foundations of canon law. Any new legal instance not foreseen by the Qur'an and the hadith remains in "suspension" pending the imam's judgment (either one of the "historical" imams or the Hidden Imam himself when he returns). Conforming to the imam's explicit instructions, any other personal method is to be rejected: analogical reasoning (*qiyas*), individual opinion (*ra'y*), personal efforts of interpretation (*ijtihad*)[3]. The focal point of this doctrine is the concept of certainty (*yaqin*); that is, the imams' teachings comprising the hadith and illuminating the Qur'an provide believers with certainty. By contrast, personal methods can produce nothing more than conjecture (*zann*), which spreads doubt and undermines faith.

Here again there is a distancing – indeed a breach – of rationalist thought from the original texts. As early as the first half of the 4th/10th century, the thinkers Abu Sahl Nawbakhti and Ibn Qiba Razi and the jurists Ibn Abi 'Aqil and Ibn Junayd Iskafi applied a rationalising form of *ijtihad* to the very notion of occultation itself. Al-Mufid adopted a more ambiguous stance in regard to the personal effort of interpretation by the religious scholar. Though his thought is wholly based on rational speculation, he rejected *ijtihad* as a disguised form of analogical reasoning. The likely explanation is that he felt uncomfortable with flagrantly contradicting the imams who were still so close in time; even so, al-Mufid's entire work left the door wide open for the later development of a genuine theory of *ijtihad*. And it is his own disciple, Sharif Murtada, who first explicitly applied a still limited concept of *ijtihad* when reasoning in cases left "in suspension" by the Qur'an and tradition.

Another great figure of the rationalist school of Buyid Baghdad, the Shaykh al-Tusi (d. 460/1067), was also, among other things, a specialist in the science of hadith and a theorist of the prerogatives of the jurist-theologian. His celebrated hadith collections seem to have two principal objectives: to provide a systematic revision of the earliest hadith and to establish law as by far the most important religious discipline of all.

The titles of his two works are revealing: "The Rectification of Principles" (*Tahdhib al-ahkam*) and "Clarification of the Differences of Opinion regarding Traditions" (*al-Istibsar fi ma'khtulifa fihi min al-akhbar*).[4] Nevertheless, Tusi made an attempt – as far as his system of thought allowed – to rehabilitate the oldest compilers of traditions, which had been severely criticized by Sharif Murtada. Moreover, insisting on the importance of tradition and on logical reasoning, Tusi systematically presented the jurists in numerous writings as the representatives of the imams during the occultation. With great intelligence, he gave nuance to the radical positions of Sharif Murtada and, in so doing, succeeded in providing the law – and consequently the jurists – with a status and range of interventions which for all intents and purposes became independent of the imam's person. Thus, the great authors of Shaykh al-Mufid's Baghdad school, and Tusi in particular, laid the foundations for two additional but essential elements of canonical law alongside the Qur'an and the hadith: on the one hand, reasoning and *ijtihad* as the field of application of reason; and, on the other, the consensus of the jurists (*ijma'*), provided that it could be corroborated by tradition.

The works of Tusi sealed the authority of the rationalist theological-juridical tradition, which became known as "Usuliyya" or the school of the *mujtahid*; that is, the practitioners of *ijtihad*. The supremacy of this tradition, which lasts to the present day, resulted in the marginalizing and, at times, violent repression of the original tradition, whose advocates – particularly among the jurists – were called "Akhbariyya" (Traditionalists).

Another example of the rationalist school's deviation from the founding texts is seen in its political activism. The occultation and its immediate consequence – the absence of an authority figure at the head of the community of believers – motivated the doctors of the Law to exercise their own authority in order to ensure that the religious life of the community remained organized. At the same time, confronted with numerous hadith of the imams warning of damnation if the faithful were to become involved in, or associated with, power circles, these same doctors were obliged to provide justification for their collaboration with the Buyid rulers and the Abbasid state.

According to the directives of tradition, since the only just power is that of the Hidden Imam, the believer is asked to accept the rule of a prevailing unjust regime and to adopt a quietist attitude until the return of the awaited Saviour and the universal re-establishment of justice.

Both philosophers and doctors of the Law would attempt to provide alternative solutions to deal with the problems associated with state power. We will examine the philosophers' solutions below. As far as the rationalist doctors are concerned, the 4th/10th century opened a new doctrinal chapter in their output, a chapter entitled "Collaboration with Power" (*al-'amal ma'a l-sultan*) or "The Exercise of Power" (*'amal al-sultan*). It is noteworthy that there had always been a close connection between the science of hadith authentication, Shi'i theories of *ijtihad* and the justification of the political power of the Islamic jurist, and that they had undergone parallel developments throughout the historical evolution of the rationalist current. The cause of this is now easy to see: hadith criticism and *ijtihad* had been explicitly rejected in the early corpus of acts and sayings attributed to the imams. But in order to resort to both in practice, and to consolidate the foundations of their authority, the doctors of the Law had no other choice but to distance themselves from the early corpus. So they established a critical science of the hadith in order to invalidate the more awkward traditions or at least to render their interpretation more acceptable through recourse to *ijtihad*.

It is a fact that already in the time of the historical imams, individual believers and groups of faithful engaged in political activity, ignoring the imams' quietist injunctions. There are examples of certain groups fomenting or participating in messianic insurrections; there are also examples of certain great families (Al Nawbakht, Al Junayd, Al Furat, Al Yaqtin, etc.) who were actively involved in the administration of the state; and there is also the example of certain doctors of the Law attempting to establish a small independent state in the region of Rayy in central Iran in the late 3rd/9th century. But these examples are not the norm. The vast majority of Shi'i faithful, including the scholars and religious authorities, seem to have rejected all forms of political activism and participation. Here again it is the work of al-Mufid that provided the first theoretical justification of the Shi'i religious authorities' massive involvement with Buyid power. Mufid sought to avoid direct contradiction of the traditional doctrine that claimed that all power was unjust until the return of the Hidden Imam. Instead he attempted to qualify the doctrine and adapt it to prevailing political circumstances. He argued that unjust power is either illegitimate (as in the case of Abbasid power and other non-Shi'i powers in general) or it is legitimate (as in the case of Buyid power since the Buyids were stalwart Shia who were well disposed to handing over the reins of power to the Hidden Imam upon his return). Shi'i jurists are authorized to collaborate with unjust but legitimate power if such involvement results in advancing the rights of the Shi'i community and avoiding repression. From this moment onward, notions of justice and injustice become the focal point of Shi'i political philosophy.

Mufid's two celebrated disciples – the brothers Sharif Radi (d. 406/1016) and Sharif Murtada (d. 436/1044) – occupied, one after the other, high positions of authority, following in their father's footsteps (chief syndic of the Shia, organizer of the pilgrim caravans to Mecca, the caliph's representative in cases of abuse by the authorities). The brothers enjoyed the personal friendship of successive caliphs. They readily appeared in their official functions in the black robes of the Abbasids. Sharif Murtada drew inspiration from Mu'tazilite concepts of evil and began to formulate a new system of thought based on notions of the justice and injustice of political power. In his aptly entitled treatise "The Collaboration with Power", he went so far as to argue that it is a duty to work with the government if it allows justice to be re-established. This was a clear reference to the need to reinstate the flouted rights of the Shia.[5] He reasoned as follows: One who assumes a responsibility to defend Shi'i rights, under the authority of an unjust or illegitimate ruler, does so by tacit order of the true sovereign, who is the Hidden Imam. And for this reason the faithful owe him their obedience. The personal ambiguity of Sharif Murtada, who was assiduous in his presence at court, emerges in full force in another work, *Epistle on the Occultation*, in which Murtada explained the duration of the occultation as a result of the tyranny of the caliphs and the persecution of the Shia.

A short while later, Shaykh Tusi lifted Murtada's thinking on political justice to its high point. According to Tusi, a ruler can be considered just if he commands Good, forbids Evil and distributes religious taxes equitably in accordance with Shi'i legal injunctions. His argument ignores the classical doctrine of the universal reign of injustice until the return of the Mahdi. Thus, just power is not the exclusive province of the imams. A ruler who governs in accordance with Shi'i canon law is also a just ruler. Tusi explained this notion with reference to his doctrine of divine Grace (*lutf*), according to which God in His justice cannot allow His servants to live indefinitely under the authority of unjust governments. Thus, the great theorist of the late Buyid period succeeded in introducing new ideas for the establishment of a "just power" during the occultation. But, as he so often did in seeking to temper Murtada's more extreme positions, he maintained that the Shi'i jurist's collaboration with government is not a duty; it is merely desirable.

The school of Hilla

The fall of the Buyids when the Seljuk Turks took Baghdad early in the second half of the 5th/11th century, the restoration of a rigorous form of Sunni Islam, and the brutal repression of the Shia were the chief reasons for the gradual relocation of the intellectual centre of Shi'ism from Baghdad to Hilla, another town in Iraq. Throughout the 6th/12th and 7th/13th centuries, the scholars of the Hilla school – who were almost to a man members of the rationalist current – continued to consolidate the theoretical foundations of Usuli theology and jurisprudence. First of all, Ibn Idris Hilli (d. 598/1202) reinstated the authority of early rationalist thinkers such as Ibn Abi 'Aqil and Ibn Junayd Iskafi even though, while asserting his own proximity to the Akhbari Traditionists, he frequently criticized Shaykh Tusi. He was apparently the first to explicitly include notions of "consensus of the jurists" and "reason" among the fundamental principles of canon law alongside the Qur'an and tradition.

After the Mongol conquest (in the middle of the 7th/13th century) and the fall of Abbasid Baghdad, the policies of the rationalist scholars gained strength. The collapse of the Abbasids and of the Isma'ilis effectively made Twelver Shi'ism the great beneficiary of the Mongol invasion. Shi'i scholars seized the historical opportunity to consolidate their faith by collaborating with the conquerors and, in some instances, converting them. This is another example of one of those critical "moments" when the rationalist jurist-theologians dramatically confronted the dilemmas of history.

The theoretical writings of the Buyid period required re-examination and renewal. Buyid power, which was Shia and therefore legitimate, had not succeeded in putting an end to the unjust caliphate of the Abbasids. Divine Grace had willed that salvation come through the Mongol infidels. The Shi'i attitude to this is summarized in the famous phrase of Ibn Tawus (d. 644/1266), one of the leading Twelver scholars of the time: "The infidel but just ruler is better than the unjust Muslim ruler".[6] Together with his illustrious contemporary, the great philosopher Nasir al-Din Tusi, Ibn Tawus lent his support to the Mongol Khan Hulagu as he attempted to restore order. Likewise, 'Allama Hilli (d. 726/1325), disciple of Nasir al-Din, and his son Fakhr al-Muhaqqiqin collaborated with Ilkhan Uljaytu (Sultan Muhammad Khudabanda), as later did Ibn Fahd Hilli (d. 841/1437), advisor to the Qara Quyunlu ruler Sepand Mirza.

In doctrinal terms, Muhaqqiq Hilli (d. 676/1277), author of the monumental work "The Canonical Laws of Islam" (*Shara'i al-islam*), was probably the first person to present the authoritative "Four Books" of Shi'i hadith, established on the model of the "Six Books" of Sunni hadith.[7] With the exception of a chapter in al-Kulayni's *Kafi* entitled "Foundations", these collections deal exclusively with canon law. Together with the Buyid-period literature relating to the science of hadith authentication (cf. the two collections by Shaykh al–Tusi), the work of Muhaqqiq represents a second decisive step in establishing the law more comprehensively at the heart of Shi'i scholarship. At the same time, the social role of the Islamic jurist and the perception that his authority is both an intellectual and spiritual *necessity* take on increasing significance.

Alongside these developments, the theory of *ijtihad* continued its evolution, reaching its apogee in the monumental work of the aforementioned 'Allama Hilli, the disciple of Muhaqqiq. According to Hilli, *ijtihad* – "a personal effort of interpretation concerning the matters of the faith" – is a logical outcome of the imamate/*walaya* since the fallibility of the doctors of the Law is the logical consequence of the impeccability of the Imams. Fallibility is one of the essential components of *ijtihad*. The jurist who makes a mistake in his "personal effort" is not guilty of sin. The reason for this is simple: Although ijtihad is an attempt at rational speculation on legal issues that are still conjectural, it is nevertheless the most effective means of leading the believer to certainty. In other words, *ijtihad* is the quickest means to certainty in legal instances that the Revelation and the Tradition had not anticipated.

The theories of two great Hilla scholars, al-Muhaqqiq and al-'Allama, provided the jurists who practiced personal interpretation – the *mujtahids* – with considerable freedom of action. For example, al-Muhaqqiq combined the notions of *faqih* (doctor of the Law) and *walaya* (in the sense of "legal authority" or "decision-taking authority", a very different sense from the usual sacred meaning it had acquired in Shi'i belief). Every doctor of the Law has his own general *walaya*, but the *mujtahid* doctor, who satisfies the necessary moral and scientific conditions, has a special *walaya*. Without specifically saying so, Muhaqqiq narrowed the gap between the position of the jurist and the status of the imam. In so doing he expanded on the ideas of the Buyid-period theorists, particularly Shaykh al-Tusi. Infallible authority, the prerogative of the Hidden Imam, was projected into an indefinite far-off future. It became the responsibility of the fallible "representatives" of the Hidden Imam – the *mujtahids* – to resolve all practical contemporary issues without hindrance from the tradition.

At the same time, al-'Allama was elaborating a corollary of *ijtihad* known as *taqlid*, literally "imitation" or "emulation". Those individuals who can not meet the requirements of personal *ijtihad* performance – a reference to the majority of believers – can place themselves in the hands of the doctors of the Law. This liberates the entire community from the strains of *ijtihad*. The ordinary believer, who is neither obligated nor qualified to perform a "personal interpretative effort", is required to look for an authority figure to whom he must surrender himself. In this way, he becomes the "imitator" of the *mujtahid* jurist-theologian.

Thus, there are now two distinct categories of Shia: the *mujtahids*, those who possess knowledge and therefore authority; and the "imitators", those who, in order to remain on the proper path, are required to heed the directives of the *mujtahid*.

Al-'Allama developed another significant argument, which had considerable historical importance; namely, that the decrees and decisions of the *mujtahid* are an obligation for his "imitators" only as long as he, the *mujtahid*, is alive. In matters of religious authority, the living always takes precedence over the dead. This daring deviation from the legacy of the past implies the perpetuation of the doctors of the Law – the "authorities for imitation" – as a class. And indeed this class gradually grew in strength.

In the 8th/14th and 9th/15th centuries, the political disintegration of the post-Mongol period together with the devastations created by Tamerlane's incursions plunged Iran, Iraq and Anatolia into great chaos. The atmosphere was apocalyptic. It was an age of several politico-religious movements promoting gnostic and messianic beliefs. Each attempted to bring a solution to the impatience of the ordinary masses living in frustrated expectation of the Mahdi's return. The leaders of these various movements offered themselves as reincarnations of the imams, as the Saviour himself if not as theophanies of God. The religious scholars denounced them all as extremists.

The successors to Tamerlane – the Timurids – and the Qara Quyunlu rulers crushed Hurufism, founded by Fadl Allah Astarabadi. Its followers are reported to have rallied to the cause of the Bektashi Turk dervishes. The Timurids also savagely repressed the followers of Muhammad Nurbakhsh. Today their followers form a small community in the valleys of the Hindu Kush. Muhammad b. Falah founded a sect in Southwest Iran based on extremist doctrines. After nearly a century, his followers, the Musha'sha' sect, began to temper his radical doctrines; some apparently joined other communities such as the Ahl-i Haqq. Among these different "Saviours", only one achieved a truly grand destiny. This was Isma'il, the founder of the Safavid dynasty. He presented himself as the reincarnation of all the imams and was deified by his followers. He imposed Shi'ism by force on Iran. Once their authority had been established, the successors to Isma'il moderated their political opinions.

From the Safavid dynasty until the present day

Another decisive turning point in Shi'i history is the rule of the Safavid dynasty in Iran (907–1135/1501–1722) and the proclamation of Twelver Shi'ism as the state religion. The Safavids, who derived legitimacy from their religious affiliation, aspired to convert all Iran to Shi'ism in order to establish a viable politico-religious opposition to the Sunni caliphate of the Ottomans. For this, they needed a rigorous religious ideology to protect themselves from their opponents. In addition to local scholars, they brought together the finest scholars and jurists from Iraq, Bahrain and Syria and especially from Jabal Amil (in present-day Lebanon) in order to elaborate the necessary conceptual framework. Thus, a religious organization – virtually an "official Church" – was founded under state control. Parallel to this, the "religious system" produced a vanguard of doctors of the Law, which gradually won its independence from state power. The nucleus of what has been called a Shi'i "clergy", it gradually consolidated its structure, hierarchy and influence.

The Safavid period and the official endorsement of the "religion of the imams" laid the groundwork for a genuine Shi'i renaissance. Twelver philosophies and mysticisms achieved their fullest expression during this period. (We will return to this below.) But yet again, the real beneficiaries of this renaissance were the religious Rationalists – the Usuli *mujtahids* with their strong intellectual traditions and roots – in spite of the fact that relations between the Twelver hierocracy and the Safavid rulers were complex and shifting.

The reformulation of the principles establishing the basis of the jurists' authority led to an expansion of their political and economic influence. It was during the Safavid period that the *mujtahid* won significant prerogatives which until then had been the exclusive preserve of the imams. Such prerogatives included the right to lead public prayer, the collection of certain religious taxes and a firm hand in legal affairs. We will return to these issues in Chapter 8. Suffice it to say here that the combination of the two notions – the *ijtihad* of the Islamic jurist and the "imitation" required of the faithful masses – was systematically established and theoretically consolidated with the help of such leading thinkers as Muqaddas Ardabili (d. 993/1585) and Hasan b. Zayn al-Din 'Amili (d. 1011/1602). One particularly important innovation was the attribution, by the ruler Shah Tahmasp I, of the title "representative of the Hidden Imam" to the Islamic jurist-theologian Muhaqqiq Karaki (d. 940/1534). This ruling was contemporary with a legal reformulation by Zayn al-'Amili, called the "second martyr" (d. 965/1557), according to which the historical "representatives" of the Hidden Imam during the Minor Occultation are called "special representatives", whereas the *mujtahids* are held to be the Imam's "general representatives" during the Major Occultation. This reformulation expanded on the theories of Muhammad Ibn Makki (d. 786/1384), known as the "first martyr", and authorized the jurist-theologians to preside over religious tribunals and to collect certain religious taxes "in the name of the Imam", as the four historical representatives had been authorized to do until then. It is hardly a coincidence that the same Muhammad Ibn Makki gave the science of hadith authentication its final form in his celebrated book, *al-Diraya*.

The legal application of these reformulations together with the administration of assets called *waqf* (plural *awqaf*) resulted in the religious class wielding tremendous social influence and vast financial autonomy. Thus, with the creation of a virtual ministry for Religious Affairs, naturally under the authority of an Islamic jurist – with men of the stamp of such scholars as Muhammad Baqir Majlisi (d. 1111/1699) as "Master of Islam" (*shaykh al-islam*), the highest religious authority in the capitol of Isfahan under Shah 'Abbas I – the Shi'i clergy appeared firmly established and fully consolidated.

Following the Afghan invasions, other decisive steps were taken under the dynasty of the Qajars (1209–1346/1794–1925). Although relations between the Shahs and the *mujtahids* were ambiguous and parlous, legitimacy was the fundamental preoccupation of both; each sought the endorsement of the other. For a while, the title of "special representative of the Hidden Imam" was held by the Shah with the agreement of the most influential doctors of the Law. But the prerogatives of the jurists, as "spokesmen of the Imam", were fully reinstated at the initiative of the leader of the *mujtahids*, Ja'far Kashif al-Ghita'

(d. 1227/1812), in Najaf (Iraq). He is the same *mujtahid* who authorized Fath 'Ali Shah, the celebrated ally of Napoleon, to lead a holy war (*jihad*) against the army of the Tsar in the name of the Hidden Imam. This was a first in the history of Shi'ism after the occultation.

Also during this period, perhaps for the first time, the jurist Mulla Ahmad Naraqi (d. 1245/1830) resorted to the expression *walaya* (or *wilaya*) *al-faqih*, referring to the delegation of power to the jurists in the name of the Hidden Imam by virtue of the privileges associated with the performance of *ijtihad*. Thereafter, the expression would appear in every major legal work by Usuli writers. It is this same expression that lies at the heart of Khomeini's political ideology, where, for the first time, it signifies the "leadership of the jurist".

Nevertheless, with Naraqi, the *walaya* of the Islamic jurist is restricted to a few limited areas of law (e.g. management responsibility for certain types of inheritance, responsibility for orphans, etc.). It does not include the authority to govern. But by placing the administration of the affairs of the community in the hands of the jurists, Naraqi effectively opened the door to a far greater politicization of their role.

Also at the beginning of the 13th/19th century, two new and complementary notions emerged in regard to the authority of the Islamic jurist: *a'lamiyyat* (the theory of the highly learned *mujtahid*); and *marja'iyyat* (the notion of a "supreme source of imitation"). According to these theories, which built on the ideas of the scholars of the Hilla school, the faithful masses must scrupulously follow or "imitate" the directives and precepts of the most learned doctor of the Law, paying strict attention to every detail in day-to-day life. The actual influence and hierarchical authority of the clerics, though theoretically grounded on "scientific expertise" (i.e. legal erudition), were based on the notion of leadership (*ri'asa*), expressed in popular acclamation and demonstrations of trust and illustrated in the payment of religious taxes. This controversial notion, vigorously rejected by the imams, depended on the effective control of the various ethnic and socio-professional groups in the community. Thus, the Twelver Shi'i community – from Muhammad Hasan Najafi (d. 1266/1849–1850) to Ayatollah[8] Borujerdi (d. 1380/1961) – experienced ten uninterrupted generations of "models of unique universal imitation". The political behaviour of these ten "most learned *mujtahids*" and their popular supporters fluctuated between apolitical quietism and militant activism, whether in the struggle against the Qajari autocracy, in resistance to foreign domination or in political engagement for and against the Iranian constitutional revolution of 1905. Nevertheless, with the rise to power of the second "model for imitation", the celebrated Sheikh Murtada Ansari (d. 1281/1864), politicization greatly intensified, owing at least partly to the ideological orientation he imposed on the institution he led. At the same time, the formation of a network of theological seminaries (*hawza 'ilmiyya*) in the holy cities of Iraq and Iran provided the religious authorities with a powerful intellectual and social base.

With the death of Ayatollah Borujerdi, the break-up of the institution resulted in the emergence of several "models" or "authorities for imitation", who quietly competed with one another. Differences of opinion in regard to political power often determined the lines of separation. The restrained anger of some religious groups who opposed the policies of secularization and modernization of Reza Shah, founder of the Pahlavi dynasty (1925–1979), took on virulent expression in the strong re-politicization of religious leadership under the influence of Ayatollah Khomeini (d. 1989). This was apparent as early as 1965 in the first uprisings against Mohammad Reza Shah.[9]

Thus it can be argued that the Khomeini doctrine, and at its core the political theory of the leadership of the Islamic jurist (*walayat/ wilayat al-faqih*), descends directly in an uninterrupted historical line from Usuli thought. In this respect we can consider them the culmination of a thousand-year-long process stretching from rationalization to political ideologization.

Though this doctrine is a logical outcome given the historical context, it is nevertheless "revolutionary" in two respects. On the one hand, it is the first time that a religious current enters into open struggle with a political authority with the firm intention of chasing it from power and assuming its place at the head of the state. Not only is this attempt in contradiction, in doctrinal terms, to the teachings of the imams as set down in the founding texts, it is also the first time in history that relations between "clergy and prince" – until then marked by a fine, if precarious, balance – are completely overturned.

Khomeini's doctrine is "revolutionary" in a second respect in that once and for all it frees itself from the classical traditions of caution and casuistry, and goes so far as to declare itself openly in rupture with the teachings attributed to the imams. In this respect, Khomeinism is without a doubt the final turning point in the development of the rationalist current. Without proper historical distance, it is difficult for us to appreciate the impact of this disruption, and all the more so as a messianic aspect seems to have come to the fore. A symptomatic expression of this is apparent in the titles given to the "Guide" of the 1979 Islamic Revolution: "Ayatollah" before the revolution and in its early days, followed by "representative of the Hidden Imam" and, finally, "imam".

The title of imam, as the reader will now appreciate, is by far the most sacred in Shi'i Islam. Until the present day, its use has been restricted to the twelve historical imams. Other than these, it has been used by only two politico-religious leaders: by Musa Sadr in the Lebanon, albeit very briefly, and by Khomeini in Iran. Another important issue is the political exploitation of the various meanings of *walaya*, the other sacred notion of Shi'i faith. Few among the faithful understand the technical, (i.e. strictly legal) meaning of the term; but every Shia understands its reference to the sacred nature and function of the imam. The *walaya* of 'Ali – the supreme imam – is even mentioned in the Shi'i call to prayer. The expression *walayat al-faqih*, the *walaya* of the supreme jurist, transmits sacrality from the imam to the jurisprudent.[10] As Heinz Halm has judiciously pointed out, the rationalist doctors of the Law, including the Ayatollahs of our modern times, are anything but fundamentalists (in spite of the fact that Usuli can be translated by the term "fundamentalist ...").[11] They are in fact the exact opposite, such is the flagrant liberty they have taken with the founding texts, including the corpus of Imami hadith.

The domination of the rationalist juridical-theological tradition ensured the uninterrupted continuity of Shi'ism as an organized religion following the eruption of a deep crisis occasioned by the end of the period of the historical Imams. The lives and work of the great thinkers of the rationalist tradition contributed hugely to an intellectual dynamism and vitality in the discussion of ideas, which continues to mark Shi'i thought up to the present day. Likewise, the "religious organization", which formed under Buyid rule and came into effect under the Safavids, instigated a "process of substitution" in the rationalist current: the doctor of the Law supplanted the imam; the law replaced the teachings of the imams; *walaya* – the love, submission and fidelity owed by every follower to his inner master – was transformed into *taqlid*, a servile "imitation" of the *mujtahid*; mystical love of the imams evolved into a morbid, dolorous cult whose violent collective expressions were tacitly approved, indeed positively encouraged, by the clerical authorities; an official institutionalized clergy ousted the "initiated companions" of the imam.

The history of rationalist clergy, especially in modern times, shows all the marks of fanaticism and exclusivism: a reduction of faith to rigid juridicism, expressions of violence against real or assumed adversaries, an instrumentalization of religion and the manipulation of the ordinary masses. The historical long view seems to suggest that, as far as the Usuli religious scholars were concerned, this process always had a direction, whether a conscious one or not: to draw Shi'ism into the political arena; to practice it as a collective religion; and to consolidate it as an ideology of power.

Notes

1 *Walayat-e faqih* in Persian. Whether spelled *walaya* or *wilaya*, it is the same concept and can be pronounced in both ways.
2 See p. 26. Nevertheless, there are exceptional instances when collaboration with the power elite is admissible; for example, specific cases of force majeure: if collaboration might lead to the protection of the lives and rights of Shia or if non–collaboration might bring with it certain death.
3 This last notion is particularly important. It would play a role in the future development of Shi'ism. The great Islamic jurists of the rationalist order would later be called *mujtahid*; that is, those who practice *ijtihad*.
4 By the 12th–13th century, these books together with *Kafi fi 'ilm al-din* (What is Sufficient in the Knowledge of the Faith) by al-Kulayni and *Kitab man la yahduruhu l-faqih* (Jurisprudence for one who has no Jurisprudent near) by Ibn Babuya form the Four Books of Twelver traditions.
5 In his commentary, al-Murtada based his arguments on a hadith attributed to Imam Ja'far al-Sadiq: "[the sin of] collaboration with power can be atoned for by providing for the needs of the [Shi'i] brothers".
6 It is noteworthy that Ibn Tawus was unable to find valid reasons for Sarif al-Radi and Sharif al-Murtada's collaboration with the authorities of their time.
7 See Note 4 (above), and corresponding text. Concerning the "Six Books" of the Sunnis, see p. 46.

8 The title of *ayatollah* (*ayat Allah*, literally sign of God) was first used in the first half of the 20th century to refer to the supreme position in the Shi'i religious hierarchy. Other titles were used, though not systematically, in reference to lesser positions; for example, *thiqat al-Islam* (the trustworthy person for Islam) or *hujjat al-Islam* (proof of Islam). Later the "supreme exemplars" (*marja' al-taqlid*), chosen from among the ayatollahs, hold the title of "grand ayatollah" (*ayat Allah al-a'zam*).

9 For information relating to the 19th and 20th centuries, we have relied on several articles published by Jean Calmard in the new edition of *The Encyclopaedia of Islam* ("Marja' al-taqlid", "Mujtahid", "Sadr").

10 It is hardly a coincidence that Khomeini, as "Father and Guide of the Revolution", became the focus of a mystical cult by his followers. This has nothing to do with his ascetic lifestyle or his philosophical-mystical work, both of which are commonplace in Shi'i religious scholarly circles. There is nothing new in this. Mysticism and messianism were frequent in the early beginnings of revolutionary-style Shi'i power (cf. the Shi'i rebels of the Ummayyad and Abbasid periods, the Shi'i rule of the Fatimids and the sect of the Qarmatians, not to forget the Safavids, the Sarbadarids in the 8th/14th century and the Musha'sha' in the 9th/15th century).

11 H. Halm, *Die Schia* (Darmstadt, 1988), p. 89.

8 Aspects of the jurist-theologian's power

As we have seen, in Shi'ism the imam is pivotal to every doctrinal issue. During the time of the occultation, the Shia in all that pertains to his individual belief and its innermost aspects, is expected to maintain a mystical relationship with the "living imam" – that is. the Hidden Imam – of the time and, more generally, with the Fourteen Impeccable Ones, to whom he is bound by intense devotion. But the absence of the physical person of the imam makes the collective exercise of religion problematical, since it requires an authorized person for proper performance. According to ancient Shi'i law, as reported in the hadith, only the imam or a person specifically designated by him by name can lead these practices. The original tradition makes clear that the prerogatives of the imam are suspended (*mutawwaqif al-ijra', saqit*) during the time of his absence as no one else has the authority to claim them. This pertains in particular to the "Four Realms of the Law" (literally the Four Precepts, *al-ahkam al-arba'a*). The theory behind this notion, probably of Yemeni Zaydi origin, pertains to the administration of religious justice and legal punishments, the collection of certain religious taxes, collective prayers (the Friday prayer and the two festival prayers: the prayer of sacrifice and the prayer ending the month of Ramadan) and the declaration of holy war.

If one were to adhere strictly to the letter and spirit of the ancient laws, then Shi'ism, by virtue of the occultation of the imam, would be in essence a personal religion. But the needs of an organized religious community – especially in regard to legal and economic matters – and the increasing importance, from the 4th/10th century onwards, of the jurist-theologians in the social and political life of the community resulted in a pressing need to amend the old laws. This process was systematically undertaken by the rationalist scholars of the Baghdad school, continued by the Hilla school and achieving tangible success under the Safavids with the establishment of a Shi'i state and clergy. It can even be argued that the rise to power of the jurists, a process that secured the transformation of the 'Ulama into an authentic clergy, occurred by means of a gradual co-optation of the imam's prerogatives. Finally, this rise to power in social and political circles, primarily in the 20th century, led to the formulation of theories of government for the first time in the history of Shi'ism. We will discuss these at the end of this chapter, but let us turn first to several issues that arise from the Four Realms of the Law.

According to ancient Shi'i law, religious magistrates are to be appointed personally by the imam. They are the only Islamic judicial authorities entitled to preside over the religious courts and to administer legal punishments. Moreover, with regard to the application of punishments stipulated in the Qur'an (the amputation of the hand of a thief, the execution of a murderer, the application of the lex talionis), the imam is held to be the only person with the authority to apply Qur'anic injunctions to individual cases. So it is easy to see how in the absence of the Imam or his personally designated representative, religious jurisdiction and the administration of legal punishments soon became subject to polemic. There was no argument about the need for justice or a judge with competence in religious affairs. The issue was whether or not the judge was required to be a religious "professional". A further complication arose from comments by the imams concerning the difficulty of dispensing fair justice. This seems to have caused scholars to speculate as to whether, in the absence of the imam, a religious magistrate is even suited to perform his role – given that he is even more prone to error since his appointment is not made by the infallible person of the imam himself – and whether he could practise his profession without compromising canon law and, indeed, religion in general.

While the Traditionalists made every effort to remain aloof from legal affairs, the Rationalists, on the other hand, given their high-profile, socio-political engagement under the Buyids, confronted the issue head-on. Nevertheless, their hesitations and ambiguous attitudes become palpable already in the writings of Sharif Murtada.

In his "Collaboration with Power", the treatise which expands on the ideas of his master Sheikh Mufid, Murtada stated quite openly that the Islamic jurist, under the orders of the Hidden Imam, is authorized to administer legal punishments and even Qur'anic punishments, which require interpretation and administration on a case-by-case basis. Nevertheless, in his treatise "The Epistle on Occultation", he declared that the administration of punishments is "suspended" in the absence of the imam:

> As regards legal punishment during the occultation of the imam, the doctrine is clear. Let us take the example of a person who requires administration of a punishment foreseen in the Qur'an. If the [Hidden] Imam "returns" while this person is still alive, and if the offence has been proved either by indictment or by confession, then the Imam will administer the agreed punishment. However, if the punishment cannot be administered owing to the death of the person [having occurred before the return of the Mahdi], the blame falls on those who frightened the Imam and caused him to go into occultation. Nevertheless, the law affecting the administration of punishments is not rescinded, for it is not possible to envisage a repeal of the law unless the hindrances to its proper functioning have been removed and the punishments are not administered. But under the circumstances we are now considering [the impossibility of administering punishments in the absence of the Imam], the law has not been abrogated.

A little later, in his treatise *al-Nihaya*, Shaykh al-Tusi listed the virtues of a good judge. He must be in full possession of his faculties of reasoning, have full knowledge of the Qur'an and of Shi'i hadith, have a firm command of Arabic and show piety and moral probity.

In order to justify the argument in favour of the Islamic jurist who assumes the function of magistrate, Tusi – and virtually every one of his successors – referred to 'Umar b. Hanzala's quotation of a famous hadith by Imam Ja'far, according to which Shi'i magistrates are the representatives and spokesmen of the imam. But the scholars neglect to note that the hadith referred to a time when the imam was still physically present; the hadith had not anticipated the occultation. Moreover, Tusi argued that magistrates could perform their function and administer legal punishments as representatives of the imam. As long as they met the established requirements, it did not matter that an unjust ruler had appointed them.

Such arguments from the grand master of the Baghdad school were not unanimously accepted. For example, the majority of doctors of the Hilla school, chiefly Ibn Idris and al-Muhaqqiq, argued that legal punishments could not be administered in the absence of the imam or his personally designated representative. In their view, during the occultation, magistrates were no more than civil magistrates (*'urfi, madani*), and their judgments were necessarily nothing but civil judgments. Nevertheless, al-'Allama, who expanded on al-Tusi's ideas, argued that the doctors of the Law, who had the ability to perform *ijtihad*, were authorized to administer legal punishments. The great figures of the Shi'i clergy, which had been established under the Safavids, naturally followed in the footsteps of al-Tusi and al-'Allama. From the 9th/17th century on, they assumed the presidency of the religious tribunals and administered legal punishments. These prerogatives, illustrations of the canonic duty to "order the Good and forbid the Evil", were taken as the natural burden of the *mujtahids*, henceforth styled the true guardians of Shi'i "orthodoxy".

From the 12th/18th century onward, they won the authority to anathematize their opponents as "unbelievers" (*takfir*). Thus, these prerogatives soon came to support acts of brutality and bloody repression. Among these were the executions of many followers of the traditionalist movement (Akhbariyya) in the 18th century by order of Wahid Bihbahani, the leader of the Rationalists or, indeed, the death sentences against the Sufis pronounced by Bihbahani's son, the massacre of the followers of Babism and Baha'ism in the 19th and 20th centuries, and the execution of intellectuals and the "henchmen of the West" following the Iranian Islamic Revolution.

Another crucial issue concerned religious taxes and, specifically, the *khums* (the payment of a fifth of one's income) and the *kharaj* (the land tax). According to ancient law, the imam, and anyone explicitly designated by him, holds the right to organize the collection and distribution of these taxes. This is why the issue constantly preoccupied the Shi'i doctors of the Law from the very outset of the occultation. The Shia consider the *khums* to be more or less an income tax. But when the occultation began in 329/940–941, the authorities of the religious hierarchy stopped collecting this tax.

According to an exegesis of verse 8:41 of the Qur'an, the *khums* consists of two equal parts. One half, called the "share of the imam", reverts to God, the Prophet and the imams. The other half, "the share of the descendants of the imams", goes to orphans, the poor and the travellers among the Sayyids. From the time of Sheikh al-Mufid and his followers, notably Shaykh al-Tusi and Abu l-Salah al-Halabi, the rationalist doctors recommended to the faithful that in expectation of the imam's return, they should either burn the first share or bury it; or indeed keep it but, before dying, hand it over to a fiduciary agent. As for the second share, they should distribute it themselves to needy Sayyids, or at the very least hand it over to a trustworthy Islamic jurist-theologian who is able to arrange proper redistribution. Other doctors, probably Traditionalists, firmly held that the *khums* was merely suspended during the entire absence of the imam.

In the 7th/13th century, Muhaqqiq Hilli was the first to argue that the continuation of the occultation and the impossibility of depositing tax monies until the return of the Hidden Imam fully justified the clerics' collection of both shares of the *khums* as well as the collection of the legal alms (*zakat*). Almost to a man, the Usuli jurists agreed that the *mujtahid* had the authority to levy this religious tax on revenues and to use it in the best interests of the faithful and the community.

Another ticklish matter concerned the collection of land tax. According to Islamic law, monies from the land tax go to the state and its civil servants. But what was to be done if the ruler was unjust and repressive? Once again it was Shaykh al-Tusi and Muhaqqiq Hilli who elaborated the complex legal arguments on the subject (a thorough discussion of these highly technical arguments is not possible here). Claiming to be the successor of these two latter authorities, Muhaqqiq Karaki (d. 940/1534) – the Safavid ruler Shah Tahmasb I called him "the representative of the Hidden Imam" – was the first to have methodically justified the 'Ulama as the beneficiaries of this tax. It is noteworthy that the rulers' donations to clerics, which at times represented rather large sums, resulted primarily from the collection of this tax. Needless to say, under Sunni rulers, Shi'i clerics received no such donations. The situation changed radically with the Safavid rise to power. The Safavids directed the proceeds of the land tax to the jurist-theologians who provided the legal arguments supporting their regime. Muhaqqiq Karaki was one of them. His personal fortune was so huge that he felt obligated to provide justification by producing an entire treatise on the legality of the collection of the *kharaj*.

Karaki was incapable of quoting a single text in support of his position. Yet he argued that the *mujtahid*, as the representative of the Hidden Imam, had an obligation to accept the donations and gifts of the ruler in order to acquire enough influence and wealth to assist his needy brothers. Karaki's arguments became the official doctrine of Shi'i clerics, though several influential personalities contradicted him, including Ibrahim b. Sulayman Qatifi from Bahrain (d. 945/1538) and Muqaddas Ardabili (d. 993/1585). Both held that the collection of the *kharaj* during the occultation was illegitimate and, indeed, illegal.

With the collection of these religious taxes combined with the proceeds from their notarial functions (wills, marriages, contracts, etc.) and the income from the many charitable foundations they administered, the clerics of the Usuli movement became an economic and financial force to be reckoned with, virtually independent of the state.

The prescribed collective prayers, especially Friday prayers, have an unquestionable political dimension. The *khutba* – the sermon delivered at Friday prayers – offers an ideal "forum" for the exposition of matters of public interest. According to Shi'i law, only the imam or his personally appointed delegate can lead these prayers. In the imam's absence, the Shi'i community apparently accepted that the conduct of collective prayers was no longer possible or should at least be "suspended" until the return of the Mahdi, at which time he would appoint new "guides" of collective prayer. It is for this reason that Twelver Shia do not perform collective prayer. It is likely that this state of affairs lasted throughout the medieval period, as Sunnis frequently denounced the Shi'i non-observance of collective prayer as one of their countless "heresies". The scholars Sheikh Tusi and Muhaqqiq Hilli produced rather confused doctrines on the topic, and Ibn Idris Hilli went so far as to declare collective prayer illegal.

Matters took a different turn with the Safavids and the establishment of a Shi'i clergy. Early in the Safavid reign, over one hundred books and treatises were written for or against the legality of collective prayers, specifically the Friday prayer. In the end, the rationalist *mujtahids* succeeded in demonstrating the indispensable nature of such prayer. Furthermore, they claimed for themselves the right to lead the prayers and to deliver the *khutba* (sermon). Once again it appears that Muhaqqiq Karaki, the supreme religious authority during the reign of the Safavid Shah Tahmasp, played a decisive role.

Karaki was from Jabal Amil (in present-day Lebanon). His victory over the ruler's two Iranian viziers, Ghiyath al-Din Dashtaki and Mir Ni'matullah – both deeply opposed to the conducting of collective prayer – illustrates the political supremacy of the immigrant scholars over the local experts, for a while at least. The fact of the matter is that the Safavid ruler appreciated the Shi'ism of the rationalist doctors of Law who had emigrated from Syrian lands. Their legal exactitude was closer to the Sunni schools and contrasted sharply with the philosophical and mystical leanings of Iranian scholars. As Safavid ruler, one of his principal concerns was to defend himself, and his religious policies, from the accusations of heresy that the Ottoman ruler and his religious scholars constantly addressed to him. Al-Karaki declared that the Friday prayer under the leadership of the *mujtahid* was not only legal, but it was in fact a duty. He founded his argument on an analysis of works by several respected Usuli scholars of the past, in particular Muhammad Ibn Makki and Muhaqqiq and 'Allama Hilli. However, none of these scholars had ever explicitly declared that collective prayers could be conducted in the absence of the imam. Henceforth, prescribed Friday prayer became a doctrine defended by the Safavid state. Karaki appointed mullahs (religious clerics) to the position of "Friday imams" and "prayer leaders" throughout Iran. Opponents of the official doctrine – jurists claiming the illegality of such prayer in the absence of the imam – were arrested, silenced or even forced to lead the prayers under the threat of injury.

On the issue of *jihad* (holy war), there were similar developments. According to the founding texts of Shi'i law, only the imam – or his personally appointed delegate – can declare and lead holy war. Authors of the classical period drew a very fine line: they declared that offensive jihad was "suspended" during the occultation, while defensive jihad was considered legal, even a duty, in the event of enemy attack. The linking of offensive jihad with the return of the eschatological Saviour gave Sunni polemicists an opportunity to compare the Shia with the Jews.

The many critical texts for and against holy war produced after the Safavids came to power in the 10th/16th century are further proof that the rationalist jurists sought to stake their claim to this additional prerogative of the imam. And this indeed did come about in the 13th/19th century. For the first time in Shi'i history, a doctor of the Law, Shaykh Ja'far Kashif al-Ghita' (d. 1227/1812), addressed an appeal to the state to engage in holy war. As *mujtahid* and representative of "the Master of the Time" (the Hidden Imam), he authorized the Qajar ruler Fath 'Ali Shah to wage holy war on the Russian Tsar. A few years later another *mujtahid* and a renowned leader of the rationalist jurists, Sayyid Muhammad Isfahani, urged the same Shah to undertake a second holy war. But the consequences for Iran were disastrous. After signing the treaties of Gulistan (1813) and Turkamanchay (1828), it was obligated to hand over all of Transcaucasia to the Russians.

To conclude this discussion of the 'Ulama's rise to power, let us turn to its culminating point; namely, its theories on the formation of the government. It is noteworthy that until Ayatollah Khomeini's notion of the "leadership of the supreme jurist", the prerogatives of the doctors of the Law never breached the walls of state power. In fact, prior to the 20th century, the jurists never once formulated a theory of government. The scholars of the Baghdad and Hilli schools never once raised the issue.

Though it was not presented as a theory of government, the first document that might be considered a governmental charter is *al-Lum'a al-dimashqiyya* (Clarity from Damascus), a commentary by Ibn Makki al-'Amili, known as the "first martyr" and executed on the orders of the Mamluks in 786/1384. Written for the Sarbadar ruler[1] Khaja 'Ali b. Mu'ayyad, the treatise granted the *mujtahid* oversight in matters of the ruler's government policies; the *mujtahid* was the ruler's "special decision-making authority as representative of the Hidden Imam". According to Ibn Makki, whose intention it apparently was to prepare the ground for the return of the Mahdi, the doctor of the Law is involved in the practical exercise of government, overseeing the justice system, collecting religious taxes, leading collective prayers and exercising the right to declare holy war.

Ibn Makki thus opened the way for the Safavid-era Usuli clerics. But his successors failed to build on his theories for the forming of a Shi'i government. On the contrary, until Khomeini, the dominant stance among the jurists in regard to the administration of community affairs was a power separation between the political authority of the ruler (*saltana*) and the religious authority of the jurist (*walaya*).

Be that as it may, a clear distinction was being made between the secular political order (*'urfi*) and the religious political order (*shar'i*). Power was now shared between the court and the clerics; but it was agreed that responsibility for government was incumbent upon the "Muslim who held power"; that is, the sovereign ruler. Throughout the Safavid and post-Safavid eras, the leading doctors of the Law upheld this doctrine in one sense or another. Shi'i dignitaries, far from promoting opposition to the rulers, simply perpetuated the widely held notion of dual royal and religious power, a concept dating from medieval times. The list of such dignitaries is long: Muhammad Baqir Sabzawari (d. 1090/1679–1680), who led the religious hierocracy in the capital Isfahan under the reign of 'Abbas II; Muhammad Baqir Majlisi (d. 1111/1699), Sabzavari's celebrated successor and highest religious authority of his age, author of the great encyclopaedia of Shi'i hadith, *Bihar al-anwar* (Oceans of Lights); Abu l-Qasim Gilani Qummi (d. 1231/1815), a major jurist of the Qajar era; Sayyid Ja'far Kashfi (d. 1267/1850–51), jurist, philosopher and theorist of the dual representation of the Hidden Imam (his temporal representation reverts to the secular ruler and his spiritual representation to the *mujtahid*); and finally Sheikh Fadlallah Nuri (d. 1327/1909), the principal opponent of the Iranian constitutional revolution of 1905.

Exponents of a distinction between the two realms, these dignitaries nevertheless supported the conceptual inseparability of the secular and religious realms, the dominions of the temporal and the spiritual. It is precisely around this fundamental notion that two important and very different personalities of pre-revolutionary Iran came together: Ayatollah Borujerdi (d. 1961), who was deeply convinced of the need for the clerics to be active in the social and political life of the community, and the Islamist intellectual Ali Shari'ati (d. 1977), who held very strong convictions against the monarchy and against the clergy; he was one of the key actors responsible for awakening revolutionary sentiments in Iran, particularly among the young.

Thus Ayatollah Khomeini's theory of the "leadership of the supreme jurist" (*walayat/wilayat al-faqih*) was the first of its kind to place the *mujtahid* at the head of the state. The result of a long historical development within the rationalist school of thought, the theory is nevertheless based on principles that are not specifically Shi'i: only an Islamic government can properly apply the fundamental precepts of Islam. Islamic government and Islamic law derive their authority directly from the founding principles of the religion; their preservation is a legal duty. The struggle against an unjust ruler, including his elimination and replacement by an Islamic government, is the responsibility of the people under the leadership of the jurists (the doctors of the Law). An Islamic government is the government of the jurist who holds the same prerogatives as the "holy legislators" (the Prophet and the Imams). This political doctrine is also called the theory of the "absolute authority of the jurist by appointment" (the jurist in a position of authority is not elected; he is appointed by other jurists "representing the Imam").

This doctrine rapidly led to the formulation of additional theories of government by other jurist-theologians. The most noteworthy of these theories were: the government of the people under the supervision of the doctors of the Law who have attained the status of "models to be imitated", formulated by Ayatollah Muhammad Baqir al-Sadr (assassinated in Iraq in 1980) and the scholars of the theological Seminary (*hawza*) in Najaf, Iraq; "the elected Islamic government", advocated in its first draft by the same Ayatollah Sadr and completed by the Lebanese scholars Muhammad Jawad Mughniya and Muhammad Mahdi Shams al-Din; the theory of the "authority of the jurist conditioned by election", developed by members of the theological Seminary of Qumm (Iran) and in particular by the Ayatollahs Mortaza Motahhari, Ja'far Sobhani, Ni'matullah Salehi Najafabadi and Husayn 'Ali Montazeri.

So, for over a thousand years, the champions of the rationalist juridical-theological tradition have dominated Twelver Shi'ism. By gradually appropriating prerogatives, which according to tradition were the special province of the historical imams, the doctors of the Usuli tradition were able to extend their authority, ultimately assuming leadership of a great state. With the Buyid dynasty, the original esoteric and non-rational tradition was censored, marginalized and finally trampled under foot. Its followers were isolated, frequently mistreated, and sometimes brutally repressed. But they did not die out. The tradition has always had its high-profile defenders. Even today it is regaining its popularity, no doubt in reaction to the exclusiveness and legalism of the rationalist clerics currently in power in Iran. Then there were the philosophers. They were the heirs to Islamic thought in general and Shi'i thought in particular, but they were also heirs to Plato, Aristotle and the Neoplatonists. They held universalist views and made efforts to stay above the fray of factions and conflict. With this distinction in mind, let us now take a closer look at some of the issues.

Note

1 "Sarbadarids" is the name given to the rulers of the region of Sabzawar in eastern Iran. They reigned for a few decades in the 8th/14th century, shortly before Timur's conquest of Iran. The Sarbadar established a revolutionary, messianic Shi'i "republic", which was supported by the local population in a climate of a disintegrating Mongol power.

9 The followers of the original tradition

The followers of the original tradition share several features in common more or less explicitly. They are markedly attached to the restoration, transmission and exegesis of the original tradition and display a resistance to the rationalistic approach, if not an openly contrary orientation; indeed, they display an avowedly mystical sensibility. This inclination expresses itself in the form of simple devotion to the Fourteen Impeccable Ones but extends as well to complex esoteric and gnostic doctrines. The teachings of the imams in the ancient corpus of the hadith lend themselves wonderfully well to this. Moreover, many of the ideas and practices shared in common by the various expressions of Muslim spirituality – devotional practices, Sufism, esotericism, occult sciences – seem to stem from one branch or another of early pre-Buyid Shi'ism; for example, the figure of the imam as archetype of the perfect man in Sufism, the concept of *walaya*, prayer rites, devotional and spiritual exercises, alchemy, the science of letters, etc.

Under the domination of the rationalist juridical-theological tradition, the followers of the original tradition adopted a more discreet attitude, especially given the increasingly obvious success of the Usuli tradition. The scholars of the Baghdad school pilloried them as "followers of outrageous thoughts" (*hashwiyya*); that is, followers of absurd teachings lacking in "reason". They were also stigmatized as "slavish imitators" (*muqallida*), meaning blind followers of the ancients with no critical sense; "anthropomorphists" (*mushabbiha*) because they held the Imam to be a theophany of divine attributes; "the people of the Delegation" (*mufawwida*), those who delegate to the imams the authority of God; "extremists and exaggerators" (*ahl al-ghuluww*); and "the people of the hadith" (*ahl al-hadith*) because they followed all hadith without any critical sense.

From the 6th/12th century on, they become known as the Traditionalists (*akhbariyya*, from *khabar*, plural of *akhbar*; in the sense of "hadith or tradition going back to the imams") in opposition to the Rationalists (*Usuliyya*, from *asl*, plural of *usul*, in the sense of "the bases of canon law"). Soon the term "Traditionalist" was used to refer to the specialists in hadith and canon law among the transmitters of the original tradition.

Theologians, exegetes, men of letters, mystics and philosophers did not give themselves any particular name and were not explicitly members of a particular current, but they did proclaim their unwavering fidelity to the tradition. Several authors of important treatises are representative of this current, which survived until the Safavid era (their literary achievements are impressive even though they worked in relative isolation): Qutb al-Din Rawandi, Abu Mansur Ahmad Tabrisi and Ibn Shahrashub in the 6th/12th century, and 'Ali b. 'Isa Irbili and Ibn Tawus in the 7th/13th century. During the period known as "the Interval" (*fatra*) – between the Mongol invasion and the fall of the Abbasid caliphate at one end and the establishment of the Sunni Ottoman caliphate and the Shi'i Safavid dynasty at the other – there occurred a phenomenon of signal significance: a gradual rapprochement between traditionalist Shi'ism and Sufism.

At the beginning of this period, several scholars – Nasir al-Din Tusi, Ibn Tawus, Mitham Bahrani – began to include references in their work to Shi'ism, a devotional mysticism close to Sufism with powerful elements of speculative thought. In agreement with the Sufis on the rich and central concept of *walaya*, they prepared the form of Shi'ism they represented to accept the thought of Ibn 'Arabi (d. 638/1240), the great theosopher from Andalusia whose ideas proved fundamental in the later development of Muslim mysticism. Even certain rationalist thinkers – 'Allama Hilli, author of the "Unveilings of the Real" (*Kashf al-haqq*), and Ibn Makki, the "First Martyr", whose view it was that the *mujtahid* and the grand Sufi master should ideally be one and the same person – were sensitive to this development. Thus the works of several theorists who succeeded in achieving a synthesis of Shi'ism, Sufism and mystical philosophy mark the end of this period. They include Haydar Amuli and Rajab Bursi in the 8th/14th century and Ibn Abi Jumhur Ahsa'i at the turn of the 9th/15th and 10th/16th centuries.

As we have seen, the Safavid era and the proclamation of Twelver Shi'ism as the state religion of Iran produced a rationalist clergy. But this Shi'i reawakening provided a stimulus for other currents of the original tradition as well. Strictly speaking, the traditionalist school made a brief but remarkable appearance in the 11th/17th and 12th/18th centuries. The founder of what can be called "neo-traditionalism" was the Iranian Muhammad Amin Astarabadi (d. 1033/1624 or 1036/1627), whose systematic critiques of the rationalist current contributed to his renown. In his important work "The Medina Teachings" (*al-Fawa'id al-Madaniyya*), Astarabadi formulated a radical criticism of the Usuli system, accusing scholars such as Ibn Abi 'Aqil, Ibn Junayd Iskafi and especially Shaykh Mufid of straying from the teachings of the imams by opening the door to analogical reasoning and *ijtihad* (personal interpretation) in matters of the faith. He directed further attacks against 'Allama Hilli and, later, against Ibn Makki and Zayn al-Din 'Amili, accusing the latter of polluting Shi'ism with his use of Sunni methods of hadith authentication. Against the Rationalists, Astarabadi argued that the hadith of the imams are the only legitimate source of the law. They provide the faithful with an infallible guide in all aspects of life. They are essential for a proper understanding of the Qur'an and the prophetic hadith, which would otherwise remain incomprehensible and could not provide the foundations of the law. He asserted that all hadith backed by confirmed sources are valid; this refers to hadith which can be traced unequivocally to the imams and to trustworthy transmitters, whatever their Shi'i doctrinal affiliation. As for the hadith of suspect origin, his recommendation was to consider them "suspended" and not act upon them. But if they conformed to the instructions of the imams, it would constitute neither an error nor a sin to put them into practice.

As Etan Kohlberg has aptly noted, Astarabadi's central argument goes like this: in respect of the religious life of the community in general and its legal system in particular, there is no difference between the periods before and after the occultation.[1] Assailing the very foundations of the rationalist movement (i.e. the notions of *ijtihad* and of the *mujtahid* jurist as a "model to be imitated"), Astarabadi maintained that from time immemorial the imams have been the sole models for imitation and that all believers without exception are their "imitators". Every believer, sound of mind, can perfect his Arabic and study the traditions in order to be able to understand the teachings of the imams. Knowledge acquired in this way does not necessarily lead to certainty, but it does ensure that all necessary legal arrangements have been taken in accordance with the instructions of the divine Guides. This line of argument is in direct opposition to rationalist reasoning, which affirms that in regard to the genuine meaning of the traditions of the imams, only conjecture is possible. Moreover, recognition of the imams as the only religious authority, supreme and legitimate, is an implicit rejection of 'Allama Hilli's thesis accepted by later *mujtahids*, who claim that the faithful are commanded to heed the directives of a living jurist exclusively.

The rehabilitation of the old corpus of hadith in the 11th/17th century appears to have been one of the major consequences of Astarabadi's work. Indeed, throughout the century, writers claiming openly to be Traditionalists produced huge hadith anthologies that accorded a very large place to the early sources. Among these were the *Wafi* by Muhsin Fayd Kashani (d. circa 1091/ 1680) and the *Tafsil* by Hurr 'Amili (d. 1104/1693).[2]

Fayd Kashani, whose oeuvre was immense, also deserves our attention for several reasons. The son-in-law and disciple of Mulla Sadra – who is held by many to be modern Shi'ism's greatest philosopher – Fayd became a link between the philosophers and followers of the traditionalist movement, following in the footsteps of his father-in-law, though in a far more intense fashion. Kashani's traditionalism was as forceful as it was moderate; though he criticized some of Astarabadi's more radical arguments, he sought to nuance them. In this way, his work helped spread neo-traditionalist ideas widely and durably among believers as well as among thinkers adhering to rationalism. Though a supporter of the traditionalist movement, Kashani strongly condemned some Akhbari followers – especially jurists and Traditionalists – for too pronounced a literalism with regard to the hadith; and he rebuked them as well for a kind of spiritual naivety in their rejection of all hermeneutics, all philosophy and all mystical theosophy. Finally, Kashani's mystical thought – and specifically his mystical epistemology – certainly permeated later mystical movements and provided them with solid intellectual credentials.

According to Fayd Kashani, there are three objects of knowledge: the core principles of faith, ethics and the law. He argued that the direct path to knowledge – and consequently the gateway to objects of knowledge, including the principles of faith – is by what he termed "inner realization". Kashani argued that, with the exception of the Impeccable Ones, only a small minority of initiated believers can achieve such realization; they constitute a mere handful of truly spiritual individuals able to gain access to the "divine knowledge and [to] realization through unveiling". True knowledge does not come from books alone, but from inspiration as well. The possessors of true knowledge – the people of the *walaya* – are the genuine successors and representatives of the imams. Kashani gave the members of this spiritual elite different names: "the ones with inner vision", "the realized ones", "the visionary ones", the "religious scholars" (*faqih*; i.e. the jurist-theologian). These individuals possess genuine wisdom and hear, with a keen inner ear, the true meaning of the traditions and the Qur'anic verses. People of this sort existed among the disciples of the imams before the occultation. They were devoted to them and initiated into their secrets. They were authorized to know the esoteric meaning of the Qur'an and the hadith, and the imams regarded them as a part of themselves. It is also obvious that such individuals existed in the time of the occultation; otherwise the spiritual teachings of the imams would have died out.

Just as with the imams, knowledge made these individuals deserving of the "holy spirit" and "holy spiritual power". It is by virtue of these sacred faculties, and not by rote learning of the chains of hadith transmissions, that such individuals succeed in penetrating to the truth of the words of God, the Prophet and the imams. Kashani applied the term *mujtahid* to this category of individuals. In his opinion, the "effort of personal interpretation" should be practiced in the spiritual realm and not in the legal realm. How far we are here from the rationalist concept of *ijtihad*! Yet the combined effect of Kashani's writing and the force of his thought had an impact that reached even the Rationalists.

From this time, in fact, pronounced mystical overtones can be detected among certain Usuli *mujtahids*. It can be argued just as easily that his efforts to "spiritualise" the law and the jurists were appropriated by the clerics and somehow turned against themselves. By referring to the "realized man" as, among other things, a "religious scholar" and *mujtahid*, Kashani was in fact indicating that the true Islamic jurist was necessarily a mystic who had attained spiritual realization. More often than not, the rationalist thinkers were clerics who borrowed Khasani's thought to claim that the true mystic – one who had attained knowledge and wisdom – could not be anything but a jurist-theologian.

There are other towering figures among the neo-Traditionalists; for example, Muhammad Taqi Majlisi, called Majlisi the First (d. 1070/1660), the father of the aforementioned Majlisi the Second; Ni'matullah Jaza'iri (d. 1112/1700); Yusuf Bahrani (d. 1186/1773; and the great religious authority Mirza Husayn Tabrisi Nuri (d. 1320/1902), author of a huge oeuvre including a work on the forbidden topic of the falsification of the Qur'an, which led to his banishment close to the end of his life. However, the neo-Traditionalists and their movement disappeared almost completely from the Shi'i religious landscape around the end of the 12th/18th century or the beginning of the 13th/19th century when the virulent leader of the rationalist doctors of Law, Muhammad Baqir Wahid Bihbahani (d. 1208/1793–1794), loosed his anathema against them, followed by the attacks of his successor, Shaykh Kashif al-Ghita' (d. 1227/1812).

Such violent reactions are comprehensible in light of the Usuli cleric's fear that the Qajari ruler Fath 'Ali Shah might convert to the traditionalist cause. At risk were the notion of *ijtihad* and everything that upheld the prerogatives of the jurists, including their extensive power and authority in economic, social and political realms. The ensuing conflicts in Iran and Iraq were bloody. Many traditionalist scholars and followers were assassinated or forced into flight and exile. Today, taking care to conceal their religious beliefs, a small number of Akhbari believers continue to live in south-west Iran and Bahrain.

At the same time, from the time of the Safavid era in Iran, a powerful current of philosophical thought which can be called "traditionalist" asserted itself. Because of the prevailing socio-political circumstances in which these thinkers lived and because of their attitude towards the rationalist current and its followers, they often found themselves embroiled in chaotic situations, and not always willingly. In the continuation of Mulla Sadra and Fayd Kashani's thought, we find philosophers such as Sadiq Ardestani (d. 1135/1722), Muhammad Bidabadi (d. 1198/1783), his disciple Mulla 'Ali Nuri (d. 1246/1830), several philosophers of the Sabzewar, Mashhad and Teheran schools and, finally, the modern philosophers Sayyid Abu l-Hasan Jelveh and Kazim 'Assar, both of whom died in the first half of the 20th century. To the present day, philosophers who combine traditionalist Shi'i thought with strands of Western philosophy, such as Mojtahed Shabestari, Mahdi Ha'eri Yazdi and 'Abdolkarim Sorush, can be considered as philosophers close to the traditionalist current. We will look more closely at Shi'i philosophy in Chapter 10.

The mystical brotherhoods were also defenders of the original tradition. Mystical sects of Twelver obedience began to emerge as such after the 11th/ 17th century. Originating in Iran, or coming out of hiding from there, these sects soon arrived in other Shi'i lands, notably in Iraq, the Caucasus and the Indian subcontinent. Of these, four are the most notable, each having several offshoots: the Dhahabiyya, Ni'matullahiyya, Khaksariyya and Shaykhiyya. The Dhahabiyya was a Shi'i branch of the great Kubrawiyya brotherhood whose namesake, Najm al-Din Kubra (d. 618/1221), was one of the leading figures of medieval Islamic spirituality. The Ni'matullahiyya brotherhood derives its name from the celebrated mystical poet Shah Ni'matullah Wali (d. 834/1431), whose followers gradually converted from Sunnism to Shi'ism. The Khaksariyya were spiritual descendants of the Qalandar, ancient wandering dervishes who arrived in Iran from India towards the beginning of the 19th century. Finally, the Shaykhiyya movement derives its name from Shaykh Ahmad Ahsa'i (d. 1241/ 1826), a celebrated Shi'i scholar from Bahrain – though the real founder of the sect was his Iranian disciple Sayyid Kazim Rashti (d. 1259/1843). The first three orders had their roots in Sufism in one form or another; they identified themselves openly as Shi'i Sufis. The Shaykhiyya, on the other hand, formed a mystico-theological brotherhood that did not wish to be considered Sufi.

Even the mystics fell victim on several occasions to clerical repression. The bloodiest episode occurred in the first half of the 19th century when the *mujtahid* Muhammad 'Ali Bihbahani launched his anathema on the dervishes, provoking a wave of assassinations. 'Ali Bihbahani, known as the "Sufi killer", was the son of the celebrated leader of the rationalist jurists of his time, Wahid Bihbahani. 'Ali's assassinations of the mystics followed hard on the heels of the massacres of the Traditionalists ordered by his father. But despite these killings, the mystical brotherhoods were not deterred. Instead they intensified their activities, even after the Islamic Revolution – doubtless in reaction to it. In any case, their popularity only continued to grow.

The Shaykhiyya were the harshest critics of the Rationalists and targeted their clerics, their methods and their institutions. The best summary of their views is without any doubt that offered by Abu l-Qasim Khan Ebrahimi (d. 1969), one of the last authorities of the Kermani branch,[3] in a book in Persian with the suggestive title "Personal Interpretation and Emulation" (*Ijtihad va taqlid*). He focused his criticism on the Rationalists' notion of *'aql* and contends that the *'aql* as discussed by the imams is a form of "holy intelligence"; that is, a faculty in the service of "inspiration" and an adequate means for the proper understanding of sacred texts. This sacred intelligence is thus fundamentally superior to – and never the mere equivalent of – the Rationalists' notion of "reason". Without referring to him explicitly, Shaykh Ebrahimi agreed with Astarabadi that all Shia, without exception, are "imitators" of the imams, who in turn are the sole "sources of imitation"; and he agreed with Fayd Kashani that the only Shia worthy of the title *mujtahid* are those who are inspired, realized and initiated into the secret teaching of the Imams.

Next, Shaykh Ebrahimi returned to the foundations of the rationalist system, to the elements that enabled rationalist thinkers to rely on *ijtihad* and to acquire their various prerogatives, and he raised the question of the criteria used to authenticate the hadith; in so doing, he made constant reference to writings by the early authorities of his school. He questioned what we know about the "problematic" hadith. The glossary of criteria used to determine the authenticity of hadith is only four or five centuries old. What system of criteria was used to accept or reject a hadith before the glossary came into being? There must have been one, he says; it is inconceivable that the religion of the imams was ever without one. By what right and in whose name should this original system, which dates back to the imams, be abandoned for the new technical lexicon and its criteria that the Rationalists promote?

In regard to the quality of the hadith transmitters, Ebrahimi claimed that the specialists compiled works that are full of contradictions. Belief and trust in the hadith of the imams, their *walaya* in the hearts of believers, are not matters for experts to accept or reject. The use of their methods will only lead to conjecture, never to genuine certainty; without certainty, a true life of spirituality is impossible. According to Ebrahimi, the authenticators of hadith place too much confidence in their own science. But then, once it is accepted that someone might have had the audacity to invent a hadith, why not suppose that he might have invented an entire chain of trustworthy persons for its transmission? Concerning this matter of the criteria of hadith authenticity, Ebrahimi identifies two paths. The first is "the exoteric path", which takes into consideration the circumstances of the narrators in order to make a judgment on the "strength" or the "weakness" of the hadith. This is the practice of the Rationalists; it will never lead to any form of certainty in regard to the deeper meaning of the hadith. The second path, "the esoteric path", aims to explore this deeper meaning of the hadith in order to discover what the imam really said. This path is not available to just any scholar. Expertise in jurisprudence or "hadith criteriology" is useless here. Only those with wisdom and the faculty of inner perception can possibly follow the esoteric path. This capacity is the fruit of pure love (*walaya*) – devotion to the imams and their cause. It is this *walaya*, and nothing else, that opens the heart of the believer to a level of reality where it is possible to come face-to-face with the imam. When this happens, the imam himself initiates his friend into the mysteries of the sacred teachings and endows him with the "gift of intuition" to recognize the authenticity of the traditions. Today, as in the past, the "presence" of the imam is precisely the same, and belief in his teaching is not contingent on an external human authority, even that of a great *mujtahid*. It is the expression of the imam's love in the heart of the perfect initiate that matters. Thus the only religious authority is the authority of the imam. And the only valid criterion of the authenticity of his teaching is the spiritual experience of a personal relationship with him, here and now.

Because they challenged the legitimacy of the Usuli institution in this manner, the Shaykhiyya fell victim to the persecutions of the Shi'i clergy. The fact that the leader of the Shaykhiyya, 'Ali Muhammad Bab, the prophet of Babism and the teacher of Baha'ullah (the prophet of Baha'ism), was a disciple of the order's founder, Sayyid Kazim Rashti, provided sufficient justification for the persecutions, which flared up once again after the Islamic Revolution.[4]

All mystics agree that the existence of a spiritual elite is necessary in the economy of the sacred. Though Shi'ism itself constitutes the esoteric aspect of Islam, all Shia are far from being initiated into the esoteric teachings of the Imams. Many hadiths recognize two types of Shia. On the one hand, there are the nominal, superficial, exoteric Shia; that is, Shia in name only who hold dearly to their devotion to the imams, but whose devotion is so tenuous that is easily lost if it comes under threat. On the other hand, there is the tiny minority of "genuine Shia" who achieve true *walaya* and are initiated into the secret doctrines of Shi'ism. The Sufi orders use an ancient expression to refer to this elite; they call them "men of mystery and the invisible" (*rejal-e ghayb*). The reasons for this are, on the one hand, that the members of this spiritual "chivalric order" are representatives of the invisible in the material world and, on the other hand, their true nature remains "invisible" to all because they are discreet and frequently conceal their level of saintliness. Among the Shaykhiyya, they

are referred to as the "fourth principle" (*rukn rabi'*), because the true men of
God – those initiated in the mysteries of the being – together with the Oneness
of God, the calling of the prophets and the vocation of the imams, constitute
the four principles on which faith is grounded. They are the "companions" of
the imams and, in particular, of the Hidden Imam. Without them, religion
would lose its inner aspect and evolve into a hodgepodge of doctrines that are
as superficial as they are rigid, plunging the faithful, in turn, into ignorance,
violence and fanaticism. The "men of the mystery" are the guardians of human
spirituality.

The mystics made another fundamental contribution to the spiritual development of Shi'ism in the process of the "internalization of the imam". The
ancient texts alluded to this notion more or less explicitly, but it was left to
modern authors to pursue it in more detail. The *walaya* is said to have an
"organic" counterpoint in man. By means of spiritual teachings and initiatory
practices, the love of the imam can crystallize in the human heart in the form
of a luminous energy called the "Light of the *walaya*".[5] Using a concentration
technique which focuses the mind on the heart, the Light opens a pathway to a
living entity within the centre of the heart, which is none other than the inner
Guide of each person, the "imam in the heart" of each pure seeker of truth,
mirroring the reality of the visible imam, who in turn is the reflection of the
Cosmic Imam, the place of God's manifestation. Thus, mystical teaching
enables each believer to discover God in his own heart by means of a theology
of successive theophanies (see p. 64ff).

A synthesis of this thought can probably best be found in a work by the
Ni'matullahi master Mulla Muhammad Sultan 'Ali Shah (d. 1327/1909) – in
his *Majma' al-sa'adat*:

> He who possesses no more than the meanings that arise from God's sensory
> kingdom can only know the imam insofar as he is a physical human being.
> But he for whom meanings arising from God's heavenly kingdom have
> been startled awake can attain knowledge of the imam insofar as he is
> Light. When the student pledges his allegiance to the teacher authorized
> by the imam (i.e. the brotherhood's rightful spiritual leader), the teacher
> takes his student's hand in his and the luminous celestial form of the imam
> penetrates the disciple's heart through this clasping of hands. This light
> form is called the Face of the imam, or the *walaya*, or indeed the Love of
> 'Ali. By means of this "Face of Light" a brotherly relationship is established
> between the imam and his devotee, which transforms the initiates into true
> brothers. But as long as the disciple who bears this form in his heart is
> entangled in the dark meshes of his own ego, that luminosity remains
> concealed. Once the curtain is raised, the light shines in its full splendour
> and radiance. In the exterior physical world, this divine manifestation is
> accomplished through the person of the Hidden Imam and his final man-
> ifestation as the Resurrector. In the inner spiritual world, it is one of the
> levels of the theophany of the Light of the imam in the heart of the

devotee. These various levels have different names: "presence", "serenity", "contemplation". This is what enlightens the disciple and enables him to recognize the Imam as Light of the heart.

A key aim of spiritual concentration exercises is to attain a vision of the Face of the Imam in one's heart; in other words, to achieve contemplation of the esoteric form of the outer Imam. It is a sign of spiritual rebirth, just as its exoteric equivalent – the manifestation of the Mahdi – is a sign of the resurrection of the world. The result is no less than the acquisition of initiatory knowledge and suprasensible powers. It is noteworthy that the earliest mention of this "vision of the heart" (*al-ru'ya bi l-qalb*), which gradually became one of the most common Sufi initiatory exercises, can be found in the earliest Shi'i hadith.

Sultan 'Ali Shah continued:

> The manifestation of the radiant Face of the Imam brings wisdom to the believer and awakens his ability to see heavenly things, opening his heart to the contemplation of heaven's inhabitants. Thus he can free himself from the bonds of time and space. He can walk on water or on the air and move miraculously from place to place.

The Sufis of the Dhahabiyya sect call this contemplative practice *vejha* (*wijha* in Arabic; "the face of something"; also "the direction of prayer" according to the Qur'an 2:148). The goal of *vejha* – the direction of initiatory prayer – is the contemplation of the Face of the Imam, which is identical to the Face of God. This "vision" is not achieved with physical eyes but with the eyes of the heart. It is accomplished by suppression of the ego and by spiritual rebirth in the *walaya* of the imam. The Light of the "imam of the heart" is made of several layers of coloured light, each revealing an aspect of the reality of the inner Guide.[6] This is the esoteric meaning of the reality of the historical physical imams.

Among the Dhahabiyya masters, Raz Shirazi (d. 1286/1869) is the author who perhaps furnishes the most useful insights into this contemplative practice, which, it must be stressed, is the most secret of all mystical practices, often involving special postures, breathing exercises and the repetition of sacred formulae. Responding to one of his disciples who asked why the Dhahabi dervishes call the eighth imam – 'Ali al-Rida – the "seventh direction of prayer", Raz Shirazi replied,

> Know, my dear son, that your question touches on one of the deepest secrets of the heart. Its mystery is only penetrable by the inner unveiling of the masters of the heart. The reason for this sublime name, like the others for this imam ("Confidant of souls", "Sun of suns"), is the streaming forth of the light of his *walaya* in the heart of his initiated followers. This holy light is clearly not his own; all imams are light descended from God. 'Ali al-Rida, the eighth imam, is the fountainhead of our order's chain of

initiation; it is his blessed Face which is manifested in this subtle centre of the heart called the "dark Concealed one". This is the seventh layer of the heart, which is manifested to the Friends [the Dhahabi mystics]. You should know that the sevenfold layers of the Friends' hearts denote the manifestations of the seven different-coloured lights and that the seventh one is the black light, which is the radiance of the most sacred Essence of the One. It is this light that is manifested for the Friends in the form of the blessed Face of the eighth imam. It is a transparent, radiant, sublime black, intense beyond measure. It is the "direction of prayer of the seventh layer of the heart". The great mystics see it as their duty to direct their true prayers towards its heart, towards this true direction of prayer: "Find first the direction of prayer then perform it". This is why we call this imam the "seventh direction of prayer".

The initiate who achieves contemplation of the "light of the *walaya*" does not become an imam; the imam has his own special theological and ontological station. But he does become a saint similar to an imam and is closely bound to him. He is a possessor of *walaya* and a *wali*, an Ally or Friend of God, a living and active example of spiritual love. In terms of Shi'i spirituality, such a Friend belongs ipso facto to the "Prophet's Holy Family". An example is the "foreigner" Salman the Persian, of whom the Prophet said: "Salman is part of us, a member of the House – the Family of the Prophet's Household".

In contrast with the "purist" Traditionists, who rejected the notion of any intermediary between the imam and his followers, the mystical movements managed to fill the void created by the occultation through the person of the initiate, in fact the spiritual master. This may explain why they were so popular with those who refused to accept that the role of intermediary could be held by the rationalist doctors of the Law – and this despite all the persecutions they underwent at the hands of powerful *mujtahids*.

Towards the end of the 3rd/9th century, the puzzling fate of the eleventh imam's putative son threw the community of the faithful into disarray. In a religion wholly focused on the figure of the imam, the absence of his authority plunged the Shia into what has been called "the period of confusion or perplexity" (*al-hayra*). Even after the establishment of an official doctrine of the occultation closed the "period of perplexity", the problem raised by the absence of a supreme authority – on the temporal level, to be sure, but perhaps even more so on the spiritual – remained intact for the Shia, henceforth to be known as the Twelvers. This explains why, for over a thousand years, the history of Shi'ism has been dominated by countless solutions and variables intended to fill the void occasioned by this absence.

Notes

1 E. Kohlberg, "Aspects of Akhbari Thought in the Seventeenth and Eighteenth Centuries".

2 The traditionalist revival and restoration of the original corpus probably influenced the writing of *Bihar al-anwar* (Oceans of Lights), a monumental encyclopaedia of hadith collected under the editorship of the famous *mujtahid* Majlisi II (d. 1111/ 1699). The last edition ran to 110 volumes. Majlisi II had an enigmatic personality. A politician and leading *mujtahid* – he was Minister of Religious Affairs – he led a perfectly rationalist way of life. Nevertheless, there is a profound traditionalist expression in much of his literary output.

3 We base our argument here on H. Corbin's presentation in his *En Islam iranien. Aspects spirituels et philosophiques*, vol. IV.

4 Although the situation has calmed down in the past few years, it should be noted that on 26 December 1979, shortly after the triumph of the revolution, the son of Shaykh Ebrahimi, 'Abd al-Rida Khan, who succeeded to the leadership of the movement, was assassinated in broad daylight in Kerman by two individuals who were never identified. The other mystical orders did not escape persecution either. Exposed to public vindictiveness, many teachers were forced into exile. Even today followers of certain movements continue to fall victim to reprisals led by "uncontrolled" members of society. A number of tombs of mystics have been profaned; some have been razed to the ground.

5 For a discussion of *walaya* as the "single and double" Light of Muhammad and 'Ali, and see Chapter 5 for a general discussion on *walaya*.

6 The literary sources of the Kubrawiyya root of the Dhahabiyya order are very rich in information concerning the visionary experience of coloured lights from the heart. Cf. the oeuvre of Najm al-Din Kubra.

10 The politics of the philosophers

The question of authority

The pursuit of the best form of government is far from absent in the works of Shi'i philosophy. This can be seen in the works of Isma'ili philosophers (4th–5th/ 10th–11th centuries) and of authors such as Farabi (d. 339/950), Nasir al-Din Tusi (597–672/1201–1274) and especially Haydar Amuli (8th/14th century) or Mulla Sadra (d. 1050/1640). These few references show that the relationship between Shi'i faith and philosophical activity assumed different expressions over the centuries and that they continued until relatively recently. Even today, the teaching of philosophy in the canonic education of Shi'i clerics emphasizes the unity of science and faith. Therefore, it is important to distinguish clearly between a long tradition of philosophical thought and the many modern-day works of ideology, the latter produced by followers of the Supreme Guide of the Islamic Revolution to justify and promote the doctrine of the "Guardianship of the Jurist" (*wilayat al-faqih*).

As we saw earlier, this doctrine, holding that the best government is that of the representative of the Hidden Imam, was brought forth in a wholly *other* doctrinal context; it was elaborated theologically in a manner quite removed from the speculations of philosophers. Furthermore, the politics of the Twelver philosophers is *fundamentally* hostile to the principle of government under the authority of the jurist-scholar. It remains detached from the political aspirations of clergy, who moved in the ruling power circles, first opposing such power and finally orchestrating its downfall. True, in the new world of the Safavid monarchy in the 9th/17th century, some philosophers, such as Mir Damad (d. 1040/ 1631–1632), defended the theological innovations of the jurists, who supported the propagation of the new doctrine of government. But though the clerics, who backed the project of an Islamic state, borrowed arguments from philosophers, more often than not this involved misconstruing certain texts and producing a meaning that was quite different from the original intention. In short, if we examine the issue in any depth, we are led to conclude that the *legal* debate relative to clerical authority is essentially missing from Twelver Shi'i philosophies.

Now this is not to say that Shi'i philosophers were not interested in the subject of power. On the contrary, various philosophers affiliated with one branch or another of Shi'ism made repeated inquiries into the foundations of *authority*. Both the course of history and the Holy Book invited them to do so. Why history? Because Shi'i philosophers, like their fellows, felt obliged to provide arguments supporting the legitimacy of the Prophet's family and his descendants, the imams. Why the Qur'an? Because it is seen as proof for every Muslim that supreme authority is in the hands of God, who decrees all things. Power, like knowledge and will, is an essential Attribute of God. A verse in the Qur'an says, "Surely His is the Creation and the Commandment" (Qur'an 7:54). The Arabic term *al-amr* means order, command, but also the imperative he who creates ex nihilo. When God decrees that something should exist, He says: "Be!" and it is.

Shi'i philosophers give considerable thought to this notion of the divine imperative. In it they see the supreme act of creation, an act establishing all corporeal and supernatural realities. It is through His command that God breaks His silence and emerges from His transcendence to reveal Himself in His act of creation. Thus God is the ultimate wielder of an order that is imperative, a creative imperative that possesses all the meanings of order. God commands and creates the best possible order, which is the perfect order of all worlds. The *world of creation* must then imitate its model, the *world of the imperative*, and the order of human communities must pattern itself, as perfectly as possible, on the ideal order of the supernatural world, the world of intelligible realities and the angels. The world that is in the process of becoming, the world of societies and peoples, has as its hidden meaning the materialization of a "history in heaven", a history that unfolds in a spiritual space located between the eternal unchanging world of the imperative and the fleeting, changing, ephemeral world of the creation, which is the space and time of the prophecy and the imamate.

In the preceding pages, we have attempted to show how Shi'ism makes sense of God's universal power. The divine order is mirrored in the actual person of the Prophet, then of the imam, who receives the divine mission to establish a just authority, which is also called "order", "command", "imperative" (*amr*) or *walaya*. According to the Qur'an, the Prophet sees himself as one endowed with a "firm power of decision" (*al-'azm*). The early Shi'i philosophers understood this power of resolution as the authority to decide, to make a ruling, to abolish an earlier scriptural revelation in order to establish a new one. Since his decisions are inspired by divine command, the Prophet establishes a figure of *shari'a*; that is. in Shi'i terminology, a symbolic form in which the concealed content of eternal wisdom lives on (*hikma*).

As for the imam, he inherits this decision-making authority, which enables him to reveal the hidden meaning of the *shari'a* and to make it prevail over blind obedience to the apparent legal meaning. In an even more audacious reading, the philosophers argue that the divine command designates an absolute and eternal reality. The two eternal figures of the Prophet and the Imam are transhistorical manifestations of this eternal reality throughout every cycle of human history. Thus the question of authority demands the existence of another world between the eternal world of God's command and the lower world of His creation. This intermediary world is both spiritual and material, a world of events announced in the Holy Book: punishment, paradise, hell, the many clashes between the forces of light and darkness. In broad brush, this is how the philosophers understood the lessons of the revelation, resorting at times to terminology and concepts that were foreign to the Qur'an, dictated by their own exegetic practices and reflecting a to and fro between the legacy of Greek philosophy and the particular contribution of the Shi'i tradition.

Who then in the community has authority over men? What is the source of such authority? What is its purpose? What are the qualities of the person who legally exercises authority? These questions are similar to the ones discussed by Greek philosophers, notably Plato and Aristotle. This is because Shi'i philosophers encountered a situation in Muslim states that recalls the political regimes that Plato criticized in his own time. The lands of Islam had fragmented into many ephemeral princedoms and kingships, offering a spectacle of injustice, strife, instability, impotence and irrationality not unlike that prevailing in the cities of ancient Greece. In this context, Shi'i philosophers could hardly pass up the opportunity to speculate on the very essence of political leadership and the necessary conditions for a well-governed state, which they did in poetry and other literary forms such as the *Mirrors for Princes*, models for virtuous conduct and instructions in practical wisdom.

In fact Shi'i philosophy is virtually inseparable from a flourishing moral literature in the Muslim Orient at this time. We might mention the importance of works such as the *Alexander Romances*, which influenced the poets Ferdowsi and Nezami; also *The Golden Prairies*, whose Shi'i author, Mas'udi, drew on the teachings of the Greek philosophers; or the position that Aristotle, that advisor in political wisdom, occupies in this literature. Or we can take the example of the work of the Shi'i philosopher Nasir al-Din Tusi, who summoned up Plato's advice on practical life, on relations between men and on a concern for the self. We could also mention the figure of Hermes and the wise kings of ancient Iran, such as Ardashir whose "testament" – quoted by such important Shi'i authors as Miskawayh (d. 421/1030) or Nasir al-Din Tusi – stresses the indispensable link between religion and royalty, respect for religious laws and temporal authority. This is where the Shi'i philosophers saw a justification for the authority of the imam.

Like Plato, Shi'i philosophers make a distinction between the concrete situation – authority as established by historical circumstances or by the intellectual blindness of the majority – and a *nomos* – a legislating order, characteristic of legitimate authority; in short, an order reflecting the divine order. Shi'ism was well suited to take up and inspire this quest for just government, an authority in alliance with knowledge and wisdom, since it held that supreme legitimacy flows from God and is exercised in the context of prophecy and *walaya*.

The interest that Shi'i philosophers took in matters of political authority cannot be separated from the theological and metaphysical speculations that preoccupied them principally. For them, political science was not what it later became in the modern Western world: a preoccupation with essential secular and profane principles of government. It could not but be a *political theology*, a philosophical reading of prophecy and an understanding of the imamate. The tools of thought familiar to the West since the Enlightenment are completely unknown in Shi'i political science. As we see, it could not be otherwise. For the Shi'i philosopher, the Good has an essence; it is an emanation of the Good par excellence which is God. This sovereign Good is the norm for all effective realities – in nature, in the arts, in the city. Against this Good, the trifling opinions of men bereft of divine inspiration can only lead to chaos and unending conflict.

The Shi'i rejection of a "common consensus" (*ijma'*) independent of the imam's directives – something that results from the deliberations of men, what the West calls parliamentarianism or debate in the public forum – is not the symptom of an unruly monarchism or of poorly disguised despotism. In Platonic fashion, it is a matter of mistrust of personal impulse, which is often ruled by emotion and the hankering after false goods (power, wealth and honours). But it is also a matter of rejecting authorities – caliphs without legitimacy or misguided princes. It is a matter of asking oneself: Who is worthy of supreme authority? Who has a lawful right to take firm decisions? Who should legislate? The answers can only come from a contemplation of the essence of Good. Philosophical reasoning, culminating in a perception of being as being, will deduce moral lessons from this act of perception as well as the very image of the master of wisdom who is the imam of the community. Philosophy is true politics because it is the high road to contemplation of the only valid principle, which is the intelligible world, the world of divine attributes.

Like Plato before them and later Hobbes and Rousseau, Shi'i philosophers posed the question of the divine legislator (of course, Western philosophers were working in very different thought systems). Their notions of freedom differed, of course, from those developed in post-Reformation Western liberal thought. Political freedom was viewed not the freedom of an abstract individual entering into a relationship with his fellow man in a social contract – the type of freedom that guarantees and respects the authority of a representative government. Theirs was a moral freedom bestowed by respect for divine norms, explained by philosophy and revealed at the highest level by the enlightened guide.

This expression of freedom was achieved through submission to the will of God and to the wisdom of the imams, but it was not the caricature of slavishness that the West imagines. Quite simply, this freedom was the freedom of the Classical world (the freedom of the Stoics); it was a liberation of the self in a watchful awareness of the self, according to a divine norm. It gradually accumulated many more complexities gleaned from Shi'i readings of Platonism and Neoplatonism; for example, the purification of the soul, the internalization of the hidden meaning of the Qur'an, knowledge of the spiritual reality of the divinely enlightened guide, the elevation of the soul from the corporeal world to union with the Divine, etc. Similarly, criticism of the city without virtue cannot be compared with the social criticism of 19th-century European thinkers. And when, in the 20th century, Marxist-trained theorists hitched their tiny cargo of socialist ideas to the rich heritage of Shi'ism, they were able only to beget monsters, as the dreams of reason always do.

The political reason that inspires Shi'i philosophers is closer to medieval Christian ideas or to Byzantine doctrines. We should not hesitate to look for the sources of inspiration of this reason in unexpected places: in metaphysical systems pertaining to the degrees of the existent; in meditations on the meaning of the oneness of the divine principle; in speculations devoted to the subject of the perfect man; and especially in an analysis of the role and function of the *shari'a*, the law revealed by the prophets. It is important too to note that there are relatively few genuinely political texts. But there are many other works of a spiritual and temporal nature which do underpin political argumentation. These works are inspired by a mystical spiritual sense and a political sense, if we understand by this a sense concerned with the legitimate authority that guides men in their communities and singularly in "the community par excellence", that of Islam. This interchangeability of thought illustrates why it is fruitless to argue that we are confronted here with a "spiritual" argument without political consequences or that we are faced with a political argument that has been distorted into a spiritual one. The meaning of Shi'i philosophical texts can be missed entirely if one tries to expunge all political intention from them or if they are treated merely as old metaphysical cloth draped over the exercise of authority.

Philosophy in confrontation with insurrection

The earliest Shi'i philosophical writings were produced in a world of constant strife among Muslims. One illustration of this is the revolt that removed the Umayyad caliphs from power and led to the proclamation of Abu'l 'Abbas as caliph in 132/749 in Kufa in southern Iraq. The new Abbasid dynasty owed its success to a coalition in which Shia participated. They were disillusioned when the Abbasids restored Sunni authority, compromised for many Muslims by a bitterness provoked by earlier Umayyad preferences. The liquidation of conspirators who had placed their hopes in a radical revolution; the establishment of a caliphate in the new capital of Baghdad, which nullified the eschatological hopes of those who had made regime change possible – such developments further encouraged the fomenting of social and religious revolt. Imam Ja'far al-Sadiq died in 148/765. His caution and political quietism were in sharp contrast with the so-called "extremist" agitation of those close to his son Isma'il (among whom was probably Abu l-Khattab, executed with his followers in 138/755). In short, a brief look at the situation at the end of the 8th and 9th centuries shows that Islamic philosophy in the widest sense was born and nurtured amidst incessant power struggles at the heart of the caliphate and on its peripheries.

The huge effort undertaken in 215–226/830–840 in Baghdad to translate the body of knowledge inherited from Greek antiquity should by no means suggest that it was a time of universal peace in the empire. For example, between 200/816 and 224/838, the uprising of Babak and the *Khurramiyya*, a so-called "communist" rebellion, took place in Azerbaijan; and between 256/869 and 270/883, the great Zanj revolt of black slaves, led by an Alid pretender, nearly brought down the caliphate. The first great names in Islamic philosophy (*falsafa*) – the Sunni al-Kindi (b. 180/796) and the Shia al-Farabi (b. 259/872) – were contemporaries of the extraordinary rise and then ouster of the Mu'tazilite theologians in Baghdad and of the slow development of "extremist" Shi'i agitations that resulted in the Qarmatian venture. Philosophy in Islam was born in a white-hot furnace.

The leading Shi'i philosophers of the 4th/10th century were also some of the earliest philosophers to appear in Islamic lands. Their philosophical writings were produced in the context of their mission, at once spiritual and political. For this reason, it may be helpful to recall the basic facts behind the Qarmatian movement, which at the end of the 3rd/9th century stood out from the rest within the Isma'il sphere of influence.

The birth of the Qarmatian movement illustrates well one of the challenges that our thinkers had to face. Under the leadership of Hamdan Qarmat and his brother 'Abdan, the Shi'i faithful established a propaganda and activist organization in expectation of the providential return of their imam, Muhammad ibn Isma'il, the grandson of Imam Ja'far. The faithful believed that their imam had disappeared only so that he could miraculously reappear on the Last Day, thereby heralding the final phase of human history, which would be marked by the end of all religious laws and the manifestation of God's reality through a spiritual dominion. The movement refused to recognize the leadership claims of another Alid descendant, the Fatimid 'Ubayd Allah – the future Mahdi – who also sought control of the community and the imamate.

This difference of opinion over the rightful claimant to the imamate was not merely political or "monarchistic". It represented a deeper division, which went to the very heart of the messianic hope placed in the successor of Muhammad and 'Ali. In essence, the issue concerned the significance of this divinely inspired person set aside by God to fulfil his *walaya*. Simplifying matters to the extreme, it can be argued that the Qarmatians – firm advocates of the providential return of Muhammad ibn Isma'il – categorically refused all commerce with the normal ways of the world, with those ways that require submission to time and to material proofs. For them, the Hidden Imam possessed an infinitely stronger symbolic authority, because his occultation signified neither his failure nor his death but his superhuman destiny and his messianic reality. Paradoxically enough, it testified to his victory over manifest history; it embodied the reversal of appearances by concealed truth, the annulment of one history and the advent of another. It made unnecessary – even ridiculous – any formal recognition of the Fatimid pretender alive and well in his residence, his "general quarter", of Salamiyya.

For these reasons, the Qarmatians moved towards a convocation, a summons for a gathering of believers. Their philosophy of history envisaged an apocalyptic, messianic event of great magnitude. The summons was an invitation not to acknowledge a master who failed to fulfil hope, a master who was merely another link in the long chain of guides issuing from the prophetic family. But if Muhammad ibn Isma'il was not the awaited "seventh prophet", it would be necessary to admit the beginning of a new cycle of time, a cycle of long and patient waiting turned by the Carmathians into a despairing renunciation. In the opposing camp, the followers of 'Ubayd Allah recognized in him a transitional figure who was both useful and even necessary in the historical time that would precede the eventual return of Muhammad ibn Isma'il.

Thus, those who ended up being called "Qarmatians" identified themselves by their refusal to believe in the death of Muhammad ibn Isma'il. They undertook to prepare and hasten his return through a series of warlike ventures in Bahrain, Yemen and central and eastern Persia (in the region of Rayy). One of these Qarmatians, Ibn al-Fadl, succeeded in capturing San'a, where he abolished the *shari'a*. It was in the midst of this messianic agitation that the first Shi'i Isma'ili philosophy evolved. Isma'ili gnosis came earlier, but philosophy in the proper sense of the word – the elaboration of thought systems worthy of the name – was contemporary with the Qarmatian uprising.

To speak of philosophy in these circumstances is also to stress the significance of another fact: the acceptance of Neoplatonist thought by al-Nasafi, the leader of the mission in Transoxania. His decision had huge consequences for subsequent Shi'i philosophy and, indeed, for Islamic thought in general. Another great philosopher, Abu Hatim al-Razi, corresponded actively with Abu Tahir al-Jannabi, a leading protagonist of the Carmatian movement, who from his base in Bahrain claimed to represent the occulted "seventh prophet", Muhammad ibn Isma'il.

The spiritual context in which all these ventures – political as well as philosophical – were steeped lay in the calling into question of an Islam based on respect for Muslim law as codified by the great nascent schools of jurisprudence. The anti-literalist movement vented its opposition through devastating campaigns in Iraq and by creating an extremist Shi'i state in Bahrain, where they decreed the community of property, the equality of all believers, the abolition of money and all traditional commerce – in sum, an ideal millenarian city. And there the return of the Mahdi would be proclaimed.

The disastrous experience of these aberrations fuelled by frustrated messianic expectations led to the following outcome: in 318/931, because Muhammad ibn Isma'il's absence continued, Abu Tahir designated a young Persian from Isfahan as the awaited Saviour and offered him the reins of power. This coincided with the supposed fifteen-hundredth anniversary of Zoroaster. Tahir's extravagant Mahdi was really no more than a "crowned anarchist". He abolished *shari'a* and imposed fire worship and the cursing of the prophets. His excesses were such that Abu Tahir was finally forced to have him executed.

In 317/930, a Qarmatian raid took place on Mecca. A wave of horsemen swept over the pilgrims in the very precincts of the Ka'ba, massacred them and carried away the Black Stone as booty in the name of Jesus as the figure of the long-awaited Mahdi. These abominations provoked horror among most

Muslims; it produced understandable unease within the messianic Qarmatian movement. It was in the midst of such chaos, shaking Muslim faith to the core, that philosophical debates on the question of authority emerged.

The unrelenting horizon of Shi'i philosophy is the enduring anxiety of messianic expectation and its recurrent disappointment in historical time. One of the lessons to be drawn from our exploration of Shi'i political philosophy is that it clarifies like no other thought the alternation of insurrectional cycles – during which the law is challenged and deemed to be superseded; and the deeper truth of hidden meaning demands an immediate manifestation in historical time – and quieter cycles – during which messianic hope is rarified, obstructed and transformed into an order that seeks to strike a balance between exterior legalistic religion and an inner spiritual religion of hope.

Our discussion of these events is meant to shed light on the philosophical elaboration of notions of political authority in early Isma'ili Shi'ism. Shi'ism had to confront insurrection, draw lessons from it, go along with it, block it and, in the end, harness it. In so doing, it applied various philosophical tools, which all fields of Shi'i philosophy gradually adopted, even those who combated Isma'ilism. Moreover, many Shi'i philosophical categories, later part of the Twelver intellectual universe, were first pondered in Isma'ili circles. The reason is simple: at that distant time, what separated the different schools of thought was not a play of philosophical concepts but the "election" of the imam and dynastic questions of legitimacy.

The Carmatian revolt posed the ultimate question in political terms – does the authority of the divinely inspired leader necessarily bring to an end, or not, the rule of the legalistic religion of Islam and the prophetic cycle of the religion of Muhammad by finally achieving what it and every religion before it proclaimed in veiled fashion: the final rule of a spiritual life freed from the physical constraints of death, the body, work and strife among men? In terms of a broad philosophy of history, there are six cycles corresponding to six major prophets: Adam, Noah, Abraham, Moses, Jesus and Muhammad. The Carmatian philosopher Abu Ya'qub al-Sijistani managed to establish a system of esoteric equivalences between the letters which form the words designating the two principles: divine Essence and these six major prophets. Each consonant of these sacred names contains the hidden meaning of the light-personality of each prophet.[1] Prophetic authority was not content to respect God's will. It was the expression of the letter composing the divine Name. When one accepts that the name expresses the reality of what it identifies, it means that prophecy is the historical unfolding of what is timeless to the highest degree; that is, the divine principles. The seventh letter designates the "seventh prophet", the awaited Qa'im. The end of history picks up again with its beginning because Adam, as Abu Ya'qub al-Sijistani argued, did not establish a rule of *shari'a*. History begins in the rule of the spirit and ends in the rule of the spirit.

The *Qai'm* symbolizes the abolition of all exoteric religions and the establishment of a purely spiritual rule. This means that the political question of authority is not merely a question of how the community should be governed, but what the city itself is *in its very essence*. Thus, when the end of historical time comes about, is the city under the leadership of the Qa'im still a city? It is not likely. No doubt it becomes a community of another type: non-political, non-social, a community embodying the ancient apocalyptic dream – the coming of the Kingdom.

After much philosophical debate, at times violent, Isma'ili philosophy reached its speculative apex in the person of Hamid al-Din al-Kirmani (d. 408/1017), a theorist close to the Fatimid imam-caliph al-Hakim in Cairo. Messianic revolt had barely subsided in his time, and Kirmani witnessed open debates – raised by certain Fatimid heads of mission – over a question that today can appear bewildering, but which had large implications; namely, the question of the Imam al-Hakim's divinity. Had God become man? Had He manifested Himself in the physical trappings of the imam? The advocates of this doctrine were a small but determined minority, and they are at the origins of a distinct branch of Isma'ili Shi'ism, the religion of the Druze.

In this context the key point is how Kirmani was able to mobilize an entire philosophical system in the service of a rationalization of Messianic hope, harnessing it to achieve social order, forestalling its inopportune millenarianism while simultaneously translating its hope. He succeeded in combining all the realities of nature, religion, the supernatural worlds, the law, the imamate and spiritual truth in a complex but nevertheless coherent system, a complex structure that in the end allowed hope for the coming of the Qa'im to be sustained while striking a balance between the exoteric law and the hidden meaning of religion, between literal and spiritual religion. This made the state possible without compromising the eschatological outlook. It rescued the spirit of revolt but forced it to submit to a policy of order. Shi'i philosophers of every school were confronted with this tension between order and hope, between observance of the *shari'a* and the hastening of spiritual truth. In the Twelver world, this tension resulted in a distinction, ostensibly in equilibrium, between exterior and inner religion. This is still the case at the present time.

It is not our intention to continue with a rehearsal of historical examples. The few we have given should provide sufficient evidence of the tenor of the original questions that more or less tacitly oriented the political thought of Shi'i philosophers – Twelvers and Isma'ilis alike – in the ages that followed. The phases of Shi'i history – the Fatimid caliphate in Egypt, which dominated a large portion of the Muslim world for over a century; the epical Isma'ili experience of the 5th/11th and 6th/12th centuries centring on the masters in Alamut; the painstaking development of a Twelver Shi'i philosophy after the collapse of the Isma'ili venture; and finally the emergent renaissance of a great Twelver Shi'i school of philosophy in the Iranian Safavid state in the 10th/18th and 11th/19th centuries – can be explored in specialized studies that are now abundant.[2] Instead we will now turn our attention to consideration of specific themes or questions and, in doing so, bring to bear references from different periods in Shi'i history and philosophical thought.

The need for a master of truth

Why does the government of men depend on access to truth? Attempting to convert a sceptical public to their cause, Shi'i thinkers were well aware that the answer to this question was hardly self-evident. The esteemed Sunni theologian al-Ghazali advanced the idea that there is no need for us to know all of truth. He argued that those who receive sufficient bounty from divine revelation to live their lives fully are content to remain blindly obedient to *shari'a*; that is, to the law and its commands. They have no need for an infallible master of truth to direct or govern them. But those who doubt the truth of the law are advised to turn to a good teacher, someone who can provide them with proofs, as a mathematics teacher provides proofs for his student. This quite profound Sunni theologian says nothing other than this: politics is not too demanding of men and it certainly does not demand absolute truth. There is only danger and folly in the conjunction of politics and truth.

Al-Ghazali adopted his moderate position in order to refute one of Shi'ism's cleverest arguments. He was responding to a short text that the great historian, commentator and philosopher (probably an Isma'ili Shia) al-Shahrastani preserved for posterity. The original text was not strictly speaking the work of a philosopher, but came from Hasan Sabbah, the celebrated Isma'ili governor of Alamut (northern Iran) in the 5th/12th century. Nevertheless, the text displays a robust philosophical cast, offering insight into the overall intention of Shia in their reflections on politics.

We are tempted to argue that Hasan Sabbah's approach was virtually Pascalian. He began with an ordinary situation: a man giving an opinion – a *doxa*. By definition, intellectual activity and reasoning are opinion (judgment or *doxa*). Sabbah does not intend to highlight the way in which every *doxa* is uncertain or questionable. This is already an established fact. Instead his aim is to focus on the silent presence of the master and even the enunciations that challenge this. Each proposition, each counterargument itself contains a lesson. Or, to put it differently, each assertion that lays claim to truth is a teaching, which can be taught to another person. Therefore, every opinion – every argument – has, nolens volens, as its master of truth either the person who speaks it or the person from whom the speaker receives it. Therefore, the act of speaking and the act of claiming truth raises the question of the authority that justifies it.

Then Hasan postulated that the master who is assumed to speak in the name of the truth is, by virtue of his speech, assumed to be a true master. And he reflected on the circumstances of this truthfulness. Though truthful discourse indeed exists, all truthful discourses are not the same. This is precisely Plato's argument. Either no discourse ranks higher than another or the authority that compels truthful discourse is itself obedient to truth. The person who speaks truth is one who is founded in speaking in truth.

Next Hasan drew a consequence from the necessary existence of the true master of truthfulness. It is the master who determines what the path should be. Therefore we require some criterion to make a choice. Hasan resorted to the familiar problem of classical philosophy: how can a master of truth be recognized?

According to Hasan, the answer to this question presupposes that men be divided into two types. This division does not separate as such those who recognize truth from those who do not – for example, those who have knowledge of divine revelation and those who do not – so much as those who are able to identify *which* person embodies truth from those who are unconcerned with the qualities of their guide. Now the identifying feature which enables the guide – that is, the imam – to be recognized is the need he arouses in the one who seeks him.

Need is the pivotal notion. Just as possible existence leads back to necessary existence, on which it is grounded, so need leads back to the master that fulfills it. The person who has already found his master by virtue of an expression of his need for him, the person who hears the calling in his restless soul to *know who* is the master of truth – such a person will recognize the master. This process illustrates the circularity of truthfulness that combines the one who speaks truth and the one who seeks a master who is a speaker of truth. The one implies the other. Spiritual guidance and political guidance follow from the need for truth and from the need for the immanent truthfulness in human words:

> By our need, we know the imam, and by the imam we know the extent of our need. Likewise, by the sheer possibility of being, we know the necessity of existence, which is to say we know the necessary Being [God] and by Him we know the extent of possiblity in all possibles. It is by the same method ("the way the arrow's feathers imitate each other") that we can establish the Oneness of God.

By sheer force of reason, Hasan's argument is designed to lead the sceptic and ordinary Muslim to accept the necessity of the imam. Once his intellectual conversion is achieved, the next step is to begin the stages of instruction itself, a spiritual exercise which the leaders of the Isma'ili missions performed with consummate wisdom.

Some Twelver philosophers offer a quite different justification. There are good examples in the hadith commentaries that deal specifically with the question of authority (cf. the exegesis of collections dedicated to the "Proof of God" written by Mulla Sadra and other thinkers of the Safavid period).

Their argument goes as follows: God needs a "proof" to be known and identified. Now there are two proofs of God: one is manifest and the other is inner and hidden. The manifest proof is for men who believe only in physical perceptible realities. The hidden proof is for "intellective" individuals (we don't speak here of intellectuals!). This is the main idea: For as long as the world exists and for as long as men live, there is need for a "proof" of God. The pedagogical model of politics is based on this conviction; namely, that man has, and will always have, need of a master and of guidance. It is folly to imagine that man can make headway using only his personal judgment. In order to progress toward "the beauty of the return to God", he requires a guide; this is the "visible proof". To instruct man in the knowledge of God, to teach him justice, an "inner proof" is necessary. In both cases, the "proof" of God is the existence of a man who assumes the burden of revelation; who bears the marks of perfection; who, in certain respects, is the human face turned towards God and the face of the Divine turned towards man.

We must also insist here on a less familiar aspect of such reasoning. It does not reject the notion of progress; nor is the Shi'i notion the opposite side of our Western post-Enlightenment thinking on progress. It is not a reactionary, fossilized body of thought. On the contrary, the entire prophetic history of humanity is a history of progress, and this progress is directed towards a return of all just men to God. The difference is between two conceptions of progress: on the one hand, a notion inherited from the Enlightenment, based on the autonomy of the individual person and his coming of age that results in his use of his faculties of reasoning and understanding; on the other, the conception of our Shi'i thinkers, whose notion of progress relies on guidance, on an internal pedagogy, but also on the maintenance and perfection of an external constraint.

Our philosophers embrace a Neoplatonist paradigm and divide all existents into three broad categories, which they call "worlds": the world of bodies, or nature; the world of souls; and the world of intangible pure intelligences. This hierarchically ordered structure of beings, inspired by the Greeks, is mirrored in anthropology. There are men, the "ordinary" masses belonging to the world of physical matter, who are unable to see beyond the horizon of the perceptible world. And there are others, an "elite", who have access to an intelligible world.

This has implications for the type of proof that God gives of Himself, since there will be a need for physical proof and for intellective proof. The revealed Books provide many examples of physical proofs; they include the miracles performed by the prophets, such as when Moses transformed the rod into a serpent. The common people need such manifestations of authority from the prophets in order to believe and obey higher authority. Common people accept obedience to legitimate authority under constraint (the power of the "sword") and through the speech and patient explanation of the prophets (the "tongue"). This is authority in the lowest sense of the word. It is a necessity as such because common man is ruled by his physical passions rather than by reason.

In contrast, the elite obey willingly and freely by intellectual conviction. They seek "luminous proof", which complements the radiance of intelligence. The reference is to an inner proof by which divine esoteric light is transformed into spiritual guidance. Constraint or guidance, physical and rhetorical proof or spiritual proof, miracle or true knowledge – such are the pairs of opposing terms that express two types of authority: the outer authority of the Prophet and the imam in their empirical physical existence in the corporeal world – what we term political authority – and a higher-order inner authority, a non-political spiritual guidance restricted to an elite capable of submission by the free exercise of intelligence.

Another argument is found at different moments in the history of Shi'i philosophy: in the 4th/10th century in al-Farabi, in the 7th/13th century in Nasir al-Din Tusi, as well as in the 10th/16th century in the philosophical writings of the Isfahan school. They take not the properties of the divine nature but the essential attributes of human nature as their starting point. Instead of beginning with God to end up with the need for an authority that is the "proof" of God, the argument begins with man in order to demonstrate that man cannot do without a unique and righteous guide inspired by divine wisdom. Such an argument manifestly results from a reading of Plato and from a profound and assiduous meditation on Aristotle's ethics and politics.

The general outline of the argument is this: man cannot exist and continue in his existence without living in a society. But every community of men requires a *sunnah* and a rule of justice. The term *sunnah*, which is often translated as "tradition", refers to a corpus of true and unquestionable doctrines. Therefore, a doctrine of truth and a rule of justice are essential for a society that aims to protect itself against the harmful effects of diverging opinions on justice and injustice, evils emanating from the illusions of personal fantasies and from the freedom that each person allows himself when he makes judgments. Without a *sunnah* and a rule, the community would be transformed into a war of each man against the other.

The same argument can be found in Sunni philosophical circles, particularly among those thinkers who were influenced by Shi'i philosophers. Avicenna offers the best example of this. He was born into a Shi'i family and was an avid reader of Farabi. The definition of *sunnah* will then be somewhat vague. It comes to denote the prophetic traditions and their conceptual heritage, or more abstractly, it will stand as a synonym for wisdom. But for the Shia, *sunnah* refers to the members of the Prophet's family and to those persons who have the legitimate authority to interpret the teachings.

There is a telling expression in use among 11th/17th-century philosophers: "the people of the prophecy and the unveiling". This is a clear reference to the prophets and the imams. In our view, it also refers to the inspired philosophers, to the spiritual Shia who practiced the "unveiling" of the hidden meanings of being, God, the world and man. Hence, authority should not devolve onto the specialists of jurisprudence alone (the "jurists" or *al-fuqaha'*) but, rather, to the imams' true disciples, the philosophers (*al-hukama'*). The conflict which raged in the courts of the Safavid kings between the jurists and the philosophers revolved around the philosopher's claim that "philosophical unveiling" is a principle of authority which belongs alongside and supports the two principles of prophecy and the imamate.

Shi'i philosophers believed that nothing is more difficult than providing a community of men with laws. Like Rousseau in his *Social Contract*, they argued that the making of laws require the purity and abnegation of a god, rather than human frailty. Unfortunately the lawmaker cannot be an angel, because angels are spiritual beings, and it is not within man's power to see an angel in its angelic purity. The prophets, the imams and the chosen few are able to see angels in a human form. But such individuals are the elite. Common men, for whom political authority exists, need a visible master who nevertheless has superhuman qualities – a lordly man or a divine man (*insan rabbani*) who is also a human lord (*rabb insani*), the caliph of God in the world. The parallel with Hobbes' "mortal God" is striking.

No doubt, Farabi's careful reading of Aristotle explains how the premises of this method of reasoning came to be accepted. It led to a certain conception of community, without which subsequent inferences would have been impossible; for example, the definition of natural man. This does not imply a theological definition of man in which nature defines the essence of Adam, the eternal servant of his Lord. Instead it is concerned with a need that characterizes every man at birth. As we saw above, this "need" is the sign of man's ontological deficiency (his "possibilty" of being). But it expresses itself simply – as Aristotle rightly observed – as the division of labour. The idea that these exchanges, stemming from the division of labour, could lead to a spontaneous civil society under the authority of the rule of law, accepted by all, and that this could lead to peace and progress was completely foreign to Shi'i philosophers. On the contrary, they saw in civil society all the seeds of civil war.

Because man needs others, he also needs the fruit of their labour, and work is divided among men according to different choices and skills. Now, division of labour inevitably leads to inequality. Politics becomes a necessity as a consequence of the inevitable inequality between men as a function of the necessities of production and the division of labour. The role of politics is to stamp out the disastrous effects of such inequality.

Man is a political animal, as our authors keep repeating, because men associate under a government's authority in order to correct, by means of just laws, the differences arising from their actions, the discords that are engendered by the different aims they set themselves – pleasure, honour, and the like. The government most worthy of the title *political* is the one that prevents each member of society from unjustly claiming the property of others, from unfairly dominating others. In short, a *political* government upholds the law and respects the rule of law. For this reason, the three main features of a political government – currency, laws and a law-giver – express an ideal of justice. But the political function does not end here. As we have seen, the perspective is historical and progressive. Therefore, governance (*tadbir*) must be in agreement with the principle and necessity of wisdom in order to be that spiritual teaching which will lead men to moral perfection. It is only then that politics is worthy to be called divine politics (*siyasa ilahiyya*).

Agreement between social protagonists does not just happen spontaneously. This is an appealing fancy, but our readers of Aristotle give it no credence. Rather, they turn towards Plato's more sombre assessment that the force of law is a necessary constraint; and in order for the law to be just and effective, there is a need for a divinely assisted person who is set apart at the pinnacle of government – a God-inspired law-giver with the authority to make the norms respected. There is, in sum, need for a royal demiurge. Classical thinkers called this person the sage organizer of the universe (Plato) or *homo politicus* (Aristotle), and it is he whom the "Moderns" (i.e. the Muslims) call the imam. Thus the notion of imamate, taken in the common sense of guidance and political government, is associated with the notion of imamate in the specifically Shi'i sense, as well as with the Greek figures of authority. One notes that Aristotle is rewarded with ownership of the concept of "political man", which resembles Plato's "philosopher king" and is no doubt modelled on Alexander, whom our authors see as the disciple of the Stagirite *in politics*.

The ideal of politics and ideal politics

The avowed aim of Shi'i philosophers is to formulate an ideal politics in the dual sense of the word: a politics guided by just ideas, a politics that does not yield to the pressure of events but, rather, adheres to a certain ideal. As the writings of al-Farabi and his followers show, the order of the universe must be reflected in the political order. Thus metaphysics plays an important role in the formulation of ideal politics. This underlines the importance of their conclusions in regard to the philosophical Attributes of God, the perfect being, the first cause of all things, immaterial, without form, unique, transcending all comparison, all oppositionality, all definition. The identification of the God of the Prophets with the Necessary Being in itself has the consequence of transforming all theological discussion into ontological discussion. Accordingly, the Attributes of God, as far as He can be known through His relations with the things emanating from Him, are to be found (albeit to a far lesser degree) in the person of the just political leader – in particular, intelligence, pre-eminently God's act, that in political man is the "acquired intellect" which nothing separates from the agent intellect that actualizes and perfects it. Linked by the activity and habit of intellection to the intelligibles emanating from God in the hierarchy of the celestial spheres, politics here below represents what each divine intelligence is in its own celestial realm and what the angel of humanity is for each prophet.

The analysis of political powers does not follow a specific historical or sociological method. It is quite astonishing that Shi'i philosophers did not confront their political ideal with particular and concrete political regimes, states effectively manifested in history. Instead, like Plato in his *Republic*, they described abstract forms of the political community using rational criteria. If the essence of God is real transcendent unity and He has the attribute of intelligence or knowledge, it will be fitting to apply these attributes to the perfect city in order to discover how its perfections may imitate those of God Himself. The perfect city is one where the highest degree of unity prevails; where actions accord harmoniously, complying with the reign of intelligence and wisdom; where the entire community, despite inevitable differences, lives and acts in concert, adhering to an ideal of unity. In sum, the political ideal of the philosophers is a politics of the *one*, and it is quick to proscribe the misdeeds of the multiple.

Opposing the perfect city is the ignorant city, in which men are deprived of the use of reason; a corrupt city, in which reason is enslaved to human weaknesses; an errant city, in which the human imagination when in power creates the rules of life. Each of these types subdivides further into other kinds of cities. Take the example of the ignorant city: we know that riches, pleasures and honours are false goods. If they are taken to be the federating principle, at the very heart of the city, they become the building blocks for several types of ignorant cities. If dominance is the ruling principle, the resulting city will be one in which mutual consent will present love and the exercise of dominance as its principle. The most admired of ignorant cities is one in which radical individualism rules. Each individual is left free to act on his own behalf. No one has more merit or more authority than his neighbour. Inevitably such cities split into diverse factions and parties which obey their respective leaders. No virtuous leader can exercise his authority there. Were he to attempt to do so, he would inevitably be put to death.

Imperfect cities are badly formed imitations of the perfect city; though for some of their forms or types, the transition to the perfect city is not inconceivable. What is necessary is to identify and limit the kinds of people who are able to block this eventual perfection: hypocrites, immoral persons, violent subversives, renegades, teachers of error, etc. Opposing these people is the virtuous imam: his rise to power is legitimate and wins the hearts of his followers. He is magnanimous and level-headed; he has the authority of firm decision; he has patience.

Ideal politics is moral politics. A detailed study of moral virtues and immoral vices helps to distinguish just politics from semblances of just politics. It suffices to run through the lists of virtues and their corresponding goods – as well as the numerous catalogues in which the "mirrors for princes" literature so delights – to find, yet again, the Aristotelian virtues. In such moral literature, the main opposition is stressed – that of the tyrant opposed to the wise and just ruler. The tyrant treats men as slaves; he provokes fear, anxiety, greed, tyranny, rivalry, treachery, slander, etc. The just ruler treats his subjects as friends, promoting freedom from fear, peace and tranquillity, mutual friendship, justice, forbearance and loyalty.

In his city, the ideal political leader is equivalent to the most vital organ of the living organism. This vision of the state serves as a model for political thinkers from al-Farabi until the 12th/18th century, reintroducing the classical commonplace of the ancients of political literature as spiritual medicine. The true sense of political authority is the healing of the world when it is sick and the safeguarding of its health when it is well. Now the origin of illness is violent tyranny and the recklessness of princes. As in the human body, the imperfections of the state go hand in hand with its weaknesses. In order to continue to exist, the state, like a living organism, must eliminate the causes of its frailties. Such causes are the misdeeds of the majority, visible in their differences of opinion and in civil strife, disorder, and injustice. If Shi'i philosophers have insisted so strongly that order and justice are the two most important political requirements in society, it is also for "medical" reasons, in order to set *unification*, the power of the one – which is conducive to health – against dissolution, the power of the many – which fosters illness. The deterioration of the state is always visible in the symptoms of greed; the desire of the common people for false goods, a languid or dissolute lifestyle, a desire for excessive comfort and a life of leisure. There are few surprises here for a reader of Plato's *Laws*.

Traces of Platonic categories are still clearly visible in the meticulous exercise of political justice. Justice is the master-principle of Shi'i thought. It rivals intelligence and wisdom in its importance, and it is in fact inseparable from them. In accordance with a rational hierarchy, political justice is exercised in mutual agreement with the social classes. Just as messianic insurrections laid claim to a kind of mystical egalitarianism of all true believers, while still deftly negotiating the hierarchy of initiatory levels, so too did Twelver Shi'i philosophy – from Farabi to the schools of the Safavid period – attach the greatest importance to this same Neoplatonic notion of hierarchy.

This notion governs every relationship within the various levels of reality, from the vilest to the noblest. Thus, the heavens are inferior in their subtle matter to the celestial souls, but they are superior to the dense and perishable physical bodies here below. By virtue of the most general conceptual pairings (being in act versus being in potency; perfection/imperfection; lightness/heaviness; immateriality/materiality), existents enter into a vast hierarchy in which each has its predetermined place. Thus, the intelligibles emanate from divine Unity; psychological realities proceed from the intelligibles; physical realities are inferior to the world of souls; and so it descends until the ultimate level of non-being, primary matter, is reached.

This preoccupation with hierarchy underpins the fondness of our philosophers for notions of rank, degree, station and grade. They share this in common with other thinkers of their age. It is only natural that their politics would be unable slip the fertile constraints of such a schema, which is hierarchical in its very essence. It holds that reciprocal and distributive justice – notions so dear to Aristotle – can only be conceived within a hierarchy of stations and degrees of perfection that men in the city attain through their personal effort and in accordance with God's decree. To be a man is not a state given once and for all. It results from a clear progression, which ascends the scale from the potentiality, weakness, and ignorance of a humble material existence to the perfection bestowed on the man who has fully realized his rational potency in action and in thought. Between these two poles there is an entire hierarchy of degrees of perfection, which differentiate men who are more or less worthy of authority. Thus political justice consists in granting power to each person according to his legitimate authority, which is an expression of the degree (or grade) of perfection he has attained; that is, his "station" on the path to God.

The concept of hierarchy, which plays a pivotal role in the Isma'ili order of esoteric "grades", assumes unusual meaning for Twelver Shia in establishing who is worthy of a place nearest the supreme authority. It is the crowning notion of the hierarchy of the social classes. Remarkably enough, at the pinnacle of society we find the important figures of specialists in knowledge, a varied cortège of individuals endowed with intelligence and literary eloquence, great masters of science and knowledge, jurists and judges, mathematicians, astronomers and poets. It is easy to identify in this list the portrait of the person who established it: an accomplished philosopher, a law-giver, a scholar, an astronomer and a politician. This is Nasir al-Din Tusi, who sees himself as an exemplar. His colleagues do likewise, always describing the sage advisor of the political leader, the imam, in the royal art in terms of their own priceless abilities. The essence of this self-affirming claim is the rightful place of the man of culture and science at the pinnacle of power. The politics of the philosophers is one in which power reverts to the philosopher. Below stretch the ranks of warriors, merchants and producers to form a model which alters the Indo-European tripartite model in which the priest, the warrior and the producer represent the major functions; it alters it by on the need for a new position in the hierarchy: the rank of the merchants.

Collective religion, inner religion

We have seen that sovereign authority was conceived in terms of a political theology. This explains why philosophical discussions bearing on the most concrete aspects of power must be deciphered in texts, which on first impression may appear to be pure metaphysical speculation on abstract notions. If one were to write a history of Shi'i political philosophy, it would be necessary to provide an account of the views of successive philosophers on one particularly important question that is always posed in varying forms: how does prophecy exceed *walaya* and the authority of the imams in its prestige?

The hierarchic ordering of prophecy and the imamate has many practical implications. The most obvious is to assume that *walaya* surpasses prophecy in importance and authority, and then ultimate authority would fall to the imam; the specific mission of the Prophet – teaching an external collective religion of laws, the *shari'a* – would be relatively discredited in favour of an inner religion and the anticipation of the return of the Imam (the Mahdi). But if the prophecy ranks higher, the *shari'a* would be the reference for all legislative practice and the law would become the normative limit of all legislative activity, and this would be the horizon of the actual lives of the faithful and of the organization of society. It would also dominate the private practice of inner religion.

It appears that, from the 8th/14th century onward, all the efforts of the philosophers were directed towards a satisfactory resolution of this problem. A very clear illustration of this is found in the work of Haydar Amuli. He distinguished between two kinds of prophecy: 1) a didactic prophecy which unveils God's Essence, Names and Attributes; it is a *theological* prophecy, the action of the Prophet in its absolute sense as the *nabi*; 2) a *legislative* prophecy, which reveals divine commands, directs moral education, teaches wisdom and determines the very existence of politics. This legislating, moral and political prophecy is the distinctive property of God's Messenger (*rasul*).

Now *walaya* is a very different kind of authority. It leads the servant towards the divine Real and awakens him to an inner path by means of a mystical path, the term for which, borrowed from Sufism, refers to the "extinction of the self" (*fana'*). In the order of *walaya*, the individual being who abandons his illusory self is led by God towards God. The divine Real seizes hold of him and leads him into the closest proximity and in so doing bestows on him a spiritual investiture, which is that of man in the true sense: man as the true servant of God. Thus, *walaya* is a power that is exercised *internally* over the private person, not over the public person; it is an authority that affects the spiritual achievement of that individual, not his political membership in the community. No earthly person, no authority can be allowed to constrain personal destiny. It is obvious that between a law-giving and political prophecy on the one hand and *walaya* on the other, there is a tension that threatens to become a contradiction. From this moment forward, there is a breach between public and private life.

In order to limit the impact of this separation, a distinction is made in the use of the two concepts. There is an absolute sense and a restricted sense, a particular sense and a common sense. The legalistic and political sense of the prophecy is its limited sense, whereas the absolute sense is found fully in the original prophecy given by Muhammad when he says, "I was a prophet when Adam was still between water and earth". Absolute prophecy is prophetic knowledge – that is, superior intelligence; God created it before all other reality. It is spirit, divine Word, divine Pen, etc. The law-giving function of the prophecy – *risala* – is therefore subordinate and limited, restricted to a specific regional territory and community, in contrast with the primordial intelligence of God, which is the absolute prophecy (*nubuwwa*).

For its part, absolute *walaya* refers to the esoteric of the absolute prophecy. In a phrase similar to Muhammad's, Imam 'Ali uttered, "I was *wali* when Adam was still between water and earth". Another of the Prophet's remarks affirms this primary conjunction of the prophecy and *walaya*, which as we have seen is a fundamental doctrine of Shi'ism: "I and 'Ali are the one and same light". In this view, all tension between prophecy and *walaya* is gone. At this metaphysical level, the two authorities are in agreement, just as knowledge is with its esoteric aspect, and just as God Himself does with the face of the perfect man, in which He unveils His epiphanies.

The concept of theophany, deeply influenced by the Sufi teachings of Ibn 'Arabi, rescues the unity of the created being and of the being of the Creator. Here is an extract from a lovely meditation by the sixth imam, Ja'far al-Sadiq – it is virtually a charter of Shi'i humanism, an expression of human dignity from the Shi'i perspective:

> In the whole of His creation, the human form is the greatest proof of God. It is the book He wrote with His own hand; the temple He built with His wisdom. It embodies the form of the two worlds. It is a summation of all the knowledge on the Preserved Tablet; the witness of all that is hidden;

the proof against all naysayers; the straight path towards all good. It is the way between the Garden and the Fire.

Absolute *walaya* is a theophanic revelation in the perfect man. It expresses in full the sense of absolute prophecy. Here man is the spiritual guide, the book and the way. There is no suggestion that prophecy, limited to legal matters and the political order, is superior.

How should the relations between the roles of the prophet, the messenger and the *wali* (the imam) be construed? How are the relations between prophetic knowledge, the legal and political order and the spiritual path to be understood? Haydar Amuli argued for a hierarchy of degrees. The *walaya* is the esoteric of prophecy; prophecy is the esoteric of the literal message. Therefore, *walaya* ranks higher than prophecy; and prophecy ranks higher than the juridical and political message. Consequently, *shari'a*, enshrined in the legal message, ranks lower than the prophetic path (the way, the *tariqa*), and the path ranks below *walaya*, whose essence is the human manifestation of divine truth (*haqiqa*). In its structure, this hierarchy is analogous to the hierarchy of the limited prophecy – that is, the prophecy of the messenger (*risala*) – and to the hierarchy of absolute prophecy (*nubuwwa*) and the unveiling, which is particular to the imam (*walaya*). Corresponding to these three levels are three modes of existence for the believer: the lesser mode is *islam* – that is, outer, physical submission to commands; the next level, the middle mode, corresponds to prophetic faith (*iman*); and, lastly, the highest level is deeply experienced certainty (*iqan*).

The theological-political proposition in these three terms is quite obvious: the public man is subordinated to the private man; or more precisely, collective Islam is subordinated to inner faith, which leads to a level of internalization in which the individual is absorbed in God, the ultimate level of certainty and spiritual unveiling. Thus, the *islam* that refers to a level of legal and political prescription is expressly devalued; it concerns the body and not the spirit.

We might be tempted to conclude that Shi'i philosophy overturns prophetic authority in favour of mystical authority. But this is not the case. Great speculative skill was necessary to safeguard the superiority of prophecy, but not the superiority of the legal-political order. Nevertheless, the question of how to reconcile the authorities – that of prophecy, that of the imamate, that of *shari'a* and that of *haqiqa*, which are one in absolute prophecy but necessarily separate in historical time – was left wide open.

This volte-face is, indeed, spectacular: if *walaya* is superior to prophecy, if prophecy itself is superior to the legal message, the implication is not that the *wali*, the man of spiritual certainty, is superior to the Prophet or that the Prophet is superior to the messenger who brings the religious law and political authority. In fact, the opposite is true; the Prophet possesses *walaya*, because *walaya* constitutes the esoteric aspect of prophecy by virtue of the principle that the exterior dimension contains the inner, as the almond contains the kernel that contains the oil.

Thus, the messenger "contains" within himself the other two levels of perfection. The *shari'a* includes both prophecy and *walaya*. It is inferior to its two "constituents", but the law-giver is by no means inferior to the custodians of the two authorities, since he is the sum of the three levels of full authority: the legal prophetic message, intellective prophecy and spiritual truth. The outer and inner *shari'a* does not imply that the law-giver is inferior to the imam. Haydar Amuli wrote:

> The subtlety is to understand this: what we mean when we say that the *walaya* is superior to the prophecy is this, that the scope of the *walaya* in a given person is superior to the scope of the prophecy, and that the prophecy is superior to the scope of the legal message.

It is indeed a subtlety in every sense of the word. Amuli was walking the tightrope here.

If it is in a particular person – viz. in a specific law-giving prophet – that the *walaya* is superior to all the other authorities, this does not mean that the legal message is inferior to inner religion, even less that *in the state* this message should be held in lower esteem. Because *walaya* is an inner phenomenon, it must be faithful to its essence and remain something inward. It is necessary to recognize Muhammad as a messenger with a mission to teach the legal-political religion, but also as an absolute prophet who possesses the *walaya* which 'Ali will himself put into practice. Amuli could not discredit the *shari'a*, nor did he wish to do so. But he proclaimed, with the same great conviction and from another perspective, the absolute supremacy of inner certainty, a life of spirituality and a religion freed from all collective submission.

Haydar Amuli was obligated to condemn vigorously the Shi'i movements that drew different conclusions from his own in regard to the existence of the inner and outer dimensions of religion. He stigmatized by name the Isma'ilis who overturned the rule of *shari'a* in order to re-establish the authority of *haqiqa* (the inner religion). He condemned the Nusayri sect, which went further and deified the historical person of 'Ali. Nevertheless, he continued to argue for the superiority of the *walaya*. He extracted himself from this theological hornet's nest with the conclusion that the *wali* is superior to the Prophet and the messenger *only* in regard to *walaya*. Otherwise, prophecy and the legal message are superior to every other level, except the level of the Prophet and the messenger.

Such, then, were the circumstances of Twelver Shi'i philosophy as it prevailed in the great schools of the Safavid period and continues to prevail today. Henceforth, the tension between *shari'a* and inner personal religion will only grow in intensity, and it will manifest itself in accord with each person's inclination either as a strengthening of *walaya* or as a fortifying of the political and legal order. It is the substratum of an inner conflict that explains the contemporary spiritual context of Shi'i Islam today. We will see in Part IV how Shi'i wisdom embarked upon a path whereby the legal message became progressively sapped and muted and was always relegated to the lower rank of an Islam narrowed to the minimal demands of pubic order. In confronting this philosophy, the jurists will base their own arguments on what is conceded by the philosophers themselves, whose leading thread we have been following. It comes down to the fact that Shi'i philosophy deserves great credit for revealing the tension in Islam as a whole from its very beginnings and in monotheism itself, torn between messianic hope and respect for the law, between inner spiritual realization and collective obedience.

Notes

1 The two principles which unveil divine Essence are KWNY and QaDaR (roughly translated as imperative and decree). Applying Cabalistic speculation to these seven syllables, we obtain the following: *Kaf* = Adam, *Waw* = Noah, *Nun* = Abraham, *Ya* = Moses, *Qaf* = Jesus, *Dal* = Muhammad, *Ra* = the Qa'im. These seven names correspond to the seven cycles of universal history.
2 See the bibliography at the end of Part III.

Bibliography for Part III

R.J. Abisaab, *Converting Persia, Religion and Power in the Safavid Empire*. London: I.B. Tauris, 2004.

H. Algar, *Religion and State in Iran, 1785–1906: The Role of the Ulama in The Qajar Period*, Berkeley; Los Angeles: University of California Press, 1969.

A. Amanat, *Resurrection and Renewal*. Ithaca, NY; London: Cornell University Press, 1989.

M.A. Amir-Moezzi, *Le Guide divin dans le shi'isme originel: aux sources de l'ésotérisme en Islam*, Lagrasse: Verdier, 1992. [The *Divine Guide in Early Shi'ism*: The Sources of Esotericism in Islam, English translation by D. Straight, Albany, NY: State University of New York Press, 1994.]

M.A. Amir-Moezzi, "Réflexions sur une évolution du shi'isme duodécimain: tradition et idéologisation", in *Les Retours aux Écritures: fondamentalismes présents et passés*, ed. E. Patlagean and A.Le Boulluec, Bibliothèque de l'Ecole des Hautes Etudes, vol. 99, Louvain: Peeters, 1993, pp. 63–82.

M.A. Amir-Moezzi, "Remarques sur les critères d'authenticité du hadith et l'autorité du juriste dans le shi'isme imamate", *Studia Islamica*, 85, 1997, pp. 539.

M.A. Amir-Moezzi (in collaboration with S. Schmidtke), "Twelver Shi'ite Resources in Europe: The Shi'ite Collection at the Oriental Department of the University of Cologne, the Fonds Henry Corbin and the Fonds Shaykhi at the École Pratique des Hautes Études, Paris. With a Catalogue of the Fonds Shaykhi", *Journal Asiatique*, 285 (1), 1997, pp. 73–122.

M.A. Amir-Moezzi, "Une absence remplie de présences. Herméneutiques de l'occultation chez les Shaykhiyya (Aspects de l'imamologie duodécimaine, VII)", *Bulletin of the School of Oriental and African Studies*, 64(1), 2001, pp. 1–18. [English trans. by A. Jacobs in The Twelver Shia in Modern Times: Religious Culture and Political History, ed. R. Brunner and W. Ende, Leiden: Brill, 2001, pp. 38–57.]

M.A. Amir-Moezzi, "Visions d'Imams en mystique duodécimaine moderne et contemporaine (Aspects de l'imamologie duodécimaine, VIII)", in *Autour du regard. Mélanges Gimaret*, ed. E.Chaumont et al., Louvain: Peeters, 2003, pp. 97–124.

S.A. Arjomand (ed.), *Authority and Political Culture in Shi'ism*, Albany, NY: State University of New York Press, 1988.

S.A. Arjomand, *The Turban for the Crown: The Islamic Revolution in Iran*, New York: Oxford University Press, 1988.

M. Arkoun, *Contribution d l'étude de l'humanisme arabe au IV–X siècle: Miskawayh philosophe et historien*, Paris: Vrin, 1970.

C. Arminjon Hachem, *Chiisme et Etat. Les clercs à l'épreuve de la modernité*. Paris: CNRS, 2013.

C. Arminjon Hachem, *Les droits de l'homme dans l'islam shi'ite*, Paris: Les Éditions du Cerf, 2017.

J. Aubin, "La politique religieuse des Safavides", in *Le Shi'isme imamite* (conference proceedings, Strasbourg, 6–9 May 1968), Paris: Presses Universitaires de France, 1970, pp. 235–249.

K. Babayan, "Sufis, Dervishes and Mullas: The Controversies over Spiritual and Temporal Dominion in Seventeenth-Century Iran", in *Safavid Persia: The History and Politics of an Islamic Society*, ed. C.Melville, London: I.B. Tauris, 1996, pp. 117–138.

K. Babayan, *Mystics, Monarchs and Messiahs: Cultural Landscapes of Early Modern Iran*, Cambridge, MA: Harvard University Press, 2002.

T. Bayhom-Daou, *Shaykh Mufid*, Oxford: Oneworld, 2005.

O. Bengio & M. Litvak (eds), *The Sunna and Shi'a in History: Division and Ecumenism in The Muslim Middle East*. Basingstoke: Palgrave, 2012.

R. Brunner, *Die Schia und die Koranfälschung*, Würzburg: Ergon, 2001.

R. Brunner & W. Ende (ed.), *The Twelver Shia in Modern Times: Religious Culture and Political History*, Leiden: Brill, 2001.

N. Calder, "Zakat in Imami Shi'i Jurisprudence", *Bulletin of the School of Oriental and African Studies*, 44(3), 1981, pp. 468–480.

N. Calder, "Accomodation and Revolution in Imami Shi'i Jurisprudence: Khumayni and the Classical Tradition", *Middle Eastern Studies*, 18, 1982, pp. 3–20.

N. Calder, "Khums in Imami Shi'i Jurisprudence from the Tenth to the Sixteenth Century AD", *Bulletin of the School of Oriental and African Studies*, 45(1), 1982, pp. 39–47.

N. Calder, "Legitimacy and Accommodation in Safavid Iran: The juristic Theory of Muhammad Baqir al-Sabzavari (d. 1090/1679)", *Iran: Journal of the British Institute of Persian Studies*, 25, 1987, pp. 91–105.

N. Calder, "Doubt and Prerogative: The Emergence of an Imami Shi'i Theory of ijtihad", *Studia Islamica*, 70, 1989, pp. 57–78.

J. Calmard, "Le chiisme imamite en Iran à l'époque seldjoukide d'après le Kitab al-Naqd", *Le Monde iranien et l'Islam*, 1, 1971, pp. 43–67.

J. Calmard, "Les olama, le pouvoir et la société en Iran: le discours ambigu de la hiérocratie", in *Le Cuisiner et le philosophe: volume d'hommages à Maxime Rodinson*, ed. J.P. Digard, Paris: Maisonneuve et Larose, 1982, pp. 43–67.

J. Calmard (ed.), *Etudes Safavides*, Paris; Teheran: Institut français de recherche en Iran, 1993.

J. Calmard, "Marja' al-taqlid", in *The Encyclopaedia of Islam*.

J. Calmard, "Mujtahid", in *The Encyclopaedia of Islam*.

J. Calmard, "Sadr", in *The Encyclopaedia of Islam*, Supplement.

P. Chelkowski (ed.), *Eternal Performance: Tazieh and other Shiite Rituals*. London: Seagull, 2010.

A. Cilardo, *Diritto ereditario Islamico delle scuole giuridiche lsmailita e Imamita*, Rome; Naples: Istituto per l'Oriente C.A.; Instituto Universitario Orientale, 1993.

L. Clarke (ed.), *Shi'ite Heritage: Essays on Classical and Modern Traditions*, Albany, NY: State University of New York Press, 2001.

J. Cole, "Imami Jurisprudence and the Role of the Ulama: Mortaza Ansari on Emulating the Supreme Exemplar", in *Religion and Politics in Iran*, ed. N.R.Keddie, New Haven, CT; London: Yale University Press, 1983, pp. 33–46.

J. Cole, "Shi'i Clerics in Iraq and Iran, 1722–1780: The Akhbari-Usuli Conflict Reconsidered", *Iranian Studies*, 18, 1985, pp. 3–33. [Also in N.R Keddie (ed.), *Shi'ism and Social Protest*, New Haven, CT: Yale University Press, 1986.]

J. Cole, *Roots of North Indian Shi'ism in Iran and Irak*, Berkeley, CA: University of California Press, 1988.

J. Eliash, "The Ithna 'Ashari Shi'i juristic Theory of Political and Legal Authority", *Studia Islamica*, 29, 1969, pp. 132–154.

Al-Farabi, *Deux Traités philosophiques: l'harmonie entre les opinions des deux sages, le divin Platon et Aristote et de la religion*, trans., introd. and notes by D.Mollet, Damascus: Institut français de Damas, 1989.

Al-Farabi, *Idées des habitants de la cité vertueuse*, trans., introd. and notes by Y. Karam, J. Chlala and A.Jaussen, Bierut: Librairie Orientale, 1986.

I. Flaskerud, *Visualizing Belief and Piety in Iranian Shiism*, London; New York: Continuum, 2010.

W. Floor, *The Afghan Occupation of Safavid Persia, 1721–1729*, Cahier 19, Paris: Association pour l'avancement des études iraniennes, 1998.

A.A.A. Fyzee, *Shi'ite Creed: A Translation of Risaltu'l I'tiqadat of Muhammad b. Ali Ibn Babawayhi al-Qummi*, Oxford: Oxford University Press, 1942.

R. Gleave, *Inevitable Doubt: Two Theories of Shii Jurisprudence*, Leiden: Brill, 2000.

R. Gleave, *Religion and Society in Qajar Iran*. London: Routledge, 2005.

R. Gleave, *Scripturalist Islam: The History and Doctrines of the Akhbari School of Shi'i Thought*. Leiden: Brill, 2007.

K.H. Göbel, *Modern schiitische Politik und Staatsidee. Nach Taufiq al-Fukaiki, Muhammad Jawad Mughniya, Ruhullah Khumaini*, Opladen, 1984.

R. Gramlich, *Die schiitischen Derwischorden Persiens*, 3 vols, Wiesbaden: Steiner, 1965; 1975; 1981.

H. Halm, *Der schiitische Islam. Von der Religion zur Revolution*, Munich: Beck, 1994. [Shi'a Islam: From Religion to Revolution, English trans. by A. Brown, Princeton, NJ: 1997.]

Y.A. Henry, *Pensées politiques de l'Ayatollah Khomeyni, présentation thématique au travers de ses écrits et discours depuis 1941*, Paris: ADPF, 1980.

D. Hermann & S. Mervin (eds), *Shi'i Trends and Dynamics in Modern Times (XVIIIth–XXth centuries)*. Beirut: Ergon, 2010.

I.K.A. Howard, *Shaykh al-Mufid, Kitab al-Irshad, The Book of the Guidance*, London, 1981.

C. Jambet, *La Grande Résurrection d Alamut. Les formes de la liberté dans le shi'isme ismaélien*, Lagrasse: Verdier, 1990.

C. Jambet, "Idéal du politique et politique idéale selon Nasir al-Din Tusi", in *Nasir al-Din Tusi, philosophe et savant du XIIIe siècle*, ed. N.Pourjavady and Z.Vesel, Tehran: Institut français de recherche en Iran, 2000, pp 31–58.

C. Jambet, *Qu'est-ce que la philosophie islamique?* Paris: Gallimard, 2011.

C. Jambet, *Le gouvernement divin. Islam et conception politique du monde*, Paris: CNRS, 2016.

C. Jambet, *La fin de toutes choses, suivi de l'Epitre du Rassemblement de Mulla Sadra*, Paris: Albin Michel, 2017.

A. Kazemi Moussavi, "The Establishment of the Position of Marja'iyyat-i Taqlid in the Twelver-Shi'i Community", *Iranian Studies*, 18, 1985, pp. 35–51.

N.K. Keddie, *Roots of Revolution. An Interpretative History of Modern Iran*, New Haven, CT: Yale University Press, 1981.

N.K. Keddie, *Religion and Politics in Iran. Shi'ism from Quietism to Revolution*, New Haven, CT: Yale University Press, 1983.

F. Khosrokhavar, *L'Utopie sacrifiée: sociologie de la révolution irannienne*, Paris: Presses de la fondation nationale des sciences politiques, 1993.

F. Khosrokhavar & P. Vieille, *Le discours populaire de la révolution islamique*, Paris: Contemporanéité, 1990, 2 vols.

P. Khosronejad (ed.), *The Art and Material Culture of Iranian Shi'ism: Iconography and Religious Devotion in Shi'i Islam*. London: I.B. Tauris, 2012.

E. Kohlberg, "The Development of the Imami Shi'i Doctrine of Jihad", in *Zeitschrift der deutschen morgenländischen Gesellschaft*, 126, 1976, pp. 64–86. [Now available in Belief and Law in Imami Shi'ism, article no. 15.]

E. Kohlberg, "Aspects of Akhbari Thought in the Seventeenth and Eighteenth Centuries", in *Eighteenth-Century Renewal and Reform in Islam*, ed. N.Levtzion & J.O. Voll, Syracuse, NY: Syracuse University Press, 1987, pp. 133–160. [Now available in a collection of articles by the author, Belief and Law in Imami Shiism, Aldershot, England: Ashgate, 1991, article no. 17.]

E. Kohlberg, *A Medieval Muslim Scholar at Work: Ibn Tawus and his Library*, Leiden: Brill, 1992.

J.L. Kraemer, *Humanism in the Renaissance of Islam: The Cultural Revival during the Buyid Age*, Leiden: Brill, 1992.

A. Lambton, "A Reconsideration of the Position of the Marja' al-taqlid and the Religious Institution", *Studia Islamica*, 20, 1964, pp. 115–135.

A. Lambton, "A Nineteenth Century View of Jihad", *Studia Islamica*, 32, 1970, pp. 45–60.

H. Laoust, "Les fondements de l'autorité dans le 'Minhaj' d'al-Hilli", in *La Notion d'autorité au Moyen Age: Islam, Byzance, Occident. Colloques internationaux de Napoule*, ed. G.Makdisi*et al.*, 1978, Paris: Presses Universitaires de France, 1982, pp. 56–72.

H. Laoust, "Les fondements de l'imamat dans le 'Minhaj' d'al-Hilli", *Revue des études islamiques*, 46, 1978, pp. 3–55.

T. Lawson, "The Dawning Places of the Lights of Certainty in the Divine Secrets Connected with the Commander of the Faithful by Rajab Bursi", in *The Legacy of Mediaeval Persian Sufism*, ed. L.Lewisohn, London: Khaniqahi Nimatullahi Publications, 1992, pp. 261–276.

T. Lawson, "The Hidden Words of Fayd Kashani", in *Iran. Questions et connaissances, vol. II: Périodes médiévale et moderne*, ed. M.Szuppe, Studia Iranica, no. 26, Paris: Peeters, 2002, pp. 427–447.

L. Lewisohn, "An Introduction to the History of Modem Persian Sufism, Part I: The Ni'matullahi Order, Revival and Schism", *Bulletin of the School of Oriental and African Studies*, 61–63, 1998, pp. 437–464.

L. Lewisohn, "An Introduction to the History of Modem Persian Sufism, Part II: A Socio-Cultural Profile of Sufism from the Dhahabi Revival to the Present Day", *Bulletin of the School of Oriental and African Studies*, 62–61, 1999, pp. 36–59.

M. Litvak, *Shi'i Scholars of Nineteenth Century Iraq. The 'Ulama' of Najaf and Karbala'*, Cambridge: Cambridge University Press, 1998.

P.J. Luizard, *La Formation de l'Irak contemporain. Le rôle politique des ulémas chiites d la fin de la domination ottomane et au moment de la construction de l'État irakien*, Paris: Éditions du Centre National de la Recherche Scientifique, 1991.

P.J. Luizard, *Histoire politique du clergé chiite: XVIIIe–XXIe siècle*, Paris: Fayard, 2014.

M. MacDermott, *The Theology of al-Shaikh al-Mufid (d. 413/1022)*, Beirut: Dar el-Machreq, 1978.

W. MacElwee Miller, *Al-'Allama Ibn al-Mutahhar al-Hilli: al-Babu'i-Hadi 'Ashar. A Treatise on the Principles of Shi'ite Theology*, London: Royal Asiatic Society, 1928.

D. MacEoin, *The Sources for Early Babi Doctrine and History*, Leiden: Brill, 1992.

W. Madelung, "A Treatise of the Sharif al-Murtada on the Legality of Working for the Government (Mas 'ala fi `l-'amal ma'a'l-sultan)", *Bulletin of the School of Oriental and African Studies*, 43, 1980, pp. 18–31. [Now available in a collection of the author's articles, Religious Schools and Sects in Medieval Islam, London: Variorum, 1985, article no. 9.]

W. Madelung, "Authority in Twelver Shiism in the Absence of the Imam", in *La Notion d'autorité au Moyen Age: Islam, Byzance, Occident. Colloque internationaux de Napoule, 1978*, Paris: Presses Universitaires de France, 1982, pp. 163–173. [Now available in Religious Schools and Sects in Medieval Islam, article no. 10.]

Y. Matsunaga, "Revisiting Ayatollah Khomeini's Doctrine of Wilayat al-Faqih (Velayat-e Faqih)", *Orient: Reports of the Society for Near Eastern Studies in Japan, Shi'i Studies* (special issue), 44, 2009, pp. 77–90.

M.M. Mazzaoui, *The Origins of the Safawids: Shi'ism, Sufism and the Ghulat*, Wiesbaden: Steiner, 1972.

C. Melville (ed.), *Safavid Persia: The History and Politics of an Islamic Society*, London; New York: I.B. Tauris, 1996.

S. Mervin, *Un réformisme chiite. `Ulama' et lettrés du Jabal 'Amil de la fin de l'Empire ottoman à l'indépendance du Liban*, Paris: Karthala, 2000.

S. Mervin (ed.), *Les mondes chiites et l'Iran*, Paris; Beirut: Karthala; Institut français du proche-orient, 2007.

Miskawayh, *The Refinement of Character*, trans. C.K. Zurayk, Beirut, 1968.

A.J. Newman, "The nature of the Akhbari/Usuli Dispute in Late Safawid Iran" *Bulletin of the School of Oriental and African Studies*, 55(1), 1992, pp. 21–51 and 55(2), 1992, pp. 250–261.

A.J. Newman, "The Myth of the Clerical Migration to Safawid Iran: Arab Shiite Opposition to 'Ali al-Karaki and Safawid Shiism", *Die Welt des Islams*, 33, 1993, pp. 66–112.

A.J. Newman, *Safavid Iran: Rebirth of a Persian Empire*, London; New York: I.B. Tauris, 2006.

R. Peters, "Idjtihad and taqlid in 18th and 19th Century Islam", *Die Welt des Islams*, 20, 1980, pp. 87–105.

D. Pinault, *The Shiites: Ritual and Popular Piety in a Muslim Community*, New York: St. Martin's Press, 1992.

Y. Richard, *Le Shi'isme en Iran: imam et révolution*, Paris: Maisonneuve, 1980.

A.A. Sachedina, "A treatise on the Occultation of the Twelfth Imamite Imam", *Studia Islamica*, 68, 1978, pp. 56–73.

A.A. Sachedina, "Al-Khums: Thé Fifth in the Imami Shi'i Legal System", *Journal of Near Eastern Studies*, 39, 1980, pp. 76–96.

M. Salati, "La Lu'lu'at al-Bahrayn... di Shaykh Yusuf b. Ahmad al-Bahrani (1107–1186/1695–1772): per Io studio della shi a di Bahrayn", *Annali ca' Foscari*, 28, 1989, pp. 111–145.

R. Savory, *Iran under the Safavids*, Cambridge: Cambridge University Press, 1980.

R. Savory, *Studies on the History of Safavid Iran*, Variorum Collected Series, London: Variorum, 1987.

G. Scarcia, "Intomo alle controversie tra Akhbari e Usuli presso gli Imamiti di Persia", *Rivista degli Studi Orientali*, 33, 1958, pp. 211–250.

K.M. Shaibi, *Sufism and Shi ism*, Surbiton: LAAM, 1991.

D. Shayegan, *Qu'est-ce qu'une révolution religieuse?* Paris: Albin Michel, 1982.

S. Schmidtke, "Modem Modification in the Shi'i Doctrine of thé Expectation of the Mahdi (intizar al-mahdi): The Case of Khumaini", *Orient*, 28, 1987, pp. 389–406.

S. Schmidtke, *The Theology of al-'Allama al-Hilli (d. 726/1325)*, Berlin: Schwarz, 1991.

S. Schmidtke, *Théologie, Philosophie und Mystik im zwölferschiitischen Islam des 9./15. Jahrhunderts. Die Gedankenwelten des Ibn Abi Jumhur al-Ahsa ï (um 838/1434-35-nach 906/1501)*, Leiden: Brill, 2000.

(La) Shi'a nell'Impero Ottomano (collective publication), Rome, 1993.

P. Smith, *The Babi and Bahai Religion. From Messianic Shi'ism to a World Religion*, Cambridge: Cambridge University Press, 1987.

D. Sourdel, L'Imamisme vu par le cheikh al Mufid (trans. of Awa'il al-maqalat by Shaykh al-Mufid), *Revue des études islamiques*, 40(2), 1972, pp. 217–296.

D.J. Stewart, *Islamic Legal Orthodoxy: Twelver Shiite Responses to the Sunni Legal System*, Salt Lake City, UT: University of Utah Press, 1998.

M. Terrier, *Histoire de la sagesse et philosophie shi'ite. "L'Aimé des cœurs" de Qutb al-Din Ashkevari*, Paris: Cerf, 2016.

D. Tsadik, *Between Foreigners and Shi'is: Nineteenth-Century Iran and its Jewish Minority*, Stanford, CA: Stanford University Press, 2007.

Nasiroddin Tusi, *La convocation d'Alamut. Somme de philosophie ismaélienne. Rawdat al-taslim (Le jardin de la vraie foi)*, trans., introd. and notes by C. Jambet, Lagrasse; Paris: Veridier; UNESCO, 1996.

V. Vakili, *Debating Religion and Politics in Iran: The Political Thought of Abdolkarim Soroush*, New York: Council on Foreign Relations, 1996.

L. Walbridge (ed.), *The Most Learned of the Shi'a. The Institution of the Marja' Taqlid*, Oxford: Oxford University Press, 2001.

R. Walzer, *Al-Farabi on the Perfect State: A Revised Text with Introduction, Translation and Commentary*, Oxford: Clarendon, 2 vols, 1985.

Part IV
Shi'ism, wisdom and philosophy

11 Moral perfection and contemplation

Shi'i Islam is not monolithic. We have said that Shi'ism, which defines itself as utter faithfulness to the imams, diversified as a result of history. It recognizes the difference between popular piety and learned religion. It confirms other variants as well. For example, loyalty to the imams can decline into rigorism which engenders social conformity. But it can also foster an inner religion and a quest for wisdom (*hikma*). Shi'i philosophy has presented various models of wisdom in competition with other modes of knowledge or in a close relation with them. Here our sole ambition is to sketch some of the traits by which Shi'i philosophy, that paradoxical figure, may be recognized.

But is there, indeed, such a thing as Shi'i philosophy? The terms that Shi'i philosophers use self-referentially vary hugely. They call themselves "sages" (*hukama'*); the wisdom they seek – and practice – is the same as the *sophia* of the Greeks, a combination of contemplative knowledge and moral wisdom. They also call themselves "mystical knowers" (*'urafa'*); their knowledge (*ma'rifa*) ranges from the most basic (the rules of discourse, reasoned argument and the canon of logic) to the most sublime and complex (the intelligences which emanate from the divine One and the cosmic order). They can also embrace the middle ranges of the world of nature and the world of the soul (both a material world and a metaphysical world).

The earliest Shi'i philosophers – Farabi, Nasir al-Din Tusi and the Isma'ili philosophers – are masters of Aristotelian science, keen practitioners of dialectic argumentation. In this respect, they scarcely differ from their contemporary Sunni and Christian counterparts. Not only do they avoid favouring a "gnostic" approach to reality, with countless references to cosmological narratives or mythologies that explain the way of the divine world and the dramas of the created world, but they also achieve a remarkable rationalization of the science of existing things. While adopting – and interpreting – the hierarchical order of the heavens and the mathematical rigor of celestial movements, they integrated the Greek legacy of astral theology with a Shi'i universe on an Aristotelian model which they smoothly combined with Platonic speculations. Plato's *Timaeus* or his theory of the World Soul in the *Laws* come to mind as well as Neoplatonic systems, avalable thanks to the Arabic translations of Plotinus and Proclus.

Shi'i philosophers were clearly involved in the effort of rationalization, the significance of which for legal scholars has been presented in the preceding pages. Evidence of this can be seen in the importance they attach in their technical vocabulary to terms such as "intellect" or "intelligence" (*al-'aql*). The intellect is what makes man truly man. He must use philosophy to enlighten and realize himself in contact with the Active Intellect, the last of the intelligences emanating from God. The life of the intellect is divine life. Moreover, God loves intelligence because He Himself is most effectively revealed in the world through His knowledge. Therefore, the words of the imams are submitted to a freely "rationalizing" interpretation, which is different from a "rationalist" interpretation. The goal of this effort of rationalization is, however, not exactly the same as the rational procedures of the jurists.

This is because, first, Shi'i philosophers have a concern for contemplation that jurists do not have. They are keen to pierce the veiled secrets concealed in scriptural revelation. They elevate philosophical contemplation to the status of an ideal in life. The good life is not blind submission to God; it is to know God and to draw from this knowledge the resources for a life of wisdom. Second, it is because they pursued a dialogue with those we call – for practical convenience – "Sufis". From them, they borrowed a certain mental attitude that emphasizes *direct* vision, putting it above dialectic argumentation and making this vision the pinnacle of the quest for knowledge, without which the search for wisdom would be vain. Shi'i philosophers paired direct vision with the essential love – the absolute love – that enables union with God and with the imams, that changes the arid prescriptions of morality into a practice of eros (*'ishq, mahabba*) that encompasses all the practices of wisdom.

This can be seen in Nasir al-Din Tusi's commentary on Avicenna, when he insists on the superior value of both profane and sacred love. Tusi's reverence for the Sufi masters resulted in a reformulation of the doctrine of love of God – borrowed initially from Aristotle (intellectual love of the divine Intelligence) – in terms of a love that consumes the lover in the searing flames of self-sacrifice and "self-effacement", an "extinction" in God according to the powerful lessons he learned from Hallaj, "the mystical martyr of Islam", as Louis Massignon calls him. Hallaj was executed on the orders of a tribunal under the decisive influence of several upstanding Baghdadi Shia. Hallaj thus becomes the inner master of a Shi'i speculative philosopher!

So, too, Mulla Sadra will write moving pages in which the perfect philosopher, the man of perfect intellect, is in the "thrall of love", overcome by an "insane love" that distracts him and makes him abandon all circumspection, in the very likeness of those angels who have been "brought near" and who prostrate themselves in everlasting prayer around the Throne of God. Such is the paradoxical situation of Shi'i philosophy sustained by Aristotle and spirited by a Platonist mysticism of love – a situation that becomes quite common in Iran after the 10th/16th century. Shi'i thinking also absorbs the ideas of Ibn 'Arabi and those of the mystical poets (e.g. Jalal al-Din Rumi and Hafiz of Shiraz, purveyors of the doctrine of "voluntary blame" – an ethics of blame and humiliation before the epiphany of God). This, then, is a form of knowledge that culminates in vision and in intense work on oneself.

How does this compare with the great Sunni philosophers; for example, Avicenna, Suhrawardi and others? From a conceptual point of view, there is no difference; but in regard to the central role of imamology the differences are absolute, particularly as regards the implications. Sometimes it is low-key, sometimes dazzling and overwhelming. It is decisive in regard to the conception of God: the Face of the revealed God, the archetype of wisdom, knowledge itself, the incarnation of the virtues of symbolic exegesis (*ta'wil*). Shi'i exegesis enables a rethinking of the world of intelligences according to a Shi'i model by introducing the authority of the Fourteen Impeccable Ones. It does the same again when imamology is made to parallel the world of intelligences in a system of subtle correspondences; and once again when the teachings of the imams inspire specific questions and philosophical problems, such as the question of divine Essence and its manifestations, the question of how to accommodate the truth of reason with the truth of faith.

The colourful names that Shi'i philosophers of the 11th/17th century give themselves ("the most astute in spiritual penetration", "the great sages of unveiling", "the masters of inmost intuition") are evidence that *sophia* (*hikma*) cannot be restricted to a few reasoned arguments. These names refer very precisely to individuals who aspire to achieve a comprehensive exegesis of the Qur'an, and in this respect Shi'i philosophy does perhaps differ from Sunni philosophy: Qur'anic exegesis plays a more central role, especially in the last three centuries. Philosophical writings contain many commentaries of the Qur'an and the imams. The Qur'anic verses serve less as illustrations, cleverly dispersed throughout the pages of pure dialectics, and more as a fundamental basis of philosophical knowledge. But, again, is it philosophy? We believe the answer is yes if one accepts that Proclus is a philosopher when he writes his *Platonic Theology*. Indeed Shi'i philosophers resemble him in many aspects. But is it knowledge? Again the answer is yes, because contemplation is never far removed from practice, and practice builds on contemplation.

A life devoted to wisdom does not stop at the observance of rituals. The Muslim ritual persists and, in time, becomes even more demanding: longer prayers, the scorn of all pleasures, increased frequency of pilgrimages, intensified solicitude for God and His commands. But the ideal of a life of knowledge is more demanding. It is unconcerned with mere physical submission and collective obedience to rituals that remain misunderstood or are taken as arbitrary. A life of contemplation demands the *understanding* of what God reveals under the symbols and narratives of the revelation; the knowledge of a moral life; an obedience illuminated by study and the practice of spiritual exercises. If the Shi'ism of the rationalist jurists can be said to be outward in orientation, it is because it concerns the individual in his obedience to social and collective interests. The Shi'ism of the philosopher is inward, allowing an individual to look within himself, to search for the presence of the imam in his own heart and to pose serious questions to himself about the meaning of his life, his death and his future destiny in the afterlife.

The concept of spiritual exercise, so essential for an understanding of Greek philosophy, can also be found in Shi'i thinking on wisdom. The lover of wisdom looks to two sources of teaching for the correction of his soul: Aristotelian moral philosophy on the one hand and the ethics of Sufism on the other. From Aristotle, he borrows the general outline of the faculties of the soul; he acknowledges vegetative powers, animal powers and the powers that are properly human. The animal powers, especially desire and anger, are a focus of constant moral attention. Spiritual exercises domesticate and lessen them, playing them off one against the other in order to safeguard the freedom of the practical intellect. From the ethics of Sufism, the Shi'i philosophers learn other types of exercises that concentrate the soul in its "innermost" "secret" abode, because there lies veiled the radiance of the divine presence which must be allowed to shine forth so that the soul can return home to itself by returning to God, according to the oft-repeated precept: "He who knows himself knows his Lord".

The philosopher takes pains to diminish the tyrannical servitudes of the "I"; he devotes his soul, stilled by spiritual exercise, to the constant interpretation of God's Word. He does not correct himself in order to satisfy some abstract, universal principle. His aim is to perfect his inner state. He doesn't seek perfection out of vanity but to improve his understanding of the mysteries of the higher realms – the world of the soul and the world of the intellect – and thereby better forget the vain entreaties of the lower realm:

> Know that Man has a body, which is the mount, and a spirit, which is the rider. It has been thus since God created him for the journey to the other world. The purpose of the journey is to meet God; this is the reason of his creation. It is in view of God that the creation exists, and this is the purpose of the spirit. As for the purpose of the body, it is to absorb all prohibitions and goods, and to purify itself of imperfections. This is the meaning of obedience to God and the authentic condition of the servant of God.[1]

Life is a journey. To know God is to know what is most pleasing to Him, since an essential aspect of God is universal knowledge. Likewise, the philosopher's love of knowledge enables him to perfect himself several more degrees, to take a further step on his homeward journey to God. Such love makes possible an understanding of the unity of divine will, divine might and divine wisdom. Thus wisdom submits to God's decree and to the destination He has ordained for each being. Wisdom represents the patient love of what God has decided for me in the knowledge of what *I am* truly when the veils and illusions cloaked by my ambitions fall away. Thus, though wisdom is a stripping away, it is also an ethics of desire and love, the focus of which is the supreme Beloved, God Himself. This love begets utmost perfection, the gradual birth of a liberated self. In the words of Nasir al-Din Tusi: "At all times be who you are to the fullest". And in the words of Jesus, which various Shi'i philosophers quote: "No one who has not been born again will enter the Kingdom". A worldly birth is followed by a spiritual rebirth, the desired destination of wisdom.

The beginning of wisdom is an awareness of suffering, the acknowledgement of a human existence cast into a world of darkness. Suffering cannot be attributed to God. Its cause is the deficiency of the mode of existence of creatures, which is a dependant and enslaved existence, an existence through *other* than self. This contrasts with divine existence, which is pure Good, because it is necessary and sufficient. Human existence is fettered in chains. The philosopher is a person who attempts to set himself free from these chains by making preparations for the journey towards the source of all Good and then undertaking it by making his fixed goal that felicity only possessed by God, which He bestows on the pilgrim at the end of his journey.

Therefore, wisdom is not resignation to the finiteness of human existence. It accepts it as an inevitable moment but attempts to go beyond it, in tension with divine infinity, with the help of metaphysical knowledge of man's origin in God and of his return to God. The circle of existence extends down from divine infinity and leads back to it. It includes the finite realities of the world created in the times and the spaces that express God's endless reality and eternity. It is in this sense that one is to understand *tawhid* – the attestation of divine Oneness and Unity.

The faithful believe that God transcends the worlds He has created. They pose the eternal being of God against the temporal being of men, thereby destroying the unity of being. Thus God becomes a judge and a lord who is utterly remote from His creation, which has no other way to recognize Him except through blind obedience to His commands. The risk is that God becomes represented in the soul of the faithful as an idol – a new insidious form of paganism – an idol that is feared and that one seeks favours from through scrupulous worship. Shi'i philosophers never ceased to struggle against the idolatry lurking under the mantle of a literalist abstract monotheism. They never gave up in the struggle against the two evils of the human soul: fear and hope. As close readers of Avicenna, Shi'i philosophers challenged degrading fear and enslaving hope. It is necessary to love God without any hope of reward so that He gives abundantly what He will, which by necessity is a Good.

There is, of course, some truth in the naïve faith that claims to uphold the creed of Islam, that claims there is no divinity but God and argues that only one truth can be said of God, the truth of His Oneness. Out of love for God's transcendence, faith can manage without knowledge. God's essence is unfathomable. He is the solid rock of Abrahamic monotheism. Shi'i philosophy understands this in a rigorous sense. Only a negative form of thought can attain the essence of God: a negative path which frees divine essence from every attribute, every name and every likeness with a living creature. The supreme Name of God – the name that signifies His *essence* – is deeply hidden. It will only be revealed at the End of Time by the Messiah, the Imam of the Resurrection. This is why certain Isma'ili texts have recourse to the biblical proclamation of the Messiah and ascribe it to the awaited One, the Resurrector: he is the "leader of Shabbat", the predestined individual who will name and reveal God in His full light on the Last Day. The Twelver philosopher Mulla Sadra placed emphasis on the figure of the Prophet, who is a paragon of earthly authority, the model of the "authority of visionary imagination" and metaphysical predestined.

Wisdom, therefore, amounts to leading the spiritual pilgrim – man – towards the Day of Judgment and towards the ultimate revelation of the effective reality of all things, in certain ignorance of the divine Essence.

But if this essence remains unfathomable, then monotheism becomes all the more difficult for our intellect to grasp. How is it possible to affirm the unity of God or insist that only He truly possesses existence – that He contains within Himself all truth and all reality – if it turns out that other creatures – other temporal existents – exist too in a lesser existence determined by God's own, but an existence that is nonetheless real? How is it possible to imagine that anything exists outside God? That outside God there is this "self", this man who lives and thinks in a world apart from his Creator? In philosophical terms, how can the one be compatible with the many?

From Farabi to Sabzawari, Shi'i philosophers have contemplated the *tawhid*, the affirmation of the Oneness of God. They first borrowed heavily from Avicenna's metaphysical framework. Then they reread Avicenna in the light of Suhrawardi's philosophy. Finally they dedicated thousands of pages to the problem of whether being can be said to be *univocal*, in the same sense of God and of His creatures, or *equivocal*, distinguishing the being of God from the being of His creatures. Most of the metaphysical treatises by philosophers of the schools of Isfahan and Qumm deal with these problems in their opening chapters. To cite but one example, this is the subject of Qadi Sa'id Qummi's brief and elegant Persian-language composition with the poetic title "The Key to Paradise".[2]

To shed light on these profound questions, Shi'i philosophers made good use of Ibn 'Arabi's ideas. Thanks to him, they were able to maintain two arguments at once: 1) there is no being except in God; 2) there exists a unity of being (*wahdat al-wujud*). Thus, the multitude of individual beings is necessarily an expression of this unity of being, and this unity of being must express the divine being. In order for the multitude of beings to be compatible with the fundamental unity of being and God, a distinction must be made between the essence of God – transcendent and apart from us – and the manifestation of God, which expresses itself in the names that God gives Himself and that He reveals in His Holy Books. If it is true that the essence of God is apart, it is also true that God reveals Himself in a multitude of names, attributes and actions, which are themselves fully known.

The consequence of this is that the well-guided human intellect can and must attain full knowledge of the properties of God; that is, the different modes that God uses to reveal Himself and make Himself known to us. It will then acknowledge that each being is one with the expression of one of God's

Names and that the many actually expresses the revealed divine Unity, while this unity of being cannot do otherwise than pour itself out into a multitude of existents.

Each person is called to attain an ambitious kind of knowledge, to know himself fully, to know *in himself* the image that mirrors – in a particular way – the Attributes of God. The ideal of wisdom is rooted in a conception in which divine Attributes and Names become man, thereby enabling man to restore within himself the original image of God. This is the goal: to return to one's original state of nature (*fitra*), to human nature, the absolute mirror of the revealed Divine (but not of the hidden God). Anthropomorphosis of God, divinization of man; wisdom leaves whole the transcendent essence of God, but involves man with the Divine, and God with man, in a suggestive play of mirrors.

This is why the theophanic function of each creature plays such an important role in Shi'i wisdom. Wisdom, in its cognitive dimension, is knowledge of the *theophanies*, knowledge of the epiphanies of God in the places where His manifestations occur, which is to say in all the created worlds and especially in man. Each man can readily understand that wisdom is not a vain pursuit when he grasps that he is not apart from God but one with God by means of a theophanic relationship, that he is in his true nature a theophany and manifestation of the divine Names. This "true nature" is the imam of each person, the face of the imam, which is given to each of us. It is the specific Shi'i feature of these philosophies.

Consequently, finiteness and suffering are temporary. They can be overcome by knowledge and practices, bringing together the mirror in which God reflects Himself – man – and the source of this reflection, which is the light of the Divine.

To quote Mulla Sadra:

> Know that the soul only attains this joy and beatitude by the constant performance of acts which purify the soul, which cleanse it of its impurities and pollutions and which polish the mirror of the heart, removing all dirt and contamination, by means of contemplation, which is the science of the forms and the essences of things. When the soul perfects itself in this way, when it progresses from the stage of material intellective power to that of pure intelligence in act, it vanquishes the need it had for the activities of the senses, the physical body and physical activities. But the body never ceases to confront the soul; it is preoccupied with the soul; it prevents it from achieving the perfection of union and the spirit of union. When the preoccupation with the body diminishes in the soul, the fruits of the deceitful imagination and the whimsical games of fantasy also diminish; the curtain is lifted; outer hindrances disappear; all that remains is the union [with God]. Indeed, the soul is eternal, as is the active principle contained within it; its outpourings are bountiful and the soul is well prepared. The two curtains – the outer and the inner – disappear.

In these few lines we have the entire programme of wisdom of Shi'ism. It matches to the letter what Socrates said in his final dialogue as set forth in Plato's *Phaedo*. The body is the origin of all the troubles of the soul; it is the hindrance and enemy of thought. The inferior powers of the soul – imagination and feelings – are deceitful powers, because they crush the soul and cloud the mirror of the heart. Thus wisdom is a real death, a longed-for death, an ascesis. But for this reason it is also a gateway to true life, to the eternity of the soul, which is the intelligible mirror of God.

The preliminary work of the moral exercises is intended to polish the mirror of the heart. This work requires cognitive activity. The knowledge of the essence of things which exist in the material world, the bonds that join them to their intelligible forms (the famous Platonic Ideas) – such speculative knowledge prepares and supports the basis for the actual act of purification, which in turn fosters and frees this knowledge. Knowledge and practice are one. The divine outpouring is generous; it never fails the individual who seeks wisdom, because for all eternity it spreads through the human soul. The soul must recognize this.

A more subtle aspect of this thinking is the inclusion of Plato's notion of the flight of the soul outside the body; that is, the metaphysical journey and its different stages. The palingenesis of the soul takes on a typically Islamic expression. Philosophical wisdom is a constantly evolving wisdom since it does not see man as a static being but as a being in perpetual transformation, on a pilgrimage already before he became flesh and blood and until such time as he will be delivered by death, after which he will await – in heavenly or hellish circumstances – the final moment of resurrection.

Death frees us from the shackles of the inferior physical body. Wisdom helps prepare us for this through a kind of philosophical death of the body. But the body is not without its usefulness. Extreme ascetics, such as certain followers of Sufism, neglect the body, torturing it with excessive trials (constant fasting, exhausting vigils). Shi'i morality is less harsh. From Nasir al-Din Tusi to Mulla Sadra, a rich morality literature rebukes or mocks those bent on destroying their mount (their bodies) to hasten their progress down the path towards God instead of exercising patience. The reference is to the Sufis, unconcerned with moral problems or forthrightly libertine and as disdainful of earthly life as pious ascetics. The struggle against the body cannot be contempt for the body. The body is the mount of the soul throughout one's life in this world. It is the outer veil that prevents the soul from seeing itself and the theophanic mirror of the divine Names within, but the body is also the mount that the soul needs. The soul demonstrates its freedom in humble exercises of moral discipline and in the struggle against the passions. The true path of wisdom is in moral purification, not in hatred of the body.

Like the net of the fisherman and the mount of the rider, our senses are useful to us. Moreover, each power of the soul has its own perfection (in this, Aristotle's influence is clearly visible). Even the senses have their own virtue and perfection. Of course, each sense is an inner veil, but somehow it is also a revelation of a lesser kind. Everything that veils God also unveils Him, and whatever unveils Him leaves Him in His mystery. In melodies, lights and colours, in the sweet taste of honey or the sight of beautiful bodies, there is some distant semblance of divine worlds.

Each face, each flower, each love reflects and imitates angelic forms, the splendours of God's Throne, and the torrents of ethereal light. All form is divine form. When the soul dominates and rules its body, it can enjoy these semblances that the imagination transfigures. They become a path to the intellective perception of the divine Names. But when the soul yields to "Satanic exhortations", it does not realize that its perceptions of this lower world are no more than distant reflections of perceptions far truer than any it has a right to expect. Then the body rules and divine forms fade away, leaving behind vain and terrifying conceits. Man's misery comes entirely from the fact that he easily succumbs to the idols of his imagination and wearily endorses that which alienates him from the truth and from himself.

Notes

1   This quotation is from the work of Mulla Sadra. We refer to various texts by Shi'i philosophers in the following pages. The translations are our own. We will not burden the reader with references to the original Arabic or Persian. There is a bibliography at the end of Part IV containing works in European languages.
2   Henry Corbin's *La Philosophie iranienne islamique aux XVIIe et XVIIIe siècles* is almost entirely devoted to these problems (see the bibliography at the end of Part IV).

12 Philosophy and syncretism

As in classical Greek wisdom, the moral doctrines of Shi'i philosophers do not neglect theoretical knowledge even as their systems of thought remain fully engaged with moral practice. This is a philosophy that encompasses both knowledges, informing moral with the light of speculative knowledge, using the intelligence in order to free man from his enslavement in a mortal body and to purify and direct him towards the Divine. By imitating and interpreting the wisdom of the prophets, Shi'i moral philosophy transfigures divine law and changes it into an inner movement of the soul, into the creative spontaneity of a new man.

If philosophy has successfully survived for better or worse in various Shi'i circles from the 4th/10th century to the present day, it was in order to reveal a hidden meaning of a special sort in the Holy Book, a meaning of a kind that only a philosophical or "theosophic" tradition could disclose. It would be a genuine mistake to see the Shi'i philosopher as a free spirit, a champion of natural reason, an intellectual using the tools of logic and science in his struggle against the naivety of faith. In Shi'ism, the need for philosophy originates in exegesis and in the attitude of a few learned individuals who believed that nobody better than they – the true philosophers – were able to unveil the most secret meanings of the divine revelation.

Quite naturally, these learned philosophers claimed authority, calling themselves the ultimate 'ulama', "those who possess knowledge". By this, they meant that the great majority of men did indeed actively participate in the macrocosm, that they unknowingly played their part in the harmony of the universe; still, they hardly rose above the level of brute beasts. It is not given to all men to take part in the life of the intellect. It is as difficult as it is rare. Either the ordinary masses hate knowledge or they pay it the attention an animal might. The philosopher, the true scholar (al-'alim), is also a world unto himself ('alam). Were it but for a single vowel, the same term would designate scholar and world. The philosopher – that world of knowledge and contemplation, a world of practical wisdom and divine knowledge – is a macrocosm in his own right, "as though he were the epitome of all the worlds". Thus, the wise philosopher imitates the imam in three ways: he is a scholar; he is a world; and he is a speaking book.

Philosophy was one mode of exegesis among several. But it succeeded in imposing its particular rigor and, in so doing, provoked the jealousy of the mystics, the theologians and the jurists. It remained an exegetic philosophy, pursuing a constant give and take between the study of scriptural revelation and the elaboration of moral, metaphysical and cosmological knowledge. Intended to lead man towards a salutary end – the future recompense for which he himself is in part responsible – Shi'i philosophy expresses little interest in collective obedience; its concern is the exact knowledge of the necessary steps to come closer to God. These inner steps correspond to the different levels of the world of creation that metaphysics and physics have a duty to explore. This is why wisdom depends on philosophical knowledge. Knowledge of the worlds is knowledge of the self. Shi'i philosophy can accommodate classical Greek science and its two masters, Plato and Aristotle. Their teachings converge and possess a value comparable to the teachings of the prophets. Similarly, Shi'i philosophy absorbs all the secret wisdom of the Abrahamic model.

Shi'i philosophy folds these ancient forms of knowledge into the exegetic, logical and rhetorical disciplines born in the land of Islam, displaying remarkable intellectual curiosity and tolerance as they do so. As long as an argument is deemed useful or respectable, it is taken into account regardless of its origin. Debated, faulted, accepted or rejected, each argument has its place in the edifice. A polite, sometimes ironical dispute can set the stage for reasoned demonstration. Thus, the most sophisticated Shi'i philosophies achieve an encyclopaedic quality.

They make use of everything in the culture of their times and apply it in the exegesis of the Revelation or work it into their own thought. Theological rigor accommodates itself very well to such tolerant assimilation of ideas. In fact, many Shi'i philosophers plumbed Sunni thought systems without any hesitancy, not to mention their taste for ideas that were foreign to Islam but nevertheless venerable in their opinion: the texts of the ancients, the other religions of the Book, the religions of ancient Iran (Mazdaism, Manichaeism) and even certain aspects of Buddhism. For them, syncretism became a method.

But the main concern of Shi'i philosophy always remained that of an *Islamic* philosophy, dedicated in essence to explaining and grounding the prophetic truths of Islam in reason. Shi'i philosophical systems are indivisible from exegesis, from interpretation of the Book and the concealed meaning of prophecy. This is the key difference with Western philosophies, which are grounded in a purely rational approach born of the sheer power of understanding. Shi'i philosophy makes rational use of philosophical *concepts* in order to give a more rational meaning to Qur'anic verses, and, conversely, it invokes the verses and the letter of the Revelation to identify the problems that philosophy should consider. Thus, revelation sheds light on reason as it lays bare problems for its attention. And reason draws out the meaning of the revelation by the demonstrative strength of its reasoned argumentation.

13 Some historical signposts

It is not possible to produce a full history of Shi'i philosophy in these pages.[1] We shall, therefore, limit ourselves to some of the milestones and landmarks of Shi'i thought.

Like Islamic philosophy in general, Shi'i thinkers benefited from the immense translation efforts that were begun in the 3rd century of the Hijra (9th century of the Common Era) when the Abbasid Caliph al-Ma'mun founded the House of Wisdom in Baghdad (*bayt al-hikma*) in 217/832. The transmission of ancient wisdom was the work of Christian Arab families. They pursued the painstaking translations of works from the Greek into Syriac. Syria, Iraq and Persia, now under Muslim domination, had once been major centres of Christian influence, and the Syriac and Aramaic communities played a key role in safeguarding and interpreting the ancient Greeks. Thus, various Christian theologies left their stamp on a legacy that still shows its mark in many works by Muslim authors. There was also a concern to provide a response to the apologetics of the Zoroastrians and, no doubt, to the presence here and there of the Manicheans. We also find exchanges between Jewish and Islamic mystics. All of the sciences, from mathematics, logic and astronomy to alchemy, medicine and physics, converged in the elaboration of thought that had no particular coherence until Islam appeared on the scene and took it up in its own particular way.

The history of Shi'i philosophic discourse is inseparable from the general course of Islamic philosophy, such as became possible when it absorbed earlier knowledge. Let us attempt to shed some light on the seminal moments of its development.

The first of these, between the 4th/10th centuries, involves the Isma'ilis. In order to reflect methodically on the elements of their faith, the propagandists of the *Da'wa* (the Call) used every available resource from Neoplatonism and achieved what the Greek Neoplatonists (excepting perhaps the Emperor Julian) were unable to do themselves: they established a theology of authority grounded in an ontological model and in speculations on the nature and qualities of the ultimate principle of the existent. From the outset, Isma'ili theorization is contemporary with the birth of Islamic philosophy among the so-called "Hellenistic" thinkers. The pinnacle of this thought is reached in the works of al-Kindi, al-Farabi and Avicenna (Ibn Sina).

After initially elaborating a theology according to the rules of a mythological discourse or even in the style of gnostic revelations, the Isma'ilis felt the need to formulate a genuine philosophical discourse. Whether in the Qarmatian movement or among the jurisprudents who prepared the conquest of spiritual and temporal authority under the Fatimids, philosophy came to the rescue of the other theoretical disciplines and gave birth to a number of magisterial works.

This is the origin of the treatises which form the "Encyclopedia" of the Brethren of Purity (*Ikhwan al-Safa*) and the works of Abu Hatim al-Razi (d. 322/933), Abu Ya'qub al-Sijistani (4th/10th century), Hamid al-Din al-Kirmani (d. circa 408/1017), Mu'ayyad al-Shirazi (d. 470/1077) and Nasir-e Khosraw (d. between 465/1072 and 470/1077). There were also numerous Iranian authors. Initially they supported the authority of leaders of clandestine organizations (they themselves were divided between the Qarmatian and Fatimid currents). Soon they shifted their allegiance to the authority of the imam in Cairo (*al-Qahira*, the Victorious), founded after the Isma'ili conquests of the Maghreb and Egypt. They wrote in Arabic, with the exception of Nasir-e Khosraw, whose works are all in Persian.

After a schism within the Isma'ili sect in 487/1094 over the succession of Imam al-Mustansir bi'llah, Isma'ili philosophy managed to survive in Yemini Isma'ili literature and in the communities of Alamut, which remained united under successive masters. But when Alamut fell to the Mongol invaders in 654/1256, the Isma'ili branch of thought gradually took the form of moral literature or of a poetic and mystical kind of thought identical to that of Sufism, first written in Persian and then in the languages of India and surviving up to the present "under the cloak" in an atmosphere of persecution. It constantly sought refuge further east in certain regions of Afghanistan and in India.

The second critical moment occurred when Twelver Shi'ism integrated practical philosophy into its own efforts of rationalization. The best observer of this was an astonishing thinker, regrettably little known in the West today, Nasir al-Din Tusi (597/1201 to 672/1274). His chequered life and the breathtaking scope of his work deserve greater attention. He was born into a Twelver Shi'i family in Khorasan and educated in Nishapur. He joined the Isma'ili organization and became an advisor to an Isma'ili prince, then the advisor to the imam of his time. During the dramatic siege of the fortress of Alamut, he betrayed his master and handed over the Isma'ili imam, who was subsequently murdered. He entered Baghdad alongside the Mongol leader Hulagu and witnessed the sacking of the Abbasid capital. It is reported that he was consulted before the execution of the caliph. He opportunistically reverted to the Twelver faith and, together with several of the leading Iranian minds, saved the civilization from being overrun by successive waves of "proletarian folk", in the words of Grousset. Such is the sort of man he was. An inspired and Machiavellian politician, he was also a scholar of universal scope. A commentator on the mathematical genius and renowned astronomer Euclid, he is credited with introducing and explaining Avicenna's philosophy into Shi'i circles.

With Avicenna, the styles and problems of philosophy as a whole henceforth loomed in importance for those scholars who were competing with rational theology (Tusi was also one of the great masters of rational theology in Twelver Shi'ism). Shi'i Avicennism, which Tusi imposed in Isma'ili circles with astonishing audacity, spread rapidly through Twelver schools of thought. But it was controversial; Tusi himself levelled criticism at Avicenna but, even more searchingly, at a revival of the philosophical sciences, which had become virtually unstoppable. In the 12th/18th century – and even today in some school curricula – Avicenna's great work, the *Book of Healing*, served as a reference for numerous commentaries. It enshrined the teaching of traditional philosophy. Even the sharp criticism of Avicenna by al-Ghazali, in his *Destruction of the Philosophers*, had little lasting effect. Indeed, curiously enough, the great Sunni doctor al-Ghazali's own teachings were soon absorbed into Shi'i Avicennism. As for the work of Averroës, immensely important in the Latin West, Shi'i philosophers had virtually no awareness of it.

Whatever the importance of Nasir al-Din Tusi, it should not overshadow that of another contemporary school of Twelver philosophy, some of whose members were in regular contact with Tusi and with the theologians of Hilla. This school flourished in Bahrain, an ancient Shi'i land that had been under Qarmatian rule for some time. Its masters – Ibn Sa'ada al-Bahrani, 'Ali ibn Sulayman, Mitham al-Bahrani – succeeded in achieving a synthesis of Imami teachings and philosophical ideas in Arabic and in Arab circles. In so doing, like Tusi, they laid the foundations for a flourishing of Shi'i philosophy in the 8th/14th century. The great figure of this movement was Haydar Amuli.

Haydar Amuli was a calm, captivating figure. He was associated with a Shi'i dynasty in the north of Iran. He became an ascetic as a result of an inner illumination. We see in him the emergence of a new synthesis, not merely a synthesis of Shi'ism and philosophy alone, but a synthesis of philosophising Shi'ism and the school of Ibn 'Arabi. With the works of 'Ali Torkeh Isfahani (d. circa 830/1426–1427), of Rajab Borsi and, above all, of Ibn Abi Jumhur (d. 906/1501), we witness the elaboration of a synthesis between speculative Shi'ism, the legacy of Suhrawardi and the inheritance of Ibn 'Arabi.

The groundwork of this synthesis was made possible by contacts and exchanges between Nasir al-Din Tusi and Sadr al-Din Qunawi, the son-in-law of Ibn 'Arabi. It is necessary to imagine here a unified cultural realm, torn by the accidents of history, but where no school of thought – Sunni or Shia, spiritual or theological – remains isolated for very long. There are many fine and subtle ties between the rational exegesis of the Sunni master Fakhr al-Din al-Razi, the legacy of Shihab al-Din al-Suhrawardi and his school (al-Suhrawardi was the "Master of Illumination" who died a martyr for philosophy in Aleppo in 587/1191), the influence of al-Ghazali, the visionary poetry of Jalal al-Din Rumi, the lessons of poets and moralists, the immense work of Ibn 'Arabi, and Avicennism. These influences enriched and transformed Shi'i thought. This is the fruit of the second "moment" of Shi'i wisdom thinking, which we are able to present here only in broad brush for lack of space.

The third moment was hastened by the founding of the Safavid state. The new dynasty, born in the eschatological climate of Shi'i Sufism, was faced with the challenge of spreading the Twelver faith throughout Iran, which it often did with extreme violence. Iran had been a constant source of adherents and great minds to Shi'iism, but it had yet to be won over to Shi'i authority. What made the difference was the "importing" of theologians from Arab Shi'i lands – Syria, Iraq and Bahrain. The newly settled families of scholars in Iran began to interact, though not always easily, with the families of Iranian Shi'i scholars. Before we explore some of the philosophies which brought fame to the reign of the Safavid rulers, we need to look more closely at the *circumstances* in which these philosophers worked. We will then highlight some of the important aspects of Shi'i thinking on wisdom that led Islamic philosophy to fruition.

The circumstances were conflictual, remaining so to this day. First, philosophers were loyal servants of royal authority, and they used their own influence to consolidate such authority. Several found themselves near the power centre, notably Mir Damad (d. 1040/1631–1632) and Sa'id Qummi (d. 1103/1691), who had been appointed *qadi* (judge) by Shah 'Abbas II. Some approved doctrines that served the interests of the jurisprudents. Others, among whom were some of the most important figures, were on guard against such doctrines; or more accurately, they held the view that the rational effort that culminates in contemplation (philosophy being its apogee) should serve spiritual knowledge or gnosis (*'irfan*), the only science able to safeguard, interpret and spread the insights of genuine Shi'i teachings.

They cared little about doctrinal theology a fortiori and even less about the law. Shi'i philosophers claimed to be the architects of what they considered true rational theology. They never questioned the major tenet of Islam: obedience to the Prophet and the imams. But they meant to lay bare its essence, to release it from the straitjacket of prescriptions. Deep down, their intention was to transform the very face of the Muslim religion. Their opponents recognized this. The Shi'i *'urafa'* – that is, genuine scholars or intellects, the *hukama'*, men of wisdom – hoped to supplant a religion that had fallen into blind obedience to religious men with a salvific wisdom that knows only God; God as only divine intelligence reveals Him to the intellects and hearts of those who have been made worthy of knowing Him.

The philosophers were convinced that they were the most genuine of believers. It was not their intention to initiate unholy innovations, but to return to an authentic exegesis of the revelation, to return to the authority of God alone. This is why they met the jurisprudents and dogmatic theologians (*mutakallimun*) on their own ground, why they had to take sides when the jurisprudents declared their own ambition to *represent* the truth. The jurisprudents aspired to speak the truth on behalf of the Hidden Imam; they were the authorities in truth. In some instances, the philosophers yielded; in others, they resisted vigorously. Inwardly they were divided by the conflict.

The philosophical argument against juridical or dogmatic authority is rather curious. Here is an example taken from one of Mulla Sadra's Qur'anic commentaries. Rather than pit human authority – his own – against the authority of his opponents, he argued that most men serve their own beliefs and not God's *as He is God*. Knowledge, which claims an absolute authority to guide others in the name of religion, is mere human belief. Authority reverts to the pronouncements of the imams because their declarations are not on the level of human belief but are *revelation*. Philosophy, by becoming a hermeneutic of revelation, does not institute a new authority which interposes itself between God's authority and the obedience of the faithful. Rather, it offers a path, a way of access to truth, which becomes the responsibility of each individual and establishes the basis of his responsibility before God.

It was in this respect that certain philosophers were persecuted or began to feel "foreign" in their own land. It is also why Shi'i philosophy is not just another discipline in the long list of those that ground religious authority. It is knowledge in excess; tolerated, taught, but always fundamentally under threat.

Philosophers were also teachers. If we know anything at all about their lives, it usually relates to aspects of their study and thinking. The transmission of knowledge from mentor to pupil was facilitated by the institution of the madrasa. The style of their works retains the aspect of oral instruction, threaded with endless commentaries and glosses on the margins of manuscripts. Commentary is the style of discourse most apt to achieve new interpretations. But its contribution is often no more than a difference or divergence from earlier expositions that the master comments on. In addition to commentary, there is also the treatise, which summarizes the doctrine under study along immutable lines. The different "schools" are in fact dynasties of scholars, sometimes with family ties between the members, but always sanctioned by an authorization granted to a pupil to teach in his turn.

Here, broadly, are some of these "lineages" of philosophers, beginning with Muhammad Baqir Astarabadi (d. 1040/1631–1632), known as Mir Damad and also called "the third master" (the first was Aristotle, the second Farabi). Aside from Mulla Sadra, he had two remarkable followers, Mulla Shamsa Gilani and, especially, Sayyid Ahmad 'Alawi (d. 1050/1640 or 1650). For his part, the philosopher Mir Fendereski (d. 1050/1640) started a dynasty of disciples that included Rajab 'Ali Tabrizi (d. 1080/1669–1670) who in turn had several renowned followers, among whom was Qadi Sa'id Qummi (d. 1103/1691– 1692). Mulla Sadra (d. 1050/1640–1641), whose work to this day towers over Islamic philosophy in Iran, had a constellation of disciples, including Mulla 'Abd al-Razzaq Lahiji (d. 1072/1661–1662), his son Agha Mirza Hasan Lahiji (d. 1121/1709) and Mohsen Fayd Kashani (d. circa 1091/1680). The "lineage" continues down to the present day by virtue of the synthesis of Mulla Hadi Sabzawari (d. 1295/1878) and the even more recent work of Sayyid Tabataba'i.

It is important to note the existence of another, relatively autonomous school, commonly called the Shaykhi school after its founder, Shaykh Ahmad Ahsa'i (d. 1241/1826) – the "Shaykh" par excellence to his followers. Their main centre was the city of Kerman (Iran). Through his place of birth, Shaykh reminds us of the importance of the Shi'i communities in Bahrain, discussed earlier. Born there in 1166/1753, Shaykh Ahmad used Bahrain as a base for his many travels to Shi'i holy places in Iraq (principally Najaf and Karbala), where he spent twenty years and enjoyed growing fame and the support of the ruling Qajar dynasty in Iran; this lasted until a regrettable incident with an "orthodox" cleric – an exemplar of the clergy's bigoted cast of mind – led to a declaration of *takfir* (similar to excommunication) against Shaykh Ahmad. Pursued by hatred, he sought to take refuge in Mecca but died on the return journey. He is interred in Medina near the family tombs of the Prophet. His principal successors at the head of his school were also prolific writers. Worthy of mention are Sayyid Kazim Rashti (d. 1259/1843), Muhammad Khan Kermani (d. 1324/ 1906) of the Kermani branch and, later, Shaykh Abu'l-Qasim Khan Ebrahimi (d. 1969).

The flowering of Shi'i thinking on wisdom, at its core an authentic practice of philosophy, reached its apogee relatively recently, from the 17th century to the end of the 20th century. This shreds the current thinking that Islamic philosophy is a so-called "medieval philosophy". Undeniably, Islamic philosophy is in the grip of problems and concepts that in the West are referred to as "medieval". But it is a mistake to judge the evolution of one philosophical tradition against another (in this instance, Western philosophy). Be that as it may, philosophy, the creative source of Shi'i wisdom, has an eminent historical and intellectual function in *modern* Islam. This paradoxical circumstance must be recognized if we hope to gain any insight whatsoever into the *contemporary* problems of Shi'i societies. This context is all the more striking if we want to broaden the horizon of philosophical problems rather than accept too easily the vulgate of "the end of metaphysics".

The word *al-'irfan*, used since the 11th/17th century to designate philosophy and mystical wisdom, means "knowledge". It is knowledge par excellence, knowledge that illuminates and saves; this sometimes makes it possible to translate the Arabic expression as "gnosis", with reference to the primary meaning of the Greek word *gnôsis*. Henry Corbin thus alluded to "Shi'i gnosis" (*'erfan-e shi'i*). This term has the virtue of stressing that knowledge is not so much a matter of abstract, disinterested knowledge in the sense of our modern positive knowledge; rather it is esoteric knowledge in the sense that it takes in a Shi'i exegesis of the Book and of the universe. It must be acknowledged, however, that the works of Shi'i philosophers bear little resemblance to gnostic systems as they are usually described. They were written according to an Aristotelian dialectical doctrine and appear in the guise of weighty tomes reminiscent of the treatises of medieval Western doctors. Thus, the title of Mir Damad's major work, the "Book of Embers" (*al-Qabasat*), for example, raises high expectations, but what the reader discovers is an austere, indeed glacial, system of metaphysics recalling the demonstrations of Leibnitz, by no means the flames of the heart.

The patient reader, however, will be rewarded with meditations in which hard dialectic becomes a vision of pure beauty; "unveilings" in which the philosopher concentrates an entire life of contemplation into visionary displays that suggest delicate painted miniatures. Mulla Sadra Shirazi (d. 1050/1640–1641), perhaps the greatest of all Shi'i philosophers, offers numerous and magnificent displays of such beauty.

The central motive of '*irfan* is a science of demonstration, which converges through its own methods with the truths won by the illumination of intelligence. '*Irfan* is philosophical and rational at the same time that it is esoteric and mystical – if what we understand by mystical is not a private exaltation of knowledge but the burning tip of contemplation experienced in an immediate and unitive vision of the revealed God. This is authentic wisdom, the consequences of which are unveiled in personal, moral and eschatological salvation.

The best way to define '*irfan* is to say that it is a contemplative science derived in the course of a process whereby God causes the knowledge that awakens this contemplation to descend into the heart of the philosopher and to guide him to the direct vision of God. This inner vision (*basira*) corresponds to Plato's idea of *opsis*, which is the climax of contemplation (theoria = '*ilm nazari*) won through speculative knowledge (episteme = *ma'rifa*). The One of Platonism is synonymous with the Good and the Beautiful, but the paradoxical focus of the Platonist philosopher's insight is replaced by all the information revealed in the Holy Book, since the vision of the pure One is denied the philosopher even for a blinding instant.

Divine Essence is – and remains forever – invisible. However, contemplation, which culminates in direct vision, does attain knowledge of the divine Names and the revelation of the divine Real in the epiphanic sites of its names. It also penetrates the esoteric meaning of the creation of the heavens and the earth in six days (which is to say the Qur'anic expression of the divine Throne and the fact that God is seated there); the esoteric meaning of the resurrection, of the tomb, of the return towards God through the body of resurrection, of paradise and hell, of the destruction of creation in the final fulfilment, of the angels of mercy and the angels of divine wrath, etc. In short, philosophic wisdom leads to the secrets of the entirety of revelation.

It is not possible to give an exact sense of all the questions broached by Shi'i philosophers over such a long period. Nevertheless, we wish simply to provide a more concrete depiction of what is included in '*irfan*. To do so, we will narrow our focus to the period starting in the 11th/17th century and restrict our inquiry to three questions, quite considerable in themselves: the question of being, the question of the destination of man and of moral practices, and the question of the mysticism of philosophical Shi'ism.

Note

1 The bibliography at the end of Part IV provides the reader with ample references to explore Shi'i philosophy in more detail.

14 From the question of being to the nature of God

Most Shi'i philosophical treatises tackle the question of being by following a particular reading of Avicenna. Philosophers had noticed that in his *Book of the Healing*, Avicenna apparently drew a distinction between two dimensions, two aspects, in every existent: the *essence* of the existent (more precisely its quiddity, its "whatness") and the concrete *existence* of the existent. Consequently, they decided to address a question that caused a certain uneasiness for the followers of Avicenna but which would become a standard question for Shia: Is the existent as such, in its broadest generality, determined in its being by *what* it is – that is, by its essence, by the fact *that it exists*, by its existence? What is dominant in every reality – the essence of a thing or its existence?

The dividing line between the followers of Mir Damad and Mulla Sadra can be read in their answers to this question. For the disciples of Mir Damad, loyal to Suhrawardi's interpretation, existence is simply the reality of existing things, and these things, which are determined to be what they are by their essence, require no sort of ontological supplement to exist. Existence is simply a point of view on the existent, a way of seeing it. What we term existence is nothing on its own; it is simply the effective reality of things.

For others, in order for a thing to exist, and for its essence to be realized, it must be established in the being. Now this is not achieved by the essence, but by the *act of existing*. The truth of being has nothing in common with the abstract term denoted by the verb "to be"; neither is it associated with the copulative sense of this verb, as in the expression "Socrates is a man". On the contrary, the act of existing precedes essence; better, it is the sole reality of all beings, and the essence of this existent is merely the shadow of its act of existing.

These two positions are rife with implications. They share in common an effort to represent God in ontological terms, in terms of a doctrine of being. All Shi'i philosophers since Nasir al-Din Tusi refer to God with the expression "the necessary in regard to being". The expression "God is the light of lights", borrowed from the vocabulary of Suhrawardi, enables an equivalence to be established with this *necessity of being*, original luminescence and divine transcendence. This interpretation of God in ontological terms naturally shocked the community of Sufis and jurists who were united in a shared mistrust of ontology.

Consequently, the two approaches to the problem of being resulted in diverging representations of God, His essence and His place in being. It would take yet another book to present the full range of hypotheses arising from the debate among our philosophers on the problem of being. But it is easy to see that the philosophical profession of faith of Mulla Sadra, who defends the absolute primacy of existence with an impressive display of demonstrations, leads inevitably to a doctrine of the *univocity* of being.

To speak of "being" – that is, to gain access to being through authentic perception – is always to perceive the immediate presence of the act of existing. What it is not is the formulation of a concept whose meaning would be the essential content of a definition. Now being as perceived in the act of immediate existence – in the auroral light in which an existence emerges – is necessarily unique; it is the same whether the being is a humble form of perceptible nature, an intelligible reality or, a fortiori, God. Indeed, God is always utmost existence, pure existence, without quiddity (without essence). His essence, therefore, is deprived of any *definition* of essence. It is absolute existence and the source of the given abundance of existence.

It is in this same sense that we say of God that He is; that we say of unnecessary things – existents emanating from God – that they are. The difference between God and the unnecessary things depends on the degree of *intensity* between these two orders: the order of the infinite and the order of the finite. All degrees of potency and weakness, luminosity and darkness, existential force and deficiency flow continuously from God (the pure being, the highest degree of intensity) outward to the material realities (the lowest level of intensity). The univocity of being is accompanied by a perception of "modulation" of being,[1] emanating from God on high, flowing down to the lower levels, to the opaque matter of the lower bodies, and thus to the limits of non-being.

Conversely, if existence is nothing in itself, then the essence of God – the light of lights – differs in every way from the essence of lights, which are inferior to Him. The being of Him who is pure light cannot be formulated in the same sense as the being of lights originating from its source. According to another hypothesis, if each thing is first determined by the defined reality of its essence and if, furthermore, one conceives its existence to be a mere attribute of its essence – an attribute which is not essential for the idea of essence, but which God adds to essence when He creates it in actuality – then the gradation of non-necessary beings does indeed ascend from the material body below to the level of the eternal intelligences. But God cannot be said "to be" in the same sense. Therefore, the sense of the word "being" is *equivocal*.

As Rajab 'Ali Tabrizi pointed out, if what we conceive of the being of God is identical to what we conceive of the being of things created by God, it follows that God has a non-necessary existence, since it resembles, in all of its aspects, the existence which is added to the essences of created things. But God is necessary existence by Himself! In sum, the univocity of being would lead to negating the transcendence and sublimity of the divine Essence. This debate is destined to go on and on, and indeed it sparks debate among Shi'i philosophers

to this day. Ontology has become their favourite discipline for debates and theoretical constructs. Shi'i ontology perpetuates to the present day a codification of
thought initially produced by al-Farabi and, especially, by Avicenna. Their
contributions firmly established the problem of the being of the existent as the
horizon of Muslim thought. This is not to say that it descends into a secularization of the Divine or a metaphysics that forgets the original sense of the
absolute. What rescues Shi'i philosophy from such "forgetfulness" is this. All
Shi'i thinkers agree on one essential point: the necessity of an apophatic
theology; that is, on the need for a philosophic and theological discourse which
leads to the essence of God by way of *negation*, which thus accepts to speak of
God only by denying all remnants of finiteness in Him. Of course, these thinkers diverge from one another in their conceptualization of this approach.
Some – Qadi Sa'id Qummi and Shaykh Ahmad Ahsa'i, for example – insist on
the rupture that exists between the being of God and the being of the realities
originating in Him. In defence of their thesis, they refer to Plotinus who, following Plato, places the One – the primary cause – "beyond being". Being, as
far as we are given to know it in existents, begins with the intelligible world. It
then pours out into the world of souls and thence into nature and bodies. But
the purity of the One is the purity of a real – an absolute real – whose mode of
reality is ineffable. Therefore, the verb "to be" cannot be used in the same
sense for this real and for the worlds that have unfurled.

But the defenders of the univocity of being are not short of arguments to
salvage negation. Sadra, for example, wrote that "the necessary Being has the
following mode: it is above infinity by virtue of what is infinite". The infinity
of divine existence is incomparable with the existence of things that we are
familiar with in the world, because it surpasses all conception of the infinite or,
rather, because we conceive of God as One Who is such that He is in no way
bound by a definition of the infinite. Because He is infinite, He is therefore
"beyond the infinite". This definition closely resembles one by Saint Anselm in
Western thought, but which Mulla Sadra took directly from Avicenna. This is
why Mulla Sadra can insist on the need for an apophatic theology, yet deny all
the predicates of the unthinkable infinity of God. In his words, existence is
never a predicate, and even less so in God than in other things.

It is obvious that a discussion of the "ontological argument" of the sort that
characterizes Western philosophy since Kant cannot emerge in this problematic
context. It has been taken for granted since Kant that rational theologians
understand existence as a predicate. Furthermore, we allow with both Avicenna
and Kant that effective and real existence is verifiable in our perceptions.
Consequently, either the philosophic argument that holds that God cannot
be without the predicate "existence" is based on an illusion of reason or existence
no longer has the least criteria of verification and is an empty concept. The
reader interested in these hoary arguments relative to the conceivable demonstration of God's existence will appreciate that the Kantian manner to conclude
the debate is entirely foreign to Shi'i thinkers and that it would most certainly
surprise them.

This is because for Shi'i thinkers, the existence of God is not conceived of in terms of a predicate that can be added to, or is absorbed in, His essence. In their reasoning: either it is necessary to conceive of the essence of the absolute Divine as "beyond" all definable subjects (which is every subject that can be given a predicate) and, indeed, even "beyond" being (in this case, created things are held to receive an existence from God – (i.e. an existence that is a predicate); or one conceives the infinity of the divine existence as *constitutive* of its essence, in which case, one thinks that existence is *constitutive* of every existent such that the precondition Kant believed should be taken for granted – that, as held by the rational theologians, existence is *always* a predicate – simply collapses. It wouldn't be such a bad thing if we took this view into account in our present understanding of ontological questions.

Negative theology opens the path to positive theology. If divine Essence is out of reach, if the necessity of the divine being can be demonstrated rationally, without the *nature* of God being resolvable, then the *revelation* of God in His Names and His Attributes does enable the elaboration of a philosophic science of being, one that begins with the study of a remarkable structure: the intelligible world.

Shi'i thinkers became familiar with the expression "the intelligible world" through their reading of Plotinus, though they attributed the notion to Aristotle, the "first master", and not to Plotinus; this is because in the 3rd/10th-century Arabic version of his six *Enneads*, the last three somehow became attributed to Aristotle! This "Arabic" Plotinus, endlessly studied, quoted and commented on, fostered a division of the non-necessary existents into three worlds: the intelligible world, the world of souls or spirits, and the world of nature. It is this vast framework that rules all Shi'i philosophy.

The intelligible world is not an abstract place formed by an accretion of universal concepts wrested by induction from empirical material realities. It is a concrete place existing by virtue of divine emanation; it is the precise equivalent of the Neoplatonic *Nous*. Intelligible realities are the eternal archetypes of all things; they are also the single individuals, the angels who have regency over the lower world, the celestial spheres and nature. Finally, they include the active principle of the human spirit, which is the abode of our soul and the limit of our destination.

In their exegetic efforts to interpret the words of the imams, Shi'i philosophers identified this intelligible world with the Fourteen Impeccables, with the timeless reality of Islam. It represents the esoteric face of all prophets and imams; it is the place of abode of the light of the prophecy and the imamate; it is the pen that God uses to write the book of the universe, the "Mother of the Book", written with the letters of the Holy Book in heaven. The inexpressible absolute reveals itself in this primeval theophany. In turn, this theophany spreads the entirety of the eternal essences throughout the worlds below, through the soul and nature. Is there any need to emphasize what such an equivalence of the intelligible and the eternal letters of the Book shares in common with the efforts of Jewish Cabbalists?

How can access to this intelligible world be gained? Reason can be used to know the forms of the existents, what Aristotle called "substantial form". Reason is formal knowledge. It is necessary, but not sufficient. Suhrawardi, the great philosopher of illuminative wisdom, had already stressed the importance of another mode of knowledge, called *presential* knowledge because it situates the knowing subject in relation to the act of presence of its object such that this presence translates in full the profound unity of the knowing subject and the known object. Whatever the particulars of the controversy concerning this unity – whether it is effective or merely a relationship, whether a union or a contact – presential knowledge is still the dawning of the light of a thing upon the intelligence, and thus it activates the light of the intelligence. The cause of this "dawning" is the agent Intelligence, an angelic reality that bears the name of the archangel Gabriel.

Classically, Islamic philosophy identified the archangel Gabriel – entrusted with responsibility for the sublunar world of nature – with the "Giver of forms", that emanation of God that gives the existents their form, safeguarding and governing them. Likewise it was what illumined intelligence in formal knowledge. Now he becomes a light in the full sense of the word; now he genuinely illuminates intelligence by revealing the concrete presence of the real, not merely its abstract form alone. It is this act of presence – of essence, according to some, of existence, according to others – that one must seize in the intelligible world in order to make an act of presence oneself at the highest level and thus to approach the ultimate presence: the revealed God seated on His Throne surrounded by a choir of angels.

Though it is illuminative knowledge, philosophic wisdom does not become a kind of "mystical" pathos. Rather it fosters an intelligence that plumbs the origin of all physical realities in its genuine metaphysical arena. This is not Aristotle's prime mover; it is a divine thought, a divine knowledge that is fully contained in the supreme Name through which the inexpressible essence reveals itself – the name *Allah*. This name designates the essence of God, but it conceals the essence as it reveals it. It establishes the limits of intelligence, its beginning and its end. The name *Allah* then disperses throughout a hierarchy of divine Names, which make an appearance throughout the microcosm and the macrocosm. Man is able to access the truth of these names because their effects aggregate in him when he is a perfect man, prophet or imam.

The perfect man, the one that Shi'i wisdom thinking embraces as its focal point, is the earthly caliph of God because he is the semblance – the image and manifestation – of the intelligible light of God in heaven. Each distinct existent – vegetal, animal or human – is in turn a place for the apparition of the divine Names, within the limits of its natural dispositions. Each existent, in its own modest measure, reflects this first likeness, this perfect man who is the mirror of *Allah*.

> Just as all the names are summarized in the meaning of the name *Allah*, so the essential realities of their places of manifestation, which are parts of the

macrocosm, come together in the mirror reflection of the name *Allah*, who is the perfect man, the microcosm from one point of view and the macrocosm from another.

The absolute unity of the manifestation of God, prophecy, the imamate, the universe and men is attested to in the presential, spiritual knowledge of the intelligible world.

Note

1 This is the translation of the technical term *al-tashkik* proposed by C. Bonmariage (see bibliography). Being is "modulated"; it is assigned an infinity of variations; it is fed by a "scepticism" which negates and produces new actualizations perpetually.

15 The destination of man

Shi'i philosophy forged its own conception of man's destiny in the philosophic interpretation of the Qur'an. The Qur'an announces the imminent apocalypse of the world and encourages men to convert to the true faith in order to avoid the tragic fate of non-believers and the disobedient. The universe has a beginning and an end in time. Man is threatened by two inescapable events: his death and the destruction of the world, which is the end of all things. Shi'i philosophers have little respect for the consoling doctrines that proclaim the eternity of the world or of nature. They take very seriously the questions of how to know whether man has a destination and an afterlife and whether creation disappears without trace when the physical universe crumbles at the End of Time. This bespeaks the importance of the theme of the *resurrection* in such a speculative context.

The Qur'an offers detailed descriptions of paradise and hell and the pleasures and tortures that await men on the Day of Judgment. Shi'i philosophers make no effort to diminish the psychological impact of these texts, nor do they hesitate to probe death in its harshest aspects. God will cause all beings to die, including the angels themselves, even the archangels Gabriel, Michael, Seraphiel and the Angel of Death himself. The time of the end of the world, like the hour of our own death, is unknown; and yet both are decreed and predestined.

Is the hoped-for resurrection (an essential doctrine of Islam) physical? Should it be taken literally? Will the mortal body be resuscitated after it has decayed beneath the earth? Will a new earth replace the one destroyed by God at the End of Time? Will a new heaven be created? Shi'i philosophers are intellectually mistrustful of naïve belief in such representations. They demonstrate that locating paradise and hell in some physical place in the universe is incompatible with reason and faith. They take issue with the hope of a physical form of pleasure as a reward for man's efforts to fulfil the law. Such pleasure, taken in the basest sense, would sanctify villainous bargaining with God, something incompatible with the grandeur of the imams' teachings. Nevertheless, Shi'i philosophers do not wish to efface the horrid or voluptuous aspects of the afterlife but, rather, to accentuate them.

Isma'ili philosophers eliminated all ties between the resurrection and physical reality. In their outlook, the resurrection is the spiritual fulfilment of man, henceforth freed from a law that loses its meaning when the cycles of history have come to an end. According to them, the imam leads men towards this liberation, delivering them from obedience to the commands, and establishes a community united in a clear understanding of the hidden meaning of religion, where all truths concealed since the creation of the world are revealed in the person of the Resurrector (*qa'im*).

The rule of the law concerns earthly existence; the rule of divine truth (*haqiqa*) concerns spiritual existence. Plentiful scholarly research can show the link between this conception of spiritual resurrection and various interpretations of Pauline Christianity (Marcionite and no doubt Manichean thought as well). On the other hand, the Isma'ilis were very discreet regarding the resurrection that follows universal death. It is unclear whether they believed in it and whether they attached any great importance to physical death. The real issue is *spiritual* life and death.

It is a different matter for Twelver philosophers. Loyal to a balance between the literal text of the Qur'an and symbolic exegesis, between apparent and hidden meanings, the Twelvers accept the truth of teachings concerning the minor and major resurrection of man. One concerns the immediate destiny of the deceased, the status of his soul detached from his body; the other concerns the final events of the life of the universe, the assembly of all the creatures when God decides on the Day of Judgment and the Hour has sounded.

The risk for philosophy would be to deny the physical resurrection of man under the pretext that the only salvation worthy of its name is the beatitude of the spirit, stripped of all ties with the material world, in contemplation of intelligible realities. Not only does this mean that only the philosopher is worthy of salvation, that therefore common man has nothing to expect from the promise of the Qur'an, but it also suggests that the commandments of the faith are not effective, because there would be no reward for remaining obedient to them and no punishment for disobeying them. Therefore it is necessary to preserve the notion of a physical resurrection, associating with it the notion of reward or punishment that awaits man after death. Moral life depends narrowly on eschatology; and the notion of the last ends determines all ethical life.

The suspicion of amorality and scepticism that affects Aristotelian doctrine and its legacy in the Islamic world focuses, oddly enough, on Avicenna's reading of it – if indeed it is true that Avicenna makes a careful distinction between the philosopher, who enjoys genuine bliss solely because his intelligence gives him access to universal and everlasting truths, and the common man, who is mired in a world of imagination and imprisoned in the ambit of a physical body. To avoid this distinction, it suffices to imagine an intermediary world (*barzakh*) between the body – composed of matter and form – and the purely immaterial, intelligible world that is a crossing over point, a place where prophecies fulfil their promise. In its use in the Qur'an, *barzakh* means "isthmus", but also "screen".

What faculty is there in man that occupies the space between sense and intelligence? In the Aristotelian tradition, this faculty can only be imagination.

It completes the task of common sense by unifying and preserving the perceptions of the external world. It communicates to the intellect the forms of things which bear certain hallmarks of physical properties, but which can jettison such impurities in order to appear in their specific universality. Imagination is dependant on the contribution of the perceptions. It is, therefore, still passive. Now Shi'i philosophers read Avicenna differently, aided in this by the insights of various great thinkers who conceptualized imagination in a more active sense. First and foremost is Suhrawardi, who emphasized the doctrine of the imagination outlined in his magnum opus, *The Book of Oriental Wisdom*. His commentators, too, boldly interpreted the function of human imagination as though it were a visionary imagination, an active imagination.

Avicenna showed the way in his treatise *On the Soul* (and in other texts). According to Suhrawardi, forms configured in the imagination have the same status as forms reflected in mirrors. The form we see in the mirror is not inherent in the substrate that casts the reflection. Similarly the form that descends from above into our imagination, when God is its inspiration, does not have the brain as its substrate. Such a form is "a citadel suspended in the air", a corporeal form without a lower, material substrate. Therefore it must belong to another world, a corporeal world that differs from the lower world revealed by our senses. This world is given the name "the world of appearances" or "the world of images" (*'alam al-mithal*) – what Henry Corbin and his followers have standardized as "the *imaginal world*".

This is not an imaginary world made of our myths and fantasies. It has nothing to do with what psychology or psychoanalysis calls the imaginary. Nor is it a poetic world created in accord with our fancy. For the disciples of Suhrawardi, it is a world which is separated from our own, where the "images in suspension" take up their enigmatic abode from whence they come to inhabit the soul predisposed to receive them. They locate this abode at the far reaches of the celestial spheres. The imaginal world filters souls as they embark on their return ascent to God in the same way that, in the Manichean myth, the sun and the moon filter the light particles.

This doctrine of the imaginal world was not without problems. Suhrawardi refused to accept that it was invested with absolute immateriality, opening the way to an extraordinary exploration of the very concept of matter. Shi'i philosophers took his ideas further when they drew a distinction between the different layers of materiality that extend from the dense matter of physical bodies to the subtle matter of imaginal forms. Better than anyone Suhrawardi recognized the usefulness of the concept in eschatological matters. It offered the faithful – those who had made at least "some progress" down the path towards wisdom – a place of reward after death.

Since the faithful had lived by norms, which were lower than pure intellective knowledge, in accordance with their imagination and what it enabled them to grasp of the Qur'an's truths, they found salvation in a world of imagination of which they had always been part. It is easy to understand why it is so important that this imaginal world not be something purely imaginary: the pleasant forms and soothing music which produce the paradise of these "midway" men are not illusions; they are a reward – no doubt middling, but nevertheless real. In the imaginal world, divine lights reverberate for them in forms befitting their imagination.

Shi'i philosophers embraced the imaginal world in full, transforming it into a major theme of Islamic philosophy during the very period that concerns us (primarily the 11th/17th century to the present day). Under the influence of Ibn 'Arabi, they placed emphasis on a divine imagination that produces perceptible forms of a higher order and shapes existents from their eternal intelligible essences. But there was no unity of opinion among Shi'i philosophers in regard to their definitions of the properties of the imaginal world. Some denied the immateriality of this world and the immateriality of human imagination. Others hesitated to identify it with the heaven and hell proclaimed in the Qur'an. Others took pains to portray its rich potentialities. It is to the thinking of the latter that we must now turn and summarize briefly.

As far as the resurrection of the body is concerned, we read that it is indeed real but that it does not occur in the physical body. The body of resurrection is a spiritual body; those who reject this idea are doomed to imagine the new birth of man as a transmigration of the soul [metempsychosis]. The philosophical doctrine of the "spiritual body" was a lively topic of controversy between Mulla Sadra's disciples and the theorists of the Shaykhi school. It is extraordinary that metempsychosis haunted so many Muslim thinkers, as though it posed a threat to prophetic truth. Ever since Suhrawardi and his disciples took it upon themselves to investigate it, palingenesis became a topic of genuine concern. One almost expects to find a return to Platonist thinking in regard to the soul's return to a new body, or indeed Buddhist notions of reincarnation. But despite obvious suggestions of this, it was not to be. In order to avoid confusion between metempsychosis and palingenesis, it was necessary to make a distinction between two bodies: the body which is born and dies in the lower world of the senses and the body which is born at the moment of the minor resurrection – the spiritual body, the imaginal body. Shi'i philosophers take great delight in interpreting, as well as arguing for and against, the existence of this body.

Without a doubt the most highly developed of the philosophical doctrines dealing with the topic of resurrection is found in Mulla Sadra. He established the foundations in Shi'i philosophy on which future conceptions of the after-world were to be built. His contribution remains influential today. Students of the Shaykhi school pushed the doctrine further still, but they also challenged it. They never tired of formulating penetrating descriptions and analyses of the imaginal realm and of the emblematic cities said to dot its allusive geography. For this reason, we offer here a brief sketch of Sadra's thought as an illustration of Shi'i thinking on wisdom at its apogee.

According to Mulla Sadra, the human soul has many modes of being and many modes of resurrection. Before descending from above into our natural body, the soul has traversed the intelligible and imaginal worlds. The soul reascends to these worlds after the body's death. The minor resurrection involves the soul leaving the body and taking its intangible, imaginative faculty with it. This faculty is the soul; it is no longer anything but imagination in action, awakened to the realities of death and aware of its destiny. In the interpretation of Ibn 'Arabi, repeated by Sadra: "sleep and death are like the sigh of resurrection".

Man's every desire, thought, action during his life on earth are incorporated into his imagination, the living memory of who he has been. The soul shapes its own imaginal body while in its physical form. When the body passes away, it becomes the substance of its own body of resurrection, a substance made of all the dreams it ever had, of all its iniquities and of all its nobility. Then this world of the soul rears up before the soul that the torments of its own imagination prey upon, and it sees itself in its true body, either a thing of youthful beauty or a hideous shrew – a dog, a pig or another animal symbolizing some passion of the soul. The paradise that the soul enters – or the hell that it is engulfed in – is only the actual projection of its own self, believing or unbelieving, a doer of Good or Evil. Each soul receives the reward or punishment it deserves as a consequence of a lifetime of desire.

As for the major resurrection, it concerns the heavens, the earth and all creation. According to a grand plan, God will destroy all the existents – from the minerals to the angels – but they will rise again in a new birth, which is a birth in the world beyond. As a function of the "substantial evolution" which moves all things, the existents are transformed and metamorphosed. The Last Day is merely the final step in a continuous transformation or revolution of the existent. Then everything returns to God in its imaginal form, ultimately achieving closeness to Him in its intelligible archetype.

All things – mineral, vegetal, animal and human – will experience their own particular resurrection; all will return to God. Hell involves only those persons who doomed themselves to nothingness because they led lives of emptiness – tyrants, speculators, oppressors of every kind, libertines, the vainglorious and others of the same stripe. Having fed on nothingness, they will become things of naught and will experience genuine hell, which is their own being in nothingness. Conversely, the person who has intensified his act of existing, reaching beyond his physical nature towards beauty, justice and truth, will experience next to God the destiny of the angels brought close to God, of whom the Qur'an speaks. As all make their return to the original light, they will be like leaves on the tree of paradise, the esoteric meaning of which lies in being the community of the awaited Imam.

16 From the visible to the invisible

We know what the basic aspects of the Shi'i mind are: a dual conception of all things split between the visible and the hidden; a dramatic perception of this duality in terms of a conflict between light and darkness, between the right-eousness of the Creator and the evil of satanic forces.[1] These attitudes can be found in Shi'i philosophy as well, but they are integrated within a perception that turns a less tormented face towards what is real. If we had to name the basic category of this thought, it would be that of *order*: providential order, order of the worlds, hierarchical order of existents.

Each person's place and lot in the world is determined by destiny. Mir Damad stated it thus:

> Is it not an elementary and manifest truth that the good is what each thing desires, what it aspires to and what it turns toward? Now it is through good that each person achieves his own degree of perfection, in the rank that is his and at his own proper level in being. Of all the God-given shares, the perfections, divine gifts and fulfilments of effective reality, essence has its own aspect, its own manner of desire, which is its lot. But Evil has no essence; it is the absence of essence, or the absence of the perfection of essence, or the absence of perfection of that which belongs to essence.

Visible nature is the manifest aspect of this order. Substances are made of given forms, which the being's movement can modify, always in the direction of a higher perfection – if such substantial movement be admitted or if one rejects the hypothesis of such motion, these same forms are said to perfect the essences of these substances. Be that as it may, natural beings are protected from the chaos of matter by the design of their deep structures, by the intelligent hier-archy of their species and their kingdoms. From the mineral to the human, the spectacle fills the soul with constant joy. Evil is the absence of both accidental and rational good. It has no substance in itself. Thus Shi'i philosophy appears to soften the gnostic sentiment of life which, nonetheless, permeates it, drawing its strength from the most vital sources of early Shi'ism.

The passage from the visible to the invisible is incessant; the journey from the world below to the world beyond is almost imperceptible. Nature's order, which nearly thwarts time itself with its mass of unpredictable and often dire events, is the visible testimony to the Creator's invisible order. As we have seen, Shia thinkers borrow heavily from the Greek Neoplatonists not only their concepts but also their general outlook. We will summarize this briefly.

The relationship between God and the worlds is analogous to the relationship between the "creator principle" and the things it creates. Here, creation is conceived of as an emanation, a procession, an outpouring. God is the "Provident" because He is the principle of everything that appears in existence. He causes the hierarchical realities of the worlds to rise up according to the level of dignity that He confers on them. He endows them with strength and firmness of being; in short, He provides them with efficacy and perfection. This type of creation cannot be compared to the craftsman who also uses matter to create some object. The craftsman's handiwork is separate from or external to him, whereas the worlds emanating from divine providence proceed from divine Essence in a sort of superabundance and outpouring which our reason cannot fathom.

These worlds express God's infinite mercy, which pours out the way a point produces ever wider circles in which its power is at work. The world visible to the physical eye is merely the furthest from the centre and derives its perfection from its likeness to the worlds that are closer to that centre. These are the world of the soul – visible with the inner eye – and the world of intelligence – visible with the heart.

Is time a denial of order? Some philosophers, like Mir Damad, distance themselves from a perfunctory representation which restricts time to a mere quantification of physical movements, a marker of transition from past to future through the ebb and flow of present states. These philosophers claim another category of time situated between time in this world below and eternity, a subtle qualitative time that marks the transition between the eternal and the temporal and so deposits a moving image of eternity in time.

Others, like Mulla Sadra, conceive of the totality of natural and mental worlds, the worlds of souls and bodies, as a vast ocean of intermingled time and space. They attempt to comprehend the real time of each of the substances, not the time that assails them from outside but the time that animates them from within the depths of their essence, their *essential* time. Each being does more than exist in time; it exists in *its own* time, which is the time devolved upon it by the internal norm of its act of existing and which depends on the rhythm of its existence, its waxing and waning. This is the real time inscribed in each being – the time of its journey.

Temporal life is not haphazard. Events that seem contingent have in fact their reason in the world of souls called the *Malakut*. Each soul is predestined by celestial design to undergo a multitude of changes, of reversals and breaches, when it has to be subject to, and govern, the body. These changes, these catastrophes, are written in the "book of effacement and establishment", which is the book of souls and the *book of time*.

It is remarkable that time is spoken of as a book. This does not mean, banally enough, that "all is written", in a vulgar deterministic manner. Rather, it means that time – with its contingencies, caprices and singularities; in short, every-thing that to us may seem barely necessary – is in fact the necessary writing of a book. Proust would have loved this idea of time as a book, while Kafka would have loved the notion of multiple times that a book dictates from forever on. It is not a stable book, but a book in effacement; not an eternal book but one in which unforeseen things happen and life's circumstances change. Such is the soul of the world, which is a place of "divine destination" in the sense of a book that predestines something to be and something else not to be.

This book is not a chaotic or insane composition. Its reason and foundations are firmly established in the world of pure intelligences called *Jabarut*, the "Mother of the Book" or the "clear Book". The written forms in this book are unchanging and unchangeable. Mir Damad described it in the following terms: "It is a divine book which contains the forms of all existents without any gradation, without concern for temporal succession, just as the supreme book of being is in respect to the realities of all essences and singularities". An atemporal book, a pure creation equivalent to and on the same level as all beings that were, are and ever will be. The first intelligence, which is the first emanation of God, is the eternal composition of each and every thing before any hierarchy is established one above the other or one before the other. God orders the temporal world according to what His intelligence dictates in the supreme book of being. History, nature and the world are like an infinite novel by a divine author.

Man's freedom does not contravene this order, nor is it constrained by it. The theologians of Islam had great difficulty preserving the notion of respon-sibility that one feels for the consequences of one's acts given the idea that God dictates all things in the book of being (what theologians refer to rather soberly as His divine decree). Experts often say that Shia are willing followers of Mu'tazili theology. This is true of the Zaydi sect and certain Twelver Shia.

A careful reading of Isma'ili authors reveals more than one surprising simi-larity with Ash'arism. This helps explain how the same author, for example al-Shahrastani, can be an Ash'ari in his theology and an Isma'ili in his exegesis of the Qur'an.

The Shia doubtless borrowed the notion of freedom of choice (*ikhtiyar*) from Mu'tazilism. The concept is not far from that of free will, differing primarily in that it is not rooted in the metaphysical conception of an *original* freedom existing at the moment of Adam's creation, which is a fundamentally Christian conception. Of course "freedom of choice" creates a problem for Islamic theology because it appears to contradict the omnipotence of the divine decree. The Mu'tazilites argue for its existence on the basis of an exegesis of various Qur'anic verses in order to justify God's promise of reward. Without free choice, how is it possible to justify paradise and hell? Al-Farabi argues that men have a free and sponta-neous choice between Good and Evil. Moral responsibility brings with it harsh punishments; this is just because the ultimate cause of man's evildoing lies solely in his misbegotten choice and in himself alone. Nasir al-Din Tusi summarized the theological position of the Mu'tazilites in the following terms: "Freedom of choice is the efficacy of producing or interrupting an action by the subject who orders it, whether or not there was any incentive to do so". Despite an Ash'ari objection that emphasizes a choice between two opposites, looking back to the necessity of a divine decree, Tusi nonetheless salvaged the possibility of freedom of choice. But he remained uncomfortable with the outcome. Given the circumstances, who wouldn't be?

Gradually Shi'i philosophers came to distrust these complex discussions and agreed that, in reality, God is the author of all things, including our acts. They did not become Ash'aris but did accept the more rational arguments, drawing no negative conclusions for the concept of our freedom of choice. Under the influence of Avicenna, Shi'i philosophers saw only necessity in existence, absolute necessity in God, secondary necessity in all created things. Even our willpower depends on a superior decision, the divine decree. Yet our will exists in and through us; it commits us and obligates us. This is why Shi'i philosophers insist on exalting the responsibility of each individual in the realization of his life after death.

Philosophers raise the study of this freedom to a higher level than dogmatic theologians, indeed to a mystical level, if it be understood as a spiritual transport profoundly experienced at every utterance of the personal pronoun "He", denoting the "essence of God". The mystics claim that the Islamic creed "there is no divinity but God" should be understood as "not Him, if not Him". The true believer repeats this formula again and again in a state of perpetual recollection; he becomes impregnated with it, and it enlivens his desire for God. In the words of Mulla Sadra, "desire is the elixir of attraction", a nice way of saying that the beloved is the sole cause of our desire and its force through the pull that it creates. But attraction is all the stronger when the beloved is absent.

Absence is a constituent of desire. The word "He" "is an awareness of those who are absent". The pronoun that designates divine Essence serves no other purpose than to awaken the pure feeling of absence and, consequently, desire in our awareness. It is an intense awareness of those who are not present stimulated by the memory of this awareness of absence. They appear in the mind as absent ones, as ones who have disappeared. Being absent does not mean being somewhere else; it is the frailty of absence within one's own being. Who other than God is the supremely Absent? Divine Essence does not exist in a world beyond our reach, but where it might be possible to know that essence if only by some miracle we could gain access to it. The divine-in-itself is disappearance; absence is its name. This is why God fosters love. In the Shi'i conception of love, it is only possible to love him who is absent – absent not by accident but by essence – he or she who constantly disappears, even in the most manifest vision. Who then, other than God, is the supreme Beloved One, the wellspring of inexhaustible desire?

Man's freedom lies wholly in his desire. It is fulfilled only in his constant desire for the absent one. The absence of the beloved does not deprive man of his freedom; rather it kindles and unfetters the liberty of the one who submits. Genuine freedom is not freedom to do whatever one chooses; it is choice made from love, exalting the soul by virtue of absence, by creating the emptiness on which the soul thrives in "Him", the absolute Other. It is in this awakening to the Other, who is absence, that man is set free. In the words of Mulla Sadra, "desire for God is the noblest of pleasures". This is a paradoxical pleasure that consists of not taking pleasure in some good but in finding one's good in the distinct pleasure of love. Echoing a splendid thought from Avicenna, Nasir al-Din Tusi believed that the highest good is found in God's love for Himself. Thus the pleasure of loving is a reflection of the divine pleasure. But only God loves Himself and achieves full satisfaction of Himself, whereas the human lover can only achieve satisfaction by loving the object of his desire infinitely in its absence because it is absent. Only the intercession and presence of the face of his imam provides him the calm to avoid pure and simple annihilation without an afterlife.

The assimilation of freedom to desire is a Platonic gesture. The virtues of the ethics of desire are strength and intensity. In the words of the *Phaedrus*, at the sight of the beloved, the soul lifts itself up and spreads its wings. When the beloved is God, freedom becomes pure attraction and self-abandonment. We are ill-prepared to grasp that freedom may lie in the most passionate state of the soul when it is most subjugated to the will of the beloved. The ethics of Stoicism, the teachings of liberal philosophy – so faithful to the rights and powers of our natural freedom – or the prerogatives of our sovereign indivi-duality persuade us that there is no freedom in the servitude of love, even if there is something moving and sublime in it.

At its mystical apogee, Shi'i philosophy is not satisfied merely to state the excellence of love and to consider the exaltation of love as the state most conducive to the feeling of God. Like Socrates in the *Phaedrus*, Shi'i philosophy deciphers the true secret of freedom there. When the soul is awakened to absence – when divine absence transforms it into a loving soul – it becomes intensified, it abandons the cares of the physical body, it rises towards the intellect, and it passes beyond the bounds of the intelligence towards the absent pole of its desire. This movement caused by God, the Absent one, becomes paradoxically the purest act of being and the most perfect liberty.

To cite an eloquent metaphor, the soul is like the white-hot iron that turns incandescent when touched by the fire of the forge. The intensification of the soul's fire – desire – is also the liquefaction of the one who loves, as in the image of the iron that loses its primary properties to become a pure flow of fire. It is this freedom, this intensity of outpouring, which burns and consumes itself without perishing. That is expressed by the two terms "annihilation in God" and "eternal being through God".

These are the two inseparable stages in the final return to the Beloved. There is no free existence, no permanence and resistance to the attractions to life in its multiple forms and diversions, if desire encounters an object which distracts it from its fundamental preoccupation, the *love without a name*. To make such "annihilation in God" palpable, we can cite Aragon, the Western poet, who knew how to express it: "I love you beyond myself where even to love you is my destruction". But at the same time there is no annihilation which is not also eternal being.

To help the "companions of the heart" achieve a deeper understanding of what that eternal being is, Mulla Sadra invoked a long-held tradition attributed to the first imam, 'Ali. When one of his followers asked him to reveal his soul, 'Ali replied, "Which of my souls would you like to see?" He then explained to the astonished disciple that man has four souls, all arrayed in a hierarchy.

The penultimate one, the intellectual soul, he said, "has no physical origin. It most resembles the angelic souls. Its two properties are purity and wisdom."

And towering above this thinking soul is the absolute divine soul, the highest soul. According to Mulla Sadra's philosophical commentary, Imam 'Ali declared that the human soul deifies itself in love and in the fulfilment of desire, culminating in intelligence at its summit. What are the potencies of this divine soul? They are pairs of correspondences symbolising the unity of absence and presence, manifestation and occultation, splendour and the greatest humility. They are the reflections in the soul of the God the Shia are searching for, the God who speaks through the mouth of their imam: immortality in annihilation; bliss in suffering; glory in disgrace; poverty in wealth; long-suffering in affliction. Gratification is submission; submission becomes bliss. The entire ethics of Shi'ism can be found in the following verses from the Qur'an: "O soul at peace, return to thy Lord, well-pleased, well-pleasing! Enter thou among My servants! Enter thou My Paradise!" (Qur'an 89:27–30).

Note

1 See p. 15ff.

Bibliography for Part IV

M.A. Amir-Moezzi, "Une absence remplie de présences. Herméneutiques de l'occultation chez les Shaykhiyya (Aspects de l'imamologie duodécimaine VII)", *Bulletin of the School of Oriental and African Studies*, 64(1), 2001, pp. 1–18. [English trans. by A. Jacobs, in *The Twelver Shia in Modern Times: Religious Culture and Political History*, ed. R. Brunner and W. Ende, Leiden: Brill, 2001, pp. 38–57.]

M.A. Amir-Moezzi, "Le combattant du ta'w'il. Un poème de Mulla Sadra sur 'Ali (Aspects de l'imamologie duodécimaine IX)", in *Islamic Thought: Papers on Historiography, Sufism and Philosophy in Honour of Hermann Landolt*, ed. T.Lawson, London: I.B. Tauris, 2004, pp. 310–341.

Sayyid Haydar Amoli, *Inner Secrets of the Path*, with introd. and notes by M.Khajavi. Trans. from the original Arabic by A.al-Dhaakir Yate, Shaftesbury: Element, 1989.

P. Antes, *Zur Theologie der Schi'a. Eine Untersuchung des Jami' al-asrar wa manba'al-anwar von Sayyid Haidar Amoli*, Freiburg: Schwarz, 1971.

C. Bonmariage, *Le Réel et les réalités: la structure de la réalité de l être chez Mulla Sadra Shirazi*, unpublished doctoral dissertation, Catholic University of Louvain, 1998.

Rajab Borsi, *Les Orients des Lumières*, trans. from the Arabic by H.Corbin, ed. and introd. by P.Lory, Lagrasse: Verdier, 1996.

J. Cooper, "Rumi and Hikmat: Towards a Reading of Sabziwari's Commentary on the Mathnawi", in *The Heritage of Persian Sufism, I: Classical Persian Sufism from its Origins to Rumi*, ed. L.Lewisohn, Oxford: Oneworld, 1999, pp. 409–433.

H. Corbin, *En Islam iranien: aspects spirituels et philosophiques*, Paris: Gallimard, 1971–1972.

H. Corbin, *Philosophie iranienne et philosophie comparée*, Tehran: Académie impériale iranienne de philosophie, 1977.

H. Corbin, *Corps spirituel et terre céleste. De l'Iran mazdéen à l'Iran shi'ite*, Paris: Buchet Chastel, 1979.

H. Corbin, *La Philosophie iranienne islamique aux XVIIe et XVIIIe siècles*, Paris: Buchet Chastel, 1981.

H. Corbin, *Histoire de la philosophie islamique*, Paris: Gallimard, 1986. [*History of Islamic Philosophy*, English trans. by L. Sherrard, London; New York: Kegan Paul, 1993.]

F. Daftary, *The Isma'ilis: Their History and Doctrines*, Cambridge: Cambridge University Press, 1990.

D. De Smet, *La Quiétude de l'intellect. Néoplatonisme et gnose ismaélienne dans l'oeuvre de Hamid ad-Din al-Kirmani (Xe-XIe siècles)*, Louvain: Peeters, 1995.

M. Fakhry, *A History of Islamic Philosophy*, 3rd rev. ed., New York: Routledge, 2004.

C.H. de Fouchécour, *Moralia. Les notions morales dans la littérature persane du IIIe/Ixe au VIIe/XIIIe siècle*, Paris: Éditions recherche sur les civilisations, 1986.

H. Halm, *Kosmologie und Heilslehre der frühen Isma'iliya*, Wiesbaden: Steiner, 1978.

T. Izutsu & M. Mohaghegh, "Mir Damad and his Metaphysics", introduction to *Mir Damad, Kitab al-Qabasat*, ed. M.Mohaghegh and T.Izutsu, Tehran: Tehran University Press, 1977, pp. 1–15.

T. Izutsu & M. Mohaghegh, *The Metaphysics of Sabzawari*. Tehran: Tehran University Press, 1983.

C. Jambet, *Se rendre immortel, Suivi du Traité de la resurrection, Molla Sadra Shirazi*, trans. from the Arabic, Montpellier: Fata Morgana, 2000.

C. Jambet, *L'Acte d'être. La philosophie de la révélation chez Molla Sadra*, Paris: Fayard, 2002.

C. Jambet, *Mort et résurrection en islam. L'au-delà selon Mulla Sadra*. Paris: Albin Michel, 2008.

C. Jambet, "'L'essence de Dieu est toute chose'. Identité et différence selon Sadr al-Din Shirazi (Mulla Sadra)", in *Le Shi'isme imamite quarante ans après. Hommage à Etan Kohlberg*, ed. M.A.Amir-Moezzi, M.M.Bar-Asher & S.Hopkins, Bibliothèque de l'Ecole des Hautes-Etudes, vol. 137, Turnhout: Brepols, 2009, pp. 269–292.

C. Jambet, *Qu'est-ce que la philosophie islamique?* Paris: Gallimard, 2011.

C. Jambet, *Le gouvernement divin. Islam et conception politique du monde*, Paris: CNRS, 2016.

C. Jambet, *La fin de toutes choses, suivi de l'Epitre du rassemblement de Mulla Sadra*, Paris: Albin Michel, 2017.

S. Kamada, "Walaya in Fayz Kashani", in *Islamic Thought: Papers on Historiography, Sufism and Philosophy in Honour of Hermann Landolt*, ed. T.Lawson, London: I.B. Tauris, 2004.

Nasir-i Khusraw, *Between Reason and Revelation: Twin Wisdoms Reconciled. An annotated English Translation of Nasir-i Khusraw's Kitab-i Jami' al-hikmatayn*, trans. Eric Ormsby, London: I.B. Tauris, 2012.

E. Kohlberg, "Aspects of Akhbari Thought in the Seventeenth and Eighteenth Centuries", in *Eighteenth-Century Renewal and Reform in Islam*, ed. N. Levtzion & J.O. Voll, Syracuse, NY: Syracuse University Press, 1987, pp. 133–160. [Now in a collection of articles by the author, Belief and Law in Imami Shi'ism, Aldershot, England: Ashgate, 1991, article no. 17.]

T. Lawson, "The Dawning Places of the Lights of Certainty in the Divine Secrets Connected with the Commander of the Faithful by Rajab Bursi", in *The Legacy of Mediaeval Persian Sufism*, ed. L. Lewisohn, London: Khaniqahi Nimatullahi Publications, 1992, pp. 261–276.

T. Lawson, "The Hidden Words of Fayd Kashani", in *Iran. Questions et connaissances, vol. II: Périodes médiévale et moderne*, ed. M.Szuppe, Studia Iranica, no. 26, Paris: Association pour l'Avancement des Études Iraniennes, 2002, pp. 427–447.

T. Lawson, "Shaykh Almad al-Ahsa'i and the World of Images", in *Shi'i Trends and Dynamics in Modern Times (XVIIIth–XXth centuries)*, ed. D.Hermann & S.Mervin, Beirut: Ergon, 2010, pp. 19–31.

L. Lewisohn, "Sufism and the School of Isfahan: Tasawwuf and 'Irfan in Late Safavid Iran", in *The Heritage of Sufism. III: Classical Persianate Sufism. The Safavid and Mughal Period*, Oxford: Oneworld, 1999, pp. 63–134.

W. Madelung, "Ash-Shahrastanis Streitschrift gegen Avicenna und ihre Widerlegung durch Nadir ad-Din at Tusi", in *Akten des VII. Kongresses für Arabistik und Islamwissenschaft* (Göttingen, 15–22 August 1974), ed. A. Dietrich, Göttingen: Vandenhoeck & Ruprecht, 1976, pp. 250–259. [Now available in a collection of articles by the author, Religious Schools and Sects in Medieval Islam, London: Variorum, 1985, article no. 16.]

W. Madelung, "Ibn Abi Jumhur al-Ahsa'is Synthesis of kalam, Philosophy and Sufism", in *La Signification du bas Moyen Age dans l'histoire et la culture du monde musulman: actes du VIIIe Congrès de l'Union européenne des arabisants et islamisants* (Aix-en-Provence, 1976), Aix-en-Provence, 1978, pp. 147–156. [Now available in Religious Schools and Sects in Medieval Islam, article no. 13.]

W. Madelung, "Nasir ad Din Tusi's Ethics between Philosophy, Shi'ism and Sufism", in *Ethics in Islam*, ed. R.G.Hovannisian, Malibu, FL: Undena, 1985, pp. 57–72.

Y. Marquet, *La philosophie des Ikhwan aliSafa: de Dieu à l'homme*, rev. ed., Paris; Milan, 1999.

G. Monnot, *Islam et religions*, Paris: Maisonneuve, 1986.

J.W. Morris, *The Wisdom of the Throne: An Introduction to the Philosophy of Mulla Sadra*, Princeton, NJ: Princeton University Press, 1981.

S.H. Nasr, "Religion in Safavid Persia", *Iranian Studies*, 7, 1974, pp. 56–89.

S.H. Nasr, *Sadr al-Din Shirazi and His Transcendent Theosophy. Background, Life and Works*, Tehran: Imperial Iranian Academy of Philosophy, 1978.

S.H. Nasr, "The Metaphysics of Sadr al-Din Shirazi and Islamic Philosophy in Qajar Persia", in *Qajar Iran: Political, Social and Cultural Change 1800–1925*, ed. E.Bosworth & C.Hillenbrand, Edinburgh: Edinburgh University Press, 1983.

S.H. Nasr, *Islamic Philosophy from its Origin to the Present*. Albany, NY: State University of New York Press, 2006.

S.H. Nasr and O. Leaman (eds), *History of Islamic Philosophy*, 2 vols, London; New York: Routledge, 1996.

A. J. Newman, "Towards a Reconsideration of the 'Isfahan School of Philosophy': Shaykh Baha'i and the Role of the Safawid 'ulama'", *Studia Iranica*, 15, 1986, pp. 165–199.

A.Q. Qara'i, "Post-Ibn Rushd Islamic Philosophy in Iran", *al-Tawhid*, 3(3), 1985, pp. 24–55.

F. Rahman, *The Philosophy of Mulla Sadra*, Albany, NY: State University of New York Press, 1975.

S.H. Rizvi, "Being (wujud) and Sanctity (wilaya): Two Poles of Intellectual and Mystical Enquiry in Qajar Iran", in *Religion and Society in Qajar Iran*, ed. R.Gleave, London; New York: RoutledgeCurzon, 2005, pp. 113–126.

S.H. Rizvi, "Between Time and Eternity: Mir Damad on God's Creative Agency", *Journal of Islamic Studies*, 12, 2006, pp. 158–176.

S.H. Rizvi, *Mulla Sadra Shirazi: His Life and Works and the Sources for Safavid Philosophy*, (*Journal of Semitic Studies*, Supplement 18), Oxford: Oxford University Press, 2007.

S.H. Rizvi, *Mulla Sadra and Metaphysics: The Modulation of Being.* London: Routledge, 2009.

S.H. Rizvi, "Hikma Muta'aliya in Qajar Iran: Hajj Mulla Hadi Sabzavari and the School of Mulla Sadra", in *Shi' Trends and Dynamics in Modern Times (XVIIIth–XXth centuries)*, D.Hermann & S.Mervin, Beirut: Ergon, 2010, pp. 51–70.

H. Sabzavari, *The Metaphysics of Sabzavari*, trans. from the Arabic by M.Mohaghegh and T.Izutsu, Delmar, NY: Caravan, 1977.

Molla Sadra and Transcendant Philosophy, 2 vols, Tehran, 2001.

B. Scarcia Amoretti, "La Risalat al-imama di Nasir al-Din Tusi", in *Rivista degli Studi Orientale*, 47, 1972, pp. 101–168.

O. Scharbrodt, "The qutb as Special Representqative of the Hidden Imam: The conflation of Shi'i and Sufi vilayat in the Ni'matullahi Order", *Shi'i Trends and Dynamics in Modern Times (XVIIIth–XXth centuries)*, ed. D.Hermann & S.Mervin, Beirut: Ergon, 2010, pp. 33–49.

S. Schmidtke, *The Theology of al-'Allama al-Hilli (d. 726/1325)*, Berlin: Schwarz, 1991.

S. Schmidtke, *Theologie, Philosophie und Mystik im zwölferschiitischen Islam des 9./15. Jahrhunderts. Die Gedankenwelten des Ibn Abi Jumhur al – Ahsa' ï (um 838/1434-35-nach 906/1501)*, Leiden: Brill, 2000.

Abu Ya'qub Sejestani, *Le Dévoilement des choses cachées*, trans. from the Persian and introd. by H.Corbin, Lagrasse: Verdier, 1988.

Shahrastani, *Livre des religions et des sectes*, introd., trans. and notes by D.Gimaret, J.Jolivet & G.Monnot, Louvain: Peeters, 2 vols, 1986–1993.

Shihaboddin Yahya Suhrawardi, *Le Livre de la sagesse orientale Kitab hikmat al-ishraq*, with commentaries by Qotboddin Shirazi and Molla Sadra Shirazi, trans. and notes by H. Corbin, ed. and introd. by C.Jambet, Paris: Gallimard, new edition, 2002.

Molla Sadra Shirazi, *Le livre des pénétrations métaphysiques*, trans. from Arabic and introd. by H.Corbin, Lagrasse: Verdier, 1988.

M. Terrier, "Le Mahbub al-qulub de Qutb al-Din Ashkevari, une oeuvre méconnue dans l'histoire de la sagesse en islam", *Journal Asiatique*, 298(2), 2010, pp. 345–387.

M. Terrier, "De l'éternité ou de la nouveautè du monde: parcours d'un problème Philosophique d'Athènes à Ispahan", *Journal Asiatique*, 299(1), 2011, pp. 369–421.

M. Terrier, "Qutb al-Din Ashkevari, un philosophe discret de la renaissance safavide", *Studia Iranica*, 40(2), 2011, pp. 171–210.

M. Terrier, *Histoire de la sagesse et philosophie shi'ite*, Paris, éditions du Cerf, 2016.

Nasir al-Din Tusi, *Contemplation and Action, the Spiritual Autobiography of a Muslim Scholar*, trans. S.J. Badakhchani, London: I.B. Tauris, 1998.

M. van den Bos, *Mystic Regimes: Sufism and the State in Iran from the Late Qajar Era to the Islamic Republic.* Leiden: Brill, 2002.

P. Walker, *Early Philosophical Shiism. The Ismaili Neoplatonism of Abu Ya'qub al-Sijistani*, Cambridge: Cambridge University Press, 1993.

Conclusion

The analyses that we have presented here have been made easier by the surge in Sh'ite studies over the past few decades. This has been due to the labours of a number of Western scholars but also to those of Shi'i researchers and research institutions – Isma'ili as well as Imami – worldwide and especially in Iran. Critical text editions are now widely available, and source material and documents are generally more accessible. We owe much gratitude to the researchers and directors of these institutions of living knowledge for their contributions.

Questions of definition always require a clear and concise formulation. But is this possible in the case of Shi'ism? Can the "essence" of Shi'ism be defined? Like every religion or religious tradition living in the flux of history, Shi'ism has changed since its origins, and its "original" features have evolved. Today, Shi'i beliefs and ritual practices are far more complicated. In this context, an essentialist definition would be risky. But by way of conclusion, we will attempt to underline certain basic constants and to note some signal points.

First, one obvious feature of Shi'ism is its pursuit of knowledge as expressed through study and learning. On various occasions we have observed that the concept of *initiation* is a constant of Shi'i thought. Wherever we look – whether to the imams or to the authors of theological, philosophical, cosmological and esoteric postulates and exegesis, or simply to the faithful – the quantity of texts available for study is phenomenal: commentaries, doctrinal treatises, mystical and polemical texts, collections of advice, prescriptions. Altogether they express the preferred attitude of the Shia, which is assiduous study of the Qur'an and the authorized commentaries (the written word dictated by the imams). This pursuit of study and learning is found among Qarmatian and Isma'ili thinkers, architects of sophisticated metaphysical systems, but also among Twelver jurists and their clerical brothers specialising in doctrinal theology, philosophy and the natural sciences. Shi'i scholars and philosophers, regardless of whether they are followers of the "Rationalist" school or esoteric mystics, are first and foremost men of study and initiation. It is through study that they attain revealed truth, a truth that is set aside for them and that is the means of their salvation. In some respects the Shi'i scholar reminds us of the Jewish scholar studying the letters of the Torah, bringing Talmudic exegesis to bear on them and quickening them through cabbalistic gnosis.

Second, it is not surprising that this pursuit of study is sustained by a passionate messianic feeling. A conception of history as battleground shapes the Shi'i vision of the world. Deep within, the Shi'i mind is haunted by time. All Muslims share this uneasiness. Both ask the same question: Muhammad being the "Seal of the Prophecy", what becomes of the revealed truth after the Prophet's death? What is the nature of the indefinite period of time that stretches from the final prophecy to the end of worldly and heavenly time? Is this time meaningful? Is it a time of spiritual, moral and eschatological struggle? Or is it a time without meaning? The Shi'i mind chooses to believe firmly in a bellicose, millenarian time.

It is incorrect to claim that Islam is less interested in history than either Judaism or Christianity. The Sunni mind is also deeply aware of the impermanence and vanity of this lower world. Again and again the Qur'an says that this world is nothing in contrast with the world beyond, the only world that matters. In general, the Sunni mind is happy to keep its distance from the lower world, either through contemplation or through strict obedience to the prescriptions of the *shari'a*. But the Shi'i mind responds differently to the injunctions of the Qur'an. For Shia, the historical time of the prophecy is followed by a time of *walaya*, a time of study but also a time directed towards the events of the return: the return in God and return to God, the announced return of the Twelfth Imam. At times the Shi'i mind seems stamped by impatience. It aspires to be unburdened of time in the lower world, and the sooner the better. The teachings of the imams make this time more bearable, though it remains a time in which injustice and the wickedness of men competes with the natural adversities of the mortal condition.

This explains the countless religious and political efforts to establish a position of authority for a true descendant of 'Ali, so that the light of *walaya* can illuminate the world. But, as we have seen, the quietist attitude of the Twelver imams stands in direct contradiction to this exasperated messianic expectation. This is experienced as inescapable necessity. Pessimistic about the world and its governance, the Shi'i mind experiences a desperate hope. It despairs at the thought of placing hope in some form of worldly power; its hope soars at the promise of the return of the Saviour, the Hidden Imam. Action in history is repugnant to the Shi'i psyche because historical time only produces useless illusions and opportunities for strife.

The world constantly summons the community of the faithful to its demands. In an ideal world, the community will live in study and meditation, united in loyalty – as ever, *walaya* – even if this means that its peoples are dispersed throughout the kingdoms of this earth. In reality, though, the ambitions and knowledge of scholars, the prerogatives of the privileged classes and the revolt of the humble effectively dictate another outcome. Under the impetus of creative and rigorous reason, the lessons of early Shi'ism were censored, encoded, transformed and re-expressed, in the ways we have discussed here, until the entire Shi'i community once again believed itself to be vested with a new messianic mission, this time vetted but travestied by the discourse of the jurist theologian.

It is surprising how reversible the concept of reason is in Shi'ism. In the original meaning of *al-'aql* – that is, intelligence of the sacred, a "non-rational" faculty – reason is neither rational nor irrational, but *super-rational*. In its other meaning of rational intelligence – an inheritance of Greek science and philosophy with contributions from Mu'tazilite theology – it becomes more ambivalent. Thus, it informed the exegetic practices of the jurist–scholars (who gradually assumed an authority which was not theirs to begin with), whilst it also illuminated the great classical works of philosophy and contemplation, and became an innovative antidote to the legalistic and political drift of Shi'ism. And so on one side we find Rationalist scholars who set Shi'ism on course to play the role it does today as a dominant force and an important religious ideology in full possession of the political reins of power, yet still inspired by a quasi-messianic spirit, which remains palpable in Iran's Islamic Revolution. On the opposite side, we find the gnostics, mystics and philosophers, who accept the challenges of the intellect and also wish for nothing but the triumph of *walaya*. But theirs is an inner-directed spirituality and is mistrustful of collective political undertakings.

Illustrating this further, among the *mujtahids*, instead of conservatism there is an imaginative effort that thrives on the living present and jeers at the past. In the vision of these scholars, death must not be allowed a hold on life. Paradoxically, these same intellectuals – the innovators, the people of light, who dare to use their reason – innovated so well that they delivered into the hands of the religious scholars themselves the authority of the state and responsibility for all aspects of community life, including responsibility for directing the conscience of the faithful.

On the other side, not innovation but respect for the traditions of the imams; not legal reasoning but contemplative intelligence; not the *fatwa* but exegesis and moral or metaphysical discourse. Here reason is synonymous with wisdom.

Every Shi'i believer is held between these two poles; a univocal position is quite rare. There are of course infinite nuances in the thinking of the characters who act out the Shi'i drama. This needs to be understood because in the end Shi'ism is a fantastic dramaturgy. This is not only because the tragedy of Imam Husayn casts a pall of mourning over the Shi'i psyche, demonstrating the truth of this world and the precarious nature of earthly life, the calamity of injustice and the short-lived triumph of the "Pharaohs" of every age; it is also because temporality is wholly experienced as drama. The believer is split between obedience and hope and the choice alienates him from himself. Should he heed only the call of his inner imam in the solitude of silent initiation? Should he become an actor in the transformation of the world in accordance with prophetic and imamological teachings? What exactly does this transformation involve? How does it come about? Is it the result of an inner transformation that gradually influences the course of history? Or is it an outer transformation, a reordering of a social or political kind? This dividedness is not unfamiliar. It lies at the very heart of the three religions of the Book.

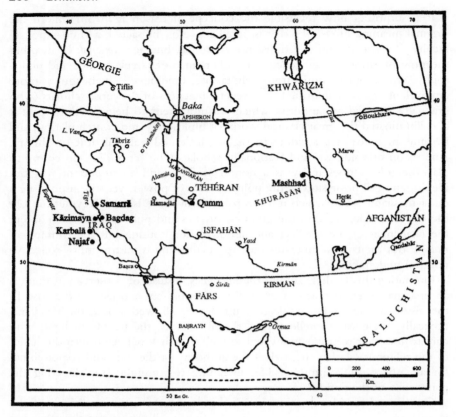

Map Main Shi'i regions today

Main dates

622: Hegira. The Muslims emigrate from Mecca to Yathrib (Medina).

632: Muhammad dies in Medina.

632–634: Abu Bakr is caliph. The Muslims conquer Palestine.

634–644: 'Umar b. al-Khattab is caliph. Egypt and Iran are conquered. The Sasanian Empire of Persia collapses.

644–656: 'Uthman b. 'Affan is caliph.

656–661: 'Ali b. Abi Talib is caliph.

656: Battle of the Camel. The enemies of 'Ali are defeated.

657: Mu'awiya, the governor of Syria, foments an uprising against 'Ali and brings about the "Great Upheaval" (al-fitna).

657: Battle of Siffin. 'Ali agrees to arbitration. Some of 'Ali's allies (the Kharijites) desert him. Battle of Nahrawan. 'Ali crushes his Kharijite opponents.

659: Adhruh's arbitration weakens 'Ali's authority.

660: Mu'awiya is recognized as caliph in Syria, Egypt and the Hijaz region. 'Ali maintains authority in Iraq and Iran.

661: A Kharijite partisan in Kufa murders 'Ali. The Umayyad dynasty is founded.

669–670: Hasan ibn 'Ali, the second imam, dies (approximate date).

671: 'Ali's faithful followers, the leaders of the Qurra' (readers of the Qur'an), are executed.

680: Mu'awiya dies. Yazid becomes caliph. Husayn ibn 'Ali, the third imam, is killed at Karbala.

684–692: The Kharijite rise in revolt.

685: Procession of the Penitents in Kufa in memory of Husayn ibn 'Ali.

685–687: Mukhtar rebels in the name of Muhammad b. al-Hanafiyya, the son of Imam 'Ali.

714: 'Ali ibn Husayn, the fourth imam, dies (approximate date).

716: The Abbasid dynasty, supporters of the Prophet's family's claim to the caliphate, is born.

737: Muhammad al-Baqir, the fifth imam, dies (approximate date).

740: Zayd b. Ali, the eponymous imam of Zaydism, dies.

744: Yazid III is caliph. The Abbasid rebellion in Khurasan begins.

748: Wasil ibn Ata, founder of Mu'tazilism, dies.

749: Abu'l 'Abbas is proclaimed caliph in Kufa. Beginning of the Abbasid dynasty.

750: Abbasid massacre of the Umayyads. Survivors flee to Andalusia.

755: Abu Muslim is executed. The Abbasid insurgents are eliminated. The new caliph adopts Sunni Islam. Rebellion in Khurasan in the name of the "occulted" Abu Muslim. An "extremist" Shi'i movement stirs up trouble in the inner circle of Isma'il ibn Ja'far, son of the sixth imam, Ja'far al-Sadiq. Abu l-Khattab, "extremist" Shi'i disciple disavowed by Imam Ja'far, is executed. The Khattabiyya Shi'i sect emerges for a short period.

762: Founding of Baghdad, capital of the Abbasid dynasty.

765: Ja'far al-Sadiq, the sixth imam, dies. The Shi'i branch splits between Isma'ilis (followers of Isma'il ibn Ja'far) and Imamis (followers of Musa ibn Ja'far al-Kazim).

799: Musa al-Kazim, the seventh imam, dies (approximate date).

816–838: Rebellion of Babak and the Khurramiyya, an extremist "communist" movement, in Azerbaijan.

817: The Abbasid caliph al-Ma'mun names Imam 'Ali al-Rida his successor.

818: 'Ali al-Rida, the eighth imam, dies.

833–842: Al-Mu'tasim is caliph. Mu'tazili theology receives the caliphate's official backing. A vast undertaking begins to translate scientific and philosophical texts from the Greek into Arabic.

835: Muhammad al-Taqi, the ninth imam, dies (approximate date).

847–861: Mutawwakil is caliph. He is assassinated. Mu'tazilism is abandoned as the official theology.

868: 'Ali al-Hadi al-Naqi, the tenth imam, dies. Muhammad al-Mahdi, the eleventh imam, is born.

869–883: African slaves rise up in Iraq (the Zanj Revolt) led by an Alid pretender.

874: Al-Hasan al-Askari, the eleventh imam, dies. Muhammad al-Mahdi, the twelfth imam, goes into "Minor" Occultation. The Sunni theologian al-Ash'ari is born.

877–899: Isma'ili Shia rise in rebellion (the Qarmatian revolt) led by Hamdan Qarmat in the name of Muhammad al-Mahdi, the imam in occultation.

875: Founding of the Samanid Emirate in Transoxiana. Bukhara is its capital.

897: Founding of the Zaydi Emirate in Yemen.

900: The Qarmatians and the Fatimid pretenders (branch of Isma'ili Shia) split.

902: The Qarmatians attack Salamiyya, the Fatimid central headquarters. The Fatimids leave for North Africa. The traditionist Imami Saffar Qummi dies.

907: Founding of the Qarmatian state of Bahrain.

910: The Fatimid Mahdi Ubaydullah makes a "messianic" entry in Kairouan.

912: The Qarmatian ruler Ibn al-Fadl occupies Yemen and abolishes religious law.

922: Al-Hallaj is tortured and executed in Baghdad.

929: The Umayyad caliphate reigns in Cordoba. 'Abd al-Rahman III is ruler.

930: The Qarmatians of Bahrain attack Mecca and remove the "Black Stone" in the Ka'ba.

931: An Iranian is proclaimed the "Messiah" in Bahrain. The Qarmatians abolish religious law.

933: The Isma'ili philosopher Abu Hatim al-Razi dies.

940: The traditionist Imami al-Kulayni dies.

941: The fourth "representative" of the twelfth imam of the Imamis (henceforth called Twelvers) dies. The twelfth imam himself goes into "Major" Occultation. Muhammad al-Nasafi, Isma'ili theologian and introducer of Neoplatonism to Isma'ili thought, dies.

945–967: The Buyid Sultanate of Mu'izz al-Dawla rules in Baghdad. This is the era of the Buyid dynasty and the school of Baghdad.

950: Abu Nasr al-Farabi, the Twelver Shi'i philosopher, dies.

957: The Twelver Shi'i Buyid dynasty strengthens its domination over the Abbasid caliphate.

962: The Buyid ruler Mu'izz al-Dawla establishes the Shi'i celebrations of 'Ashura and Ghadir Khumm in Baghdad.

969: The Fatimids conquer Egypt. Cairo is founded. The Fatimid Empire is born.

974: Qadi Nu'man, Isma'ili philosopher and jurist, dies.

980: The philosopher Abu Ali ibn Sina (Avicenna) is born.

991: Caliph al-Qadir takes the lead in the Sunni struggle against Shi'ism. Hanbalism becomes the official position. Ibn Babawayh dies.

993: The vizier Sabur founds the Shi'i library Dar al-ilm (the "House of Knowledge") in Baghdad.

995–1055: Hanbali Sunnism expands in Baghdad.

998–1186: The Sunni Ghaznawid Sultanate reigns in Iraq and in the east of Iran.

999: New Sunni celebrations are inaugurated in Baghdad to counter Shi'i influence.

1005: The Samanid Emirate comes to an end.

1008: The Fatimid imam al-Hakim destroys the Church of the Holy Sepulchre.

1012: The Sunnis and the Twelver Shia in Baghdad jointly condemn the Fatimids. The Buyid sultan Baha al-Dawla dies.

1016: The Imami thinker al-Sharif al-Radi dies.

1020: Al-Kirmani, a high official at the Fatimid court, finalizes Isma'ili Shi'i doctrine in Cairo.

1022: The Imami jurist and theologian Shaykh al-Mufid dies.

1030–1039: The Umayyad caliphate in Andalusia collapses.

1037: Avicenna dies.

1038: Miskawayh, a prominent Shi'i philosopher in the service of the Buyid, dies.

1041–1186: Seljuk Emirates.

1044: The Imami jurist and theologian al-Sharif al-Murtada dies.

1050: The Seljuk Turks overthrow the Shi'i Buyid regime of Baghdad.

1059: Abu Hamid al-Ghazali, the great Sunni theologian and mystic, is born.

1065: Nizam al-Mulk is Seljuk vizier of Baghdad.

1067: The madrassa Nizamiyya, a centre of Sunni teaching, is founded in Baghdad. Shaykh al-Tusi, Imami jurist and theologian, dies.

1076: Seljuk Sunnis take over control of Damascus from the Fatimids.

1079–1082: The Almoravid dynasty conquers central Maghreb. Oujda, Tlemcen (now Tilimsi) and Algiers are seized.

1094: The Fatimid caliph al-Mustansir bi'llah dies. Isma'ili Shi'i Islam splits between the partisans of al-Musta'li and Nizar. Hasan Sabbah establishes a Nizari Isma'ili state in Alamut.

1098: The Crusaders capture Antioch.

1099: The Crusaders capture Jerusalem.

1106: The Almoravid dynasty takes control of Andalusia.

1109: The Crusaders found the County of Tripoli.

1111: Al-Ghazali dies.

1124: Hassan Sabbah dies.

1125: The Crusaders take Tyre.

1147: The Almohad dynasty triumphs in Marrakesh and Seville.

1164: The Nizari Isma'ili imam Hasan proclaims the "resurrection" in Alamut. Religious law is abolished.

1167: Temudjin, the future Genghis Khan, is born.

1169: Saladin seizes power in Egypt.

1171: Saladin, founder of the Ayyubid dynasty, puts an end to the Fatimid caliphate of Cairo.

1187: Saladin takes Jerusalem from the Crusaders.

1190: The Third Crusade.

1191: Saint John of Acre falls. In Aleppo the philosopher Suhrawardi is executed by order of Saladin.

1192: Saladin loses the battle of Jaffa against Richard the Lionheart. The Imami thinker Ibn Shahrashub dies.

1201: The philosopher Nasir al-Din Tusi is born.

1202: Ibn Idris Hilli, Imami jurist and theologian, dies. The Hilla school is founded.

1229: After reaching agreement with the Ayyubid sultan al-Malik al-Kamil, Frederick II, leader of the Sixth Crusade, reinstates the Latin Kingdom of Jerusalem.

1234: In Baghdad the Mustansiriyya madrassa is inaugurated. It accommodates teaching of the four schools of Sunni jurisprudence on an equal footing.

1236: Frederick III of Castile takes Cordoba.

1238: The Alhambra is founded in Grenada.

1242–1258: Al-Mu'tasim, the last Abbasid caliph of Baghdad, is ruler.

1250: Saint Louis concedes defeat at al-Mansura.

1256: Alamut fort falls into the hands of the Mongols. The Nizari Isma'ili imam dies. The Mongols rule over Western Iran.

1266: Ibn Tawus, the Imami thinker, dies.

1277: Muhaqqiq Hilli, Imami jurist and theologian, dies.

1258–1512: The Kingdom of Granada thrives.

1320: Haydar Amuli, Imami thinker, is born.

1325: 'Allama Hilli, Imami thinker, dies.

1334: The founder of the Sufi order of the Safavid dynasty, Safi al-Din, dies.

1406: The theologian and historian Ibn Khaldun dies.

1453: Constantinople falls to the Ottoman Sultan Muhammad III.

1501: The leader of the Safavid religious brotherhood, Shah Isma'il, is enthroned in Tabriz. Twelver Shi'ism is enshrined as the state religion of Iran.

1508: The Safavid state captures Baghdad.

1511: The Ottomans persecute and deport the Shia of Asia Minor.

1516: The Ottomans conquer Syria.

1517: The Ottomans conquer Egypt.

1524: Shah Isma'il dies.

1534:The Ottomans reconquer Iraq. The Imami jurist Muhaqqiq Karaki dies.

1576: Shah Tahmasp dies.

1588–1629: Shah 'Abbas I is ruler.

1598: Isfahan becomes the capital of the Safavid state.

1627: Muhammad Amin Astarabadi, founder of Imami neo-traditionalism, dies (approximate date).

1631–1632: Mir Damad, Imami philosopher and theologian, dies.

1640–1641: Mulla Sadra, Imami philosopher and theologian, dies.

1642–1666: Shah 'Abbas II is ruler.

1680: Fayd Kashani, Imami thinker, dies (approximate date).

1699: Muhammad Baqir Majlisi, Imami thinker and Traditionist, dies.

1722: The Afghans take Isfahan. Sadiq Ardestani, Imami philosopher, dies.

1729: The Safavid dynasty is re-established in Isfahan. Shah Tahmasp II is ruler.

1736–1747: Nadir Shah is ruler.

1792: Ibn 'Abd al-Wahhab, the eponymous founder of Wahhabism, dies.

1795: The Qajar dynasty is founded. Tehran becomes the new capital of Iran.

1802: The Wahhabis pillage the Shi'i shrines of Karbala.

1812: Persia and Russia go to war. The Shi'i "clergy" declare jihad.

1830: Mulla 'Ali Nuri, Imami philosopher, dies.

1850: The Bab is executed in Tabriz.

1878: Mulla Hadi Sabzawari, Imami philosopher and theologian, dies.

1891: Shi'i "clergy" lead popular movement against the tobacco monopoly awarded to the British.

1902: Mirza Husayn Nuri, Imami thinker and Traditionist, dies.

1906: First National Assembly in Iran is held. Constitutional monarchy is established.

1921: Iraq becomes a kingdom.

1923: Reza Shah founds the Pahlavi dynasty in Iran.

1926: Ibn Sa'ud is proclaimed King of the Hijaz. The Wahhabi dynasty rules in Arabia.

1941: Reza Shah abdicates in favour of his son Muhammad Reza Pahlavi.

1951: Mosadegh nationalizes Iran's oil.

1953: Mass riots in Tehran. The Shah flees to Italy. Mosadegh falls. The Shah returns.

1962: The Zaydi Kingdom comes to an end in Yemen.

1963: The "White Revolution" begins in Iran (land reforms, political modernization, including the right to vote for women, and numerous other measures). Khomeini is arrested.

1964: Khomeini is expelled to Turkey, then Iraq.

1967: The official coronation of Muhammad Reza Pahlavi and his spouse, Farah Diba.

1971: Festivities in Persepolis.

1978: Mass riots in Qumm, Tabriz, Isfahan and Tehran. General strike and insurrection.

1979: The Shah leaves for Egypt. The imperial regime falls. Ayatollah Khomeini is victorious. The Islamic Republic of Iran is proclaimed.

Index